, What people are sa

BrexLit

Dulcie's writing pulses with an assured rhythm that is attuned both to the larger vision she is seeking to articulate and the local nuances of the works under discussion. To write so powerfully and well is an achievement to be commended.

Steven Shoemaker, PhD, Professor of English at Connecticut College and Director of the Roth Writing Center.

outstanding...its scale and scope are remarkable; its originality is unmistakable; its interdisciplinarity (spanning political science, history, and literary studies) is rare; the quality of its close readings is a continual pleasure; the polished elegance of its prose is like nothing I've seen from an undergraduate; and its timeliness and importance argue for its wider dissemination.

Julie Rivkin, PhD, Author of *False Positions: The Representational Logics of Henry James's Fiction.*

The Financial Times may have coined the term 'BrexLit', but Dulcie Everitt has written the book on it.

Jeff Strabone, PhD, Author of *Poetry and British Nationalisms in the Bardic Eighteenth Century: Imagined Antiquities.*

I read with pleasure *BrexLit: The Problem of Englishness in Pre- and Post-Brexit Referendum Literature.* I was struck by its skillful intertwining of theories of nationalism, post-war British history and recent literature on Englishness. I was moreover impressed by Dulcie's ability to tie together scholarship on nationalism, the UK-EU relationship, peripheral nationalism in the Celtic fringe, rising English nationalism and a sophisticated analysis of different literary genres.

David Patton, PhD, Author of *In Out of the East: From PDS to Left Party in Unified Germany* and *Cold War Politics in Postwar Germany.*

Nationalism is an increasingly worrying phenomena. Dulcie gets to the heart of this issue with an academic review of the literature centred on Brexit and the English people's understanding of their own identity and how it sits alongside the concept of being British.

Mark Glover, FPRCA, Chief Executive, Newington Communications; Executive Director, SEC Group

BrexLit

The Problem of Englishness in Pre- and
Post-Brexit Referendum Literature

BrexLit

The Problem of Englishness in Pre- and Post-Brexit Referendum Literature

Dulcie Everitt

Winchester, UK
Washington, USA

JOHN HUNT PUBLISHING

First published by Zero Books, 2021
Zero Books is an imprint of John Hunt Publishing Ltd., No. 3 East St., Alresford,
Hampshire SO24 9EE, UK
office@jhpbooks.com
www.johnhuntpublishing.com
www.zero-books.net

For distributor details and how to order please visit the 'Ordering' section on our website.

Text copyright: Dulcie Everitt 2020

ISBN: 978 1 78904 737 0
978 1 78904 738 7 (ebook)
Library of Congress Control Number: 2020949085

A CIP catalogue record for this book is available from the British Library.

Design: Stuart Davies

UK: Printed and bound by CPI Group (UK) Ltd, Croydon, CR0 4YY
Printed in North America by CPI GPS partners

We operate a distinctive and ethical publishing philosophy in
all areas of our business, from our global network of authors to
production and worldwide distribution.

Contents

Contents

Note on Usage

Throughout this book, I have chosen to follow the conventional usage of terms relating to England and the United Kingdom. I have used 'UK' and 'Britain' interchangeably although a more precise definition of each is available. Having said this, I specifically use 'Britain' or 'British' when I am referring to the British Empire or the British people at large acknowledging that Britain, even today, is dominated by England in terms of politics and power. Where I use 'the UK' I indicate towards the purportedly equal political union between England, Scotland, Wales, and Northern Ireland. I would also like to make clear that 'England' is not the name of the polity of the United Kingdom. When I refer to England, I refer specifically to the subnational territorial unit that lies south of the Kershope Burn and east of the River Wye. When I refer to Englishness, I refer specifically to a national identity that is distinct from 'British' and that represents a constituent part of the United Kingdom— an identity that forms itself in opposition to other national identities within the UK in Scotland, Wales, and Northern Ireland.

Introduction

Over the past 2 decades, the Western world has collectively experienced a resurgence of nationalist sentiment that has deeply disturbed the political landscape. Throughout Europe, nationalist, right-wing political parties have begun to capture a larger number of supporters, while in the United States, Donald Trump's presidency has brought to light some of the ugliest facets of American self-conceptualization. However, nowhere else have the effects of resurgent nationalism been more crippling than in England. In the 4 years since the United Kingdom voted to leave the European Union on June 23, 2016— a movement dubbed 'Brexit'—a seismic shift has occurred towards a collective effort and desire to (re)discover the meaning of Englishness among those who consider themselves a part of this national group.

Although what is happening in England is, as journalist Fintan O'Toole suggests, 'a local version of a global phenomenon...it is also different' (O'Toole x). Unlike other Western countries experiencing a resurgence of right-wing nationalism, England is not a sovereign state, but rather a constituent part of the United Kingdom of Great Britain and Northern Ireland. Therefore, English nationalism is a form of nationalism that does not directly correlate to the existing nation-state. English nationalists are attempting to define and assert Englishness as distinct within the larger polity—an attempt that has struggled to find firm ground and has in fact submerged England in a crisis of identity. Given the stark contrast between how the English voted (Leave, with the notable exception of London), how Wales voted (Leave, by a smaller majority), and how Scotland and Northern Ireland voted (Remain), speculation surrounding what 'Englishness' means as opposed to 'Britishness' has been rife among scholars, politicians, and artists.

1

Such speculation has displayed not only the vast array of theories on English nationalism; the splintering of opinion and explanation has also demonstrated just how incapable of defining itself England actually is. Discussions of Englishness inevitably bring to the fore how history (and the dearth of accurate historical knowledge), political rhetoric, and the international liberal order, which the UK had a major hand in creating, have worked together to produce the contemporary manifestations of English nationalism.

The debate over whether to remain a member of the EU or not was among the most polarizing political debates that Britain has ever seen, not just among individuals, but among the constituent parts of the UK as well. Like most seismic events in our world, Brexit immediately triggered a literary movement that sought to make sense of our reality through fiction. This still-emerging genre of literature has been named 'BrexLit' by the *Financial Times* in 2016 ('Brexit' + 'Literature'). For those readers unfamiliar with what the political phenomenon of Brexit is, it refers to the UK's decision, made via a referendum vote, to withdraw from the European Union. A referendum is a political vote determined by the people rather than the government; it is defined by the *Oxford English Dictionary* as 'The process or principle of referring an important political question (e.g. a proposed constitutional change) to be decided by a general vote of the entire electorate' (*OED*). Sometimes, referenda are non-binding, meaning that the result does not have to be acted upon by the government. However, in the case of Brexit, the results were accepted by the government, and Parliament began the legal process of disentangling the UK from the EU.

The literary works that I cover in this book are a non-exhaustive list of BrexLit texts, and given the immediacy of my own project I am also likely to leave out some that haven't quite reached publication yet. However, I believe they provide the best possible opportunity to gauge the immediate chaos, confusion, and tension that followed the referendum. They are also well-suited to answering the question that this book raises on the problem of Englishness in both pre- and post-Brexit Britain, and how that problem might be solved.

In order to comprehend what literature is telling us about Englishness, it is vital to first understand the historical background that either constitutes or informs the backdrop for these texts. For this reason, I use the first part of this book to delve into the theoretical and historical context necessary for understanding how and why Brexit came to be. I have done so as concisely as possible to allow for maximum understanding in minimum time. Then, in the second part I go on to analyse how literature published both pre-referendum and post-referendum considers the problem of Englishness, which is to say the problem of a fractured sense of English identity.

Part one of this book is by no means a complete guide to English nationalism, UK membership of the EU, or insurgent nationalisms in the UK. What I discuss is what I believe is most relevant for understanding the BrexLit texts discussed in part two. I acknowledge that I may skim over or skip altogether elements of history or politics that to others might seem more important or equally so. I also recognise that my discussion might simplify some of the events, people, or movements that I consider. For example, when I discuss Irish nationalism I focus specifically on the Irish Republican Army (IRA). However, I do not do this to suggest that all Irish nationalists support terrorism or that this is the sole expression of Irish nationalism. Rather, I aim to outline where the surge in peripheral nationalisms across the UK has been most visibly expressed, as well as to provide context to some of the literature that I cover later that specifically refers to the IRA and its attacks. For those readers who wish to delve even deeper into the historical and political context that I grapple with in part one, please refer to the section at the end of this book for further reading, where I have listed more expertly written sources.

I acknowledge that the works I cover in part two come from what I read to be a Remain perspective—some are dystopian, and all of them criticize both the campaign and projected aftermath of the vote. However, I sincerely believe that despite their, in certain instances, rather obvious biases, they are all valuable documents of how Brexit has divided a nation in two, and how the insecure underpinnings of English identity have been revealed and confronted.

I write this book from the perspective of a young student living through events it details. I was home in London for the Brexit referendum of 2016, before I left the UK to study in the US, placing me in-country for Donald Trump's presidential election of the same year. Watching the growth of right-wing nationalism in both countries sparked in me an urgent desire to understand the present moment—how we got here as a nation and where we go now.

My intention for this book is not to force my analysis and the conclusions I draw from current events and literature on my readers. After all, the literary fiction I cover takes an almost maddening joy in leaving the conclusion-drawing to the person holding the book, rather than the one who wrote it. I have sought to impartially analyse all that I have found throughout my research—both on the politics and literature surrounding Brexit and Englishness—to draw conclusions that inevitably end up being somewhat partial. Of course, we all draw conclusions differently, and I encourage my readers to do the same with this book—draw your own conclusions by analysing and critiquing mine! I hope to inspire reflection, and to make the first contribution to what I know will become a topic of deep interest to many over time.

PART ONE

PART ONE

Chapter One

Theories of Nationalism and the English Case

The Romans first with Julius Caesar came,
Including all the nations of that name,
Gauls, Greeks, and Lombards; and by computation,
Auxiliaries, or slaves of every nation.
With Hengist, Saxons; Danes, with Sueno came,
In search of plunder, not in search of fame.
Scots, Picts, and Irish from th' Hibernian shore;
And conquering William brought the Normans o'er.
All these their bar'brous offspring left behind,
The dregs of armies, they of all mankind:
Blended with Britons, who before were here,
Of whom the Welch have blest the character.
From this amphibious ill-born mob began
That vain ill-natured thing, an Englishman.
Daniel Defoe

Theories of Nationalism

To tackle the problem of Englishness in contemporary Britain, we must first understand what nationalism is and how it came about. Nationalism is a word we hear and use regularly with little reflection, primarily because in an age when the existence of distinct nations defines the way that our world operates, it appears to be a natural and universal phenomenon. According to the *Oxford English Dictionary*, the word 'nationalism' was first recorded in 1798 by Augustin Barruel, a French publicist and Jesuit priest. He used it as follows: 'Nationalism, or the love for a particular nation, took place of the general love' (*OED*). Barruel's use of the word nationalism might seem vague, but it

7

is actually very useful for understanding why this was the first time the word is recorded in use. Barruel first briefly defines what the word nationalism means as 'love for a particular nation', which suggests that a love of one's nation was not necessarily a widespread sentiment before the turn of the nineteenth century. His phrasing of how nationalism 'took place of the general love' is unspecific but useful in its implication that other forms of identity attachment had, until that time, traditionally been more important than one's nationhood. There are many possible identity attachments that come to mind, but one's religious beliefs seem to be the most obvious one, especially in the English case where sectarian violence is historically rife. The shift that Barruel describes suggests that around the time of the Enlightenment, national attachment became a more robust and prevalent phenomenon. In the two hundred years since this first use of the word 'nationalism', this is still typically how political scientists understand how contemporary nationalism functions: as a predominant identity attachment shared by a group of individuals living in the same region or territory.

Despite the consensus on what nationalism means in terms of how it impacts the identity and selfhood of citizens, there are a plethora of theories on how to truly define the word nationalism, how it develops (or is developed), and how it is expressed over time. These debates take place mostly among academics—whose intention is generally to simply understand—and politicians—whose intention is to use this understanding to appeal to the people and to advance their agenda—but they also reach into literature and visual art, which I explore in the second part of this book. One of the leading academic scholars in the field, Benedict Anderson, wrote a book titled *Imagined Communities* in which he defines nationalism—as his book title suggests—as 'an imagined political community—and imagined as both inherently limited and sovereign' (Anderson 6). Anderson locates the rise of modern forms of nationalism as simultaneous with the rise of print capitalism, the novel, and the newspaper, arguing that 'these forms provided the technical means for "re-presenting" the kind of imagined community that is the nation' (Anderson 25). Indeed, the rise of print capitalism in the eighteenth century provided a new opportunity for those in power to disseminate identical information across entire nations. Where information had chiefly spread by word of mouth, now stories and ideas were received almost simultaneously and in identical form. When a population located within the same geographical area is reading the same texts, its people are inevitably tied together in new and significant ways, and this forms a basis for the 'imagined community'. It doesn't seem so special to us now that we might meet a stranger and share things in common—a TV show we watched, a book we read—but in those times, it must have been incredible to know that people you never met before had shared experiences from reading the same newspapers and books. Print capitalism, Anderson argues, was transformative in creating a people with shared ideas, experiences and beliefs, and thus a national community. Anderson's argument neatly corresponds with and affirms Barruel's statement in 1798 that nationalism 'took place of the general love'; for as print capitalism emerges, it forms invisible bonds throughout a politically bordered region which results in national identity becoming more important than other identity attachments.

Anderson's theory becomes even more persuasive when one considers how the definition of words related to nationalism have changed over time. For example, 'nationalist' appears in 1715 and 1716 as 'An adherent or advocate of a national church', but just over a century later in 1817 it reappears as 'A person considered as belonging to a particular nationality; a typical representative of a particular nationality' (*OED*). As I alluded above, religious attachment in England in particular was extremely important during the Reformation of the sixteenth century, and the violent struggle between Protestants and Catholics within its borders is a prime example of how national attachment—one's 'Englishness'—was considered less important than one's relationship to the Church. Anderson's theory suggests that as imagined communities began to form throughout the eighteenth century, while religion certainly did not disappear, a person introducing themselves might become more inclined to say that they were 'English' rather than 'Catholic'.

Unlike Anderson, some scholars focus less on the mechanisms through which modern nationalisms came to be, and more on how modern nationalisms are experienced. Jeremy Black states that 'Nationalism is a feeling as much as a principle' (Black 1), suggesting that there is something more emotional than logical about nationalism. Similarly, Tom Nairn suggests that ''Nationalism' is the pathology of modern developmental history, as inescapable as 'neurosis' in the individual, with much the same essential ambiguity attaching to it, a similar built-in capacity for descent into dementia, rooted in the dilemmas of helplessness thrust upon most of the world (the equivalent of infantilism for societies) and largely incurable' (qtd. in Anderson 5). Describing nationalism as being like a disease suggests that there is something irresistible and inescapable about it, as though it is a lifelong virus that flares up in the right environmental conditions—rather an apt description. In this definition, Nairn also touches on some of the key characteristics of modern nationalism: its 'ambiguity', its capacity to eradicate accurate historical knowledge ('descent into dementia'), and its inescapability ('largely incurable'). All three of these characteristics affect the experience of nationalism at both the collective national level, and at the individual level.

Despite the fact that scholarly analysis of nationalism is a fairly recent phenomenon (the majority of this work was carried out in the twentieth century) and often focuses on the world of nations since the seventeenth century at the earliest, many scholars use 'nationalism' to describe a phenomenon in England specifically that is purported to have existed for far longer. Eric Hobsbawm, for example, suggests that nationalism is a phenomenon that *can* exist in the absence of the modern nation-state and Anderson's print capitalism. He writes: 'nationalism comes before nations. Nations do not make states and nationalisms but the other way around' (Hobsbawm 10). Hobsbawm's argument here is a version of the chicken and the egg; in order to create a nation-state, one first requires a group of people (nationalists) to actively create, perform, and assert their collective identity as a nation. On this understanding, nationalism does not require a territory—and certainly does not require print capitalism and the novel—to be experienced, and therefore suggests that England could have been privy to the experience of nationalism long before the eighteenth century. Black similarly argues that England experienced nationalism long before other states, claiming that it met many of the modern conditions for nationalism discussed in scholarship: 'Nationalism is frequently discussed as a product of the last quarter-millennium...many characteristics of nationalism, including a collective name, shared history, a distinctive shared culture, an association with a specific territory, and a sense of solidarity, can be seen earlier, and certainly so with England' (Black 36). Black similarly undercuts Anderson's requirement for print capitalism and the novel, suggesting that 'A sense of national consciousness [in England] did not require mass support, nor indeed an audience' (Black 63). If this is true, then English nationalism might be an exceptional case of nationalism, where the desire to belong and co-exist with those who share your space, language, and, in many cases, ethnicity, came before a regional effort to convince people that they had such a desire.

However, even if both Hobsbawm and Black suggest that nationalism has been, and can be, experienced in England without modern innovations, they also both acknowledge the

11

problematic nature of the very term 'English nationalism'. England today is not, in actual fact, a sovereign state in its own right at all. English nationalism is a 'proto-nationalism...because there is currently no English state within the United Kingdom, which is the United Kingdom of Great Britain and Northern Ireland' (Black 1). Although what Black says is true, England has not always been a part of the United Kingdom. England was among the first nations to exist in its recognizable territorial form, emerging as a distinct kingdom even before the Norman conquest of 1066, and its long history provides it ample space to have developed some form of cohesive identity before the formation of the UK. Throughout the Middle Ages, particularly at the end of the Hundred Years' War, England was on track to develop a 'greater degree of national identity and uniformity' (Black 75) — a precursor perhaps to the form of nationalism rife during the rise of the British Empire, which I will discuss later. However, as early as the sixteenth century, under Tudor rule, England began to define itself through expansion across the island on which it lies. King Henry VIII (r. 1509–1547), who was partly Welsh-descended, sought to align the English and Welsh through the Laws in Wales Acts (1535, 1542), which politically incorporated Wales into the Kingdom of England. Notably, this law incorporated Wales into England, rather than merging them as equals. A unitary British kingdom — the beginning of the end for England as a self-contained nation — truly commenced with the Act of Union in 1707, whereby England joined with Scotland to create the Kingdom of Great Britain (of which Wales was automatically a part as well). Ireland, which is of course itself an island, was the last member of the current United Kingdom to join the conglomerate. In 1801, Ireland officially became a part of the United Kingdom, despite having been subject to English, and later British, monarchical rule for over 600 years. It was not until the Anglo-Irish Treaty of 1921, when the Irish Free State (which became the Republic of Ireland in 1949) broke away from the United Kingdom leaving Northern Ireland behind, that the United Kingdom of Great Britain and Northern Ireland was finally formed.

The English Case: Challenges to the Post-Empire Quest for Identity

So how can England, which no longer exists as a sovereign nation-state, but rather as a part of the larger polity of the UK, experience its own nationalism? And does Hobsbawm's suggestion that nationalisms precede nations make the case of English nationalism less confusing? Perhaps so, for if England has, for all intents and purposes, lost its nation-state, then the nationalist push to reclaim it seems extremely predictable. However, it was England that spearheaded the formation of the UK in the first place, arguably in an attempt to exert control over all the people and resources in its vicinity (or perhaps debate would be too generous). Furthermore, if nationalist movements tend to stem from a desire for national self-determination—a Wilsonian principle dating back to World War I—then the English case is even more confusing. England's lack of a sovereign nation-state does not mean that it lacks political power or necessarily self-determination. In fact, it continues to dominate politics across the entire UK, with the government operating out of Westminster in London, led by a prime minister who is typically—though not always—English. Anglo-centrism in the UK may in part be down to the fact that decision-making in many cases stems from Westminster, but it may also reflect the distribution of the population, as just under 84 per cent of the British population lives in England (*World Population Review*). Furthermore, in a table comparing the Aggregate Labour Productivity Index in different regions of the UK (excluding Northern Ireland) Christopher Rocks demonstrates that the average contribution of labour to the generation of goods and services, which is a major factor behind GDP per capita, is much higher than the rest of the UK (Rocks 7). With this unequal distribution of power in mind, if nationalist movements arise out of a desire to assert political independence and power, then neighbouring Scottish, Welsh, and Irish nationalisms, which are formed in opposition to an Anglo-centric framework of government, appear far more natural. The only convincing argument that England has somehow lost sovereignty as a result of UK politics is the West Lothian question, which is the argument over whether MPs from Scotland, Wales, and Northern Ireland should be able to vote in matters concerning only England when English MPs are unable to vote on exclusively Scottish, Welsh, and Northern Irish matters because they have their own regional assemblies.

Having said this, the paranoia and protectionist rhetoric emerging among English nationalists in recent years suggests that a more complicated explanation is required to fully understand what has triggered this surge of nationalism. One explanation is that Englishness has historically been formed in response to, and as a consequence of, international pressures, whether those be positive for the nation's status as a global power, as with the rise of the British Empire, or negative, as with the fall of Empire and the rise of insurgent Scottish, Welsh, and Irish nationalisms. In other words, Englishness is 'reliant on opposition to others' (Black 14). Although the rise of the British Empire was not a uniquely English pursuit, to the English, and indeed to many foreign nationals, 'England' and 'Britain' are often viewed as essentially coterminous (Black 83), meaning that both the fallen Empire and the geographical territory of the UK is often associated specifically with England as opposed to Scotland, Wales, or Northern Ireland. As Anthony Barnett points out in his book *The Lure of Greatness: England's Brexit and America's Trump*, even supposedly British newspapers demonstrate this bias; in February 2016 the Daily Mail printed a front page headline reading 'WHO WILL SPEAK FOR ENGLAND?', printing underneath: 'and, of course, by "England"...we mean the whole of the United Kingdom' (Barnett 114–115). The blurring between Englishness and Britishness further complicates conceptions of English nationalism. 'English' and 'British' becomes a hybrid, and 'British' seemingly excludes the Scot, Welsh, and Irish citizens it should represent.

One explanation for the hybridity of English and British nationalism, and thus for the root of contemporary Englishness, is that as the British Empire expanded and gained global power and significance, so did what Arthur Aughey calls English 'exceptionalism' (Aughey, *The Politics* 23). As Anglo-centric Britain became a global superpower, 'Englishness was of universal, not just local significance—an exemplary exception—and so did not have to adopt...cultural distinctiveness' (Aughey, *The Politics* 94). The notion of exceptionalism is significant because many modern nation-states have developed their nationalism in the post-colonial era as a way of redefining and reasserting themselves on the global stage, having previously been dominated by Britain and similar powers. England did not have to do this; it was never oppressed but was, rather, the oppressor, which meant that the only self-conceptualization it needed during the rise of Empire was to imagine itself as the superior nation. Indeed, the song 'Rule Britannia', a patriotic homage to Britain's military strength and exceptionalism, links 'national destiny, naval strength and personal liberty' (Black 8) and is still frequently played during events of national significance. Similarly, according to Jeremy Black, during the Victorian era 'Britain displayed attitudes of national uniqueness, nationalist self-confidence, and a xenophobic contempt for foreigners...seen as backward and illiberal' (Black 9–10). Though these Victorian attitudes were not directly related to Britain's military prowess, the notion of British exceptionalism, and therefore of Englishness as equivalent to greatness, was imagined in terms of English opposition to others—to other nations and superpowers, and to the 'backward and illiberal' people from across the Empire. The imagery of the uncivilized 'savage' comes to mind, conveniently placing England on an imagined pedestal of intellect and importance that only existed in the mind of the nation. Perhaps inevitably, a collective belief in British distinctiveness and exceptionalism did rise up and take root at the height of the British Empire, though many English people ironically thought of exceptionalism as a 'norm' (Aughey, *The Politics* 23), rather than something exclusive to England, perhaps unable to recognize their own privileged position in the global order. This made it all the more difficult, when the Empire fell, for England to define itself in a meaningful way. Still exceptional, but now in a problematic position, England was left entirely bereft of identity. Global power created an identity based on domination and unchecked power, so in the absence of Empire debate and confusion surrounding what it meant to be English *now* emerged—a question we are still struggling to answer.

Fast forward to the twentieth century as war grips Europe; the international landscape began to change drastically, forcing England into a new and profound experience of identity-based confusion. World War I initially seemed to bolster British global supremacy, but Britain also suffered tremendous loss of life and resources. World War II then constituted a major turning point for Britain. Despite demonstrably winning the war with the help of its allies, Britain suffered major economic and social trauma that drastically depleted its assets and capital. The year 1945 ushered in a concentrated period of decolonization as the British Empire began to steadily decline. At the same time, in a collective effort to prevent future world wars, countries throughout the world began to collaborate in liberal international projects whereby the creation of new institutions created a rules-based international order. The UK was a founding member of both the United Nations in 1945, and the

North Atlantic Treaty Organisation (NATO) in 1949, willingly placing itself in organizations where it was simply one nation among many. Meanwhile, Europe engaged in its own regional project named the European Coal and Steel Community (ECSC) (1951 Treaty of Paris), and had six member states: France, West Germany, Luxembourg, Belgium, Italy, and the Netherlands. The ECSC existed as a standalone entity until 1967, when the Treaty of Brussels led to the assimilation of the ECSC into the European Economic Community (EEC), which was established in 1957 by the Treaty of Rome. The six founding states of the ECSC were the same six states that belonged to the EEC, so even as the functions merged there was little change to the dynamic within the bloc. New members steadily began to join the EEC over the next half-century, but the European Union as we know it did not exist until 1993 and the Treaty of Maastricht.

Despite Winston Churchill leading the charge for a united European entity from the outset, even calling for the creation of a 'United States of Europe' in 1946, he never suggested that the UK would actually be a part of it. Churchill aligned the UK with the US and the USSR at the end of his speech: 'Great Britain, the British Commonwealth of Nations, mighty America — and, I trust, Soviet Russia, for then indeed all would be well — must be the friends and sponsors of the new Europe and must champion its right to live. Therefore I say to you "Let Europe arise"!' (Churchill, 'United States of Europe'). Here, Churchill places the UK and its Commonwealth on a pedestal with two other global superpowers and implies that the UK is somehow above entering into this European project — that it remained exceptional. Of course, the UK did join in 1973 under Edward Heath, proving this to be a rather aloof statement. However, it is absolutely true that unlike its European neighbours, the UK's entry into the EEC represented not a gaining of significance, but rather 'a contraction of power now that Britain, whose influence was spread across the globe, has returned to the condition of a medium-sized European power' (Aughey, *The Politics* 88). The UK entered based on the economic benefits that the EEC would offer them, and never strongly supported the aim of an 'ever closer union' that was enshrined in the Treaty of Rome in 1957 (Miller). Yet, the overwhelming sense that the UK (England in particular) had lost some of its exceptionalism in the global arena meant that almost immediately after it joined the EEC there was widespread angst about the European project. Importantly, the UK did manage to retain some facets of its own political and economic culture over time that other EU members have not—for example, the UK did not adopt the euro, instead keeping its own currency, the pound sterling. In this way, the UK (and by default England) did preserve some of its exceptionalism even as it entered the EEC on a supposedly level playing field. However, ultimately, the shift from global superpower to one-among-many powers proved to be a stressful transition in terms of defining Englishness in particular, since it had not only been the political powerhouse of the UK but of a large percentage of the Earth. As Fintan O'Toole points out, 'In reality, Britain went from being an imperial power to being a reasonably ordinary but privileged Western European country. In the apparition conjured by Brexit, it went straight from being the colonizer to being the colonized' (O'Toole 86). Indeed, the depletion of English influence within the EEC meant a collapsing of identity where identity traditionally meant global dominance. Although the void that was left may have been unnoticeable to many, it was undeniably present, and has driven anti-EU sentiment ever since.

Aside from membership of the EU, another more local threat to English national identity and exceptionalism has begun to emerge in the last 3 decades in particular: devolution of the United Kingdom itself. Scholars analysing the resurgence of English nationalism post-referendum have asserted that it is the insurgent nationalisms of neighbouring Ireland, Scotland,

and Wales that have truly driven contemporary versions of Englishness. Indeed, Jeremy Black argues that, 'nationalism, or at least a distinctive nationalism, has been precipitated, and, in part, forced upon England, by the development in the British Isles of strident nationalisms that have contested Britishness, and with much success. Irish nationalism was the first, but it was followed by those of Wales and, more prominently, Scotland' (Black 2). As Ireland, Scotland, and Wales engaged in their own attempts to reassert their identities—movements triggered by disillusionment with the Anglo-centric axis of power in Britain—the possibility that England's power could further diminish loomed large. This novel concern, as Aughey describes it, was 'not the end of empire but the end of the United Kingdom or the anxiety that, while the other nations are coming out from under the "safety blanket" of Britishness, the English will be smothered under its folds' (Aughey, *The Politics* 97). The growing strength of insurgent nationalisms within the UK was and remains a serious wake-up call for England; either it must follow suit and reassert a viable and cohesive version of its own identity, or it must be prepared to lose its last glimmer of exceptionalism on the international stage.

English nationalists' attempts to repatriate themselves with a lost English identity over the past 2 decades in particular have allowed for the introduction of new nationalist narratives into the mainstream political discourse. One such narrative is nostalgia—an appeal to a better, more glorious past. The word 'nostalgia' can be defined as both an individual and a collective experience—the latter being more relevant to the discussion of nationalism. The *OED* defines nostalgia as a 'sentimental imagining or evocation of a period of the past', or 'a collective term for things which evoke a former (remembered) era' (*OED*). In recent Western political rhetoric, the invocation of nostalgia has especially been used by xenophobic politicians and leaders to bolster their platforms. Donald Trump's slogan 'Make

America Great Again' is an invocation of past greatness that, regardless of whether that greatness ever existed as imagined, appealed to a large swathe of the country that felt left behind or angry with their current situations. The same was true of the Brexit referendum campaign slogan—'Take back control'— which implied that control had been not only lost but *taken* from the UK. The invocation of nostalgia is not a new political device, nor one exclusive to Britain. As David Lowenthal outlines:

> There always appears a time when 'folk did not feel fragmented, when doubt was either absent or patent, when thought fused with action, when aspiration achieved consummation, when life was wholehearted; in short, a past that was unified and comprehensible, unlike the incoherent, divided present'. The only thing missing in this past, of course, is its own nostalgia for an undivided, coherent past. (qtd. in Aughey, *The Politics* 83)

Indeed, the appeal to a 'great' past where one had 'control' suggests that the current political and economic situation— which is tremendously divided and divisive—is 'new' and can be reversed by imitating the world as it existed in the past—the opposite of what we would typically describe as progress. The greatest deception of nostalgia, as Lowenthal points out, is that every generation feels it; at no time in history has any nation or territory—England in particular—been completely at ease with itself and the state of the world in the contemporary moment.

Having said this, appeals to nostalgia are most successful when a significant percentage of the country feels disenfranchised by the current political environment, and when going back in time means returning to a period of greater stability and prosperity in their lives. Immediately following the Brexit referendum, three political scientists, Steven Winlow, Steve Hall, and James Treadwell, sought to understand how the Leave campaign was so successful in England in particular. They spoke with several fervent Brexit supporters—specifically those associating themselves with the English Defence League, a far-right political group that describes itself as having 'risen from the English working class to act, lead and inspire in the struggle against global Islamification', and 'respects English tradition' (*English Defence League*). The authors link the 'rise of the right'—the title of their book—to the 'palpable sense of lack' (Winlow, Hall, and Treadwell 2) being experienced by the people, and suggest that:

> many ordinary people...often see for themselves a life of unending struggle, a life in which the pleasures of community life have been withdrawn, a life of frustration, interrupted all too briefly by occasional flurries of consumerist hedonism. They can sense life only as a backward step, the loss of things deemed valuable and important. The benefits of our allegedly open, marketised society are the privileges of successful others. Those trapped in the lower echelons can see no forward step in their own lives. They are convinced that for them the best times have now been left behind. As a result of all this, a growing number of these people are now very angry. (Winlow, Hall, and Treadwell 3)

The anger described here is borne of individuals feeling marginalized and frustrated by the political and social environment in which they find themselves, and it explains, in part, why Leave was as successful as it was. Leave's campaign offered a change that Remain didn't and gave its supporters hope for a better future—one that could only be rediscovered by taking back control and returning to the 'glory days', pre-EU, when England truly was exceptional on the world stage.

While the political weaponization of economic lack was a key tactic that the Brexit campaign used to gain widespread support among the more rural areas of England, a more disturbing, yet related, tool was used as well: racism and xenophobia. Nigel Farage, leader of the UK Independence Party (UKIP), is often seen as the ringleader of xenophobic rhetoric during the campaign. He expertly tapped into existing fears of foreigners—of refugees, immigrants, and asylum seekers—and used them as scapegoats for many of the problems that white British people are faced with—for example unemployment and low income levels. In one instance, Farage used the side of a London bus to exhibit an image of hundreds of Middle Eastern asylum seekers waiting to enter the UK border, drawing on what was at the time an almost world-wide anxiety about the influx of Syrian refugees in particular, and suggesting that upon their inevitable arrival, they would steal jobs and services from the 'true' British people (see Appendix, Figure 1). Farage's rhetoric sparked vicious debate about race and ethnicity in the UK, and the kindling was especially flammable in England.

To understand the appeal of Farage's rhetoric, one must understand the historical place of racism within English and British nationalism. Often, nationalisms expressed in our contemporary moment are defined by a desire for a shared ethnic identity—a phenomenon unsurprisingly called ethnic nationalism. Ethnic nationalism is often viewed in opposition to civic nationalism, which holds that regardless of race or ethnicity, those who value the nation's institutions and civic life belong to it. England was initially built more on ideas of civic nationalism than on the idea of a single ethnic identity. The territorial space that constitutes the British Isles has been invaded several times, including by the Romans, the Vikings, the Normans, the French, and the Dutch. Over time, as new invasions brought new people, the population became significantly mixed and led to an amalgamation of ethnicities.

Interestingly, as recently as the eighteenth century 'the English were quite exceptional in boasting of their mongrel origins (Britons, Anglo-Saxons, Scandinavians, Normans, Scots, Irish, etc.)' (Hobsbawm 108). However, even if many did boast of the ethnically diverse origins of Britain, that is not to say that racism and xenophobia were entirely absent from political or everyday rhetoric. Daniel Defoe's satirical poem *The True-Born Englishman* that begins this chapter was written in 1701 to defend King William of England, who was from the Netherlands, against xenophobic attacks from his own people. The poem has gained significant popularity particularly in the past few decades for 'its exposure of the fallacies of racial prejudice' (Mutter) in England—the same racial prejudice that was incited for political gain during the Brexit campaign. Defoe's poem describes the process of ethnic amalgamation within Britain; from the Romans to the Normans, all have 'Blended with Britons' and produced the mixed generations to come. His defence of the foreign King amounts to the accusation that the 'vain ill-natured thing, an Englishman' despises the very 'amphibious ill-born mob' of which they are a direct result. The hyperbolic language he uses is both amusing and endearing. The reader is encouraged to feel kindly towards the 'bar'brous offspring left behind' and to laugh as we realize that Defoe's deep scepticism towards any definition of the 'true-born Englishman' lies in the fact that there is no such thing.

Having said all this, while frequent invasion did lead to a 'mongrel' nation, England was still predominantly white. Therefore, by the time national consciousness truly began to take hold in the eighteenth century, Englishness was—and still is—subconsciously synonymous with whiteness. When we think academically about the creation of the white subject, we often do so in an American context—a nation built on the foundations of white supremacy. However, quick to criticize the US, we often need to be reminded that the UK has also been built on a foundation of white supremacy, and in many ways is no different from the United States. Paul Gilroy's book *There*

Ain't No Black in the Union Jack published in 1987 did just that at a time when very few had the ears for what he had to say. He shed light on the attitudes towards race relations within the UK in the 1980s, and although in an introduction to the 2002 edition of the text he notes: 'Britain's black and other minority settlers still constitute a problem, but its dimensions have altered... "race" is rendered differently' (Gilroy xii), much of his original text remains deeply relevant in post-Brexit referendum Britain. Indeed, despite Gilroy's attempts to invite deep reflection and offer a newfound understanding of race relations in Britain, the topic remains an uncomfortable one for many. In his book *Natives: Race & Class in the Ruins of Empire* published in 2019, hip-hop artist, writer, educator and social entrepreneur Akala discusses how his own life has been shaped by race and class, and he too acknowledges the ongoing difficulties of discussing race in Britain. He writes:

> discussions about race in the UK are rather fascinating and often coloured by what I am going to call 'A Very British Brand of Racism'; polite denial, quiet amusement or outright outrage that one could dare to suggest that the mother of liberty is not a total meritocracy after all, that we too, like so many 'less-civilized' nations around the world, have a caste system. (Akala 23)

Akala's description of the Briton unable or unwilling to acknowledge the faults of the nation provides insight into why little has changed in the last 50 years. It is the resistance to discussions such as those led by Gilroy and Akala which allows racist discourse to continuously enter the mainstream narrative with little challenge, and which thus allows it to remain woven into the fabric of what it means to be British. In the wake of George Floyd's murder in Minnesota and the Black Lives Matter protests that erupted across the globe, white people in Britain have certainly become more aware that these conversations urgently need to be had, and many have become more open to having them. However, it still remains a deeply uncomfortable process for many people, and Akala's point about 'A Very British Brand of Racism' certainly still holds true.

Both Akala and Gilroy link the 'ruins of Empire' to modern manifestations of racism and reveal how the link between them perpetuates an Englishness rooted in whiteness. While Akala takes a more personal approach to his book, Gilroy focuses almost exclusively on the theorizing of racism and its place in Britain. He makes the case that the waning of Empire and racist discourse are interrelated phenomena—that the framing of Englishness as white is a way of maintaining the comfort of white Britons who have nowhere else to latch their national identity. In the introduction to his book, Gilroy writes: 'Britons have come to need "race". They may even rely upon its sham certainties as one way to keep their bearings in an increasingly confusing and vertiginous world' (Gilroy xxiii). Here, Gilroy reminds us that race is not a natural divider, but rather a social construct intentionally built to suppress one group and elevate another. To those already elevated equality feels less like raising up others and more like being pulled down themselves. It is exactly the same logic as is used to imagine that England has been dragged down by both loss of Empire and through its membership of the EU—an organization of equals. Once again, the overlap between a declining Empire and the lack of a cohesive English identity leads to an almost desperate and morally void quest to unify the nation. Gilroy later reiterates his point: 'The black presence is thus constructed as a problem or threat against which a homogenous, white, national "we" could be unified' (Gilroy 49). In other words, race is relied upon to maintain white English exceptionalism and superiority.

In Gilroy's introduction to the 2002 edition of *There Ain't No Black in the Union Jack*, he uses several examples of events occurring between the original publication and the newest version that reaffirm his original argument.

One that many will be familiar with is the murder of Stephen Lawrence. In 1993, Stephen Lawrence, a black teenager from Greenwich, London, was killed in an 'unprovoked attack by a gang of white youths', and the police response to the murder has been heavily criticized in the decades since ('Stephen Lawrence murder: A timeline of how the story unfolded'). In the 6 years after the attack, Stephen's murderers had been put on trial twice and were acquitted—first an investigation on behalf of the Crown prosecution fell through and then a trial took place in a private prosecution led by Stephen's parents which led to a not-guilty resolution. The government response was better—after the acquittal of Stephen's murderers the law of 'double jeopardy', which states that the same person cannot be tried for the same case twice (even if they confess after they are released), was repealed, which gave Stephen's family another chance to convict their son's killers. The then-Home Secretary Jack Straw also requested that the case be reinvestigated, and brought in judge Sir William Macpherson, who in 1999 published a 350-page report accusing the police of institutional racism preventing a fair inquiry. Still, it took until 2012 for just two of the five men implicated in the attack to be sentenced for Stephen's murder, and their sentence was only 15 years because although they were now adult men, they were tried as juveniles. Twenty-seven years on, the Metropolitan Police has suggested that all lines of inquiry have been exhausted, and now labels the case 'inactive' (Grierson). Just before referring to the Macpherson Report, Gilroy writes that 'intermittent racial tragedies' like Stephen Lawrence's death have 'become part of an eventful history' in Britain. He writes:

They punctuate the chronic boredom of national decline with a functional anguish that combines the psychological dynamics of denial and displacement. The loss of empire and the additional loss of certainty about the limits of racial identity in which it results, sustain people, providing them with both pleasure and distraction. (Gilroy xxiii)

In this frankly disturbing passage, Gilroy suggests that racist attacks in Britain function to allow white citizens to cling to the small sliver of exceptionalism and superiority that they imagine increasingly slips from their grasp. Before jumping to offence at the implications of this passage, it is important to note that Gilroy does not suggest that white Britons are revelling in racially-motivated tragedies such as this one. On the contrary, they are to most vile instances of bigotry that make us question the humanity of our fellow people. However, what he is suggesting is that on a much more subconscious level, racist attacks reinforce what many still feel is the order of our society—an order where whiteness is valued more than blackness. He goes on to write: 'The learned judge's well-publicized adjustments to the concept of institutional racism acknowledged that prejudice was present but emphasized the idea that it was unwitting', and 'provided a definition of what counted as racist that was so narrowly and tightly drawn that it excluded almost everybody and left the sources of these mysterious failures inaccessible to all but management consultants' (Gilroy xxiii). Here, Gilroy sheds light on how the way the word racism is used can shift public perception of a situation, or at least shift the blame in a tragedy such as this one. If the racism inherent in the trial of Stephen Lawrence's murderers can be 'unwitting' then it follows that racism is a subconscious aspect of Englishness and English systems.

Where overt and covert forms of racism remain prolific throughout the UK, so does the interrelated and widespread disdain for foreigners in general. In an eerily foreboding passage, Gilroy continues to link xenophobia with Britain's waning power, arguing that England's diminished relevance in the post-imperial era is often blamed on the arrival of foreign immigrants. While he remains focused on how blackness informs who is 'foreign', he writes that 'Alien groups' are:

> judged to be incompatible with authentic forms of Englishness (Lawrence, 1982). The obviousness of the differences they manifest in their cultural lives underlines the need to maintain strong and effective controls on who may enter Britain. The process of national decline is presented as coinciding with the dilution of a once homogenous and continuous national stock by alien strains. Alien cultures come to embody a threat which, in turn, invites the conclusion that national decline and weakness have been precipitated by the arrival of blacks. The operation of banning blacks, repatriating them to the places which are congruent with their ethnicity and culture, becomes doubly desirable. It assists in the process of making Britain great again and restores an ethnic symmetry to a world distorted by imperial adventure and migration. (Gilroy 46)

In this paragraph, one can hear the reverberations of Trump's call across the Atlantic to 'Make America Great Again', alongside the 'go back to where you came from' rhetoric instigated by the Leave campaign in 2016. That Gilroy wrote this in the early 1980s makes it frankly embarrassing that much of the Western World never saw the events of 2016 coming. The logic Gilroy outlines here, which resonates with many, was weaponized by the Leave campaign and applied to Eastern Europeans and all other immigrants who either look or sound different from what is imagined as quintessentially British. He says in a short passage what many struggle to say at all: that blackness and 'otherness' is often scapegoated for England's waning power and the failures of government and capitalism that leave people lacking in the first place. Whether it be within the UK, within the EU, or in the world at large, England's steady decline into a like-sized power is lamented by nationalists and regarded as the product of interference by the foreign 'other'.

The success of the Leave campaign is a harsh reminder that the work to disentangle racism and xenophobia from the political landscape of the UK and from Englishness in particular is far from over. While Farage and Johnson, who spearheaded the campaign, never explicitly took aim at the black citizens of the UK, the 'Take Back Control' mantra does effectively the same thing. As Gilroy writes, the decline of Empire is often associated with the arrival of blacks into Britain, and 'take back control' suggests that our imperial control has been stolen by them. While the bell has tolled on Brexit, learning from these expressions of nationalism allows a unique opportunity to do better. We certainly need new systems, leaders that seek to unite rather than to divide, and perhaps most of all, we need to unlearn the harmful lessons that seek to instil in us the belief that the British Empire was a time of greatness and global liberation. In a chapter of his book titled 'Empire and Slavery in the British Memory', Akala writes that 'The ability for collective, selective amnesia is nowhere better exemplified than in the manner that much of Britain has chosen to remember transatlantic slavery in particular, and the British Empire more generally' (Akala 126). Indeed, as he recalls the way his former teacher told him that William Wilberforce single-handedly brought down the transatlantic slave trade in Britain, Akala reminds us of those commonly touted slight un-truths that make the British feel better — we were the first ones to ban slavery after all! In a similar passage, Gilroy sums up what he sees as the problem with our collective memory. Referring to our continued admiration — our nostalgia — for Britain's triumphant victory in the Second World War and the era before the European Union, Gilroy writes:

the memory of World War II has been stretched so thin that

it cannot possibly accomplish all the important cultural work it is increasingly relied upon to do. A generation for whom knowledge of that conflict arrives on a long loop via Hollywood are nonetheless required to use a cheaply-manufactured surrogate memory of it as the favoured means to find and restore their ebbing sense of what it is to be English. Devolution and disintegration have intensified a nagging uncertainty as to the cultural content of national identity. Is it morris dancing or line dancing? Gosford Park, Finsbury Park or park and ride? The failure to just know or rather to just feel what that favoured filling should be, feeds the melancholic outlook which is compounded by the shrinkage of the national community and the disturbing news that the newly-devolved are evidently having a better time. (Gilroy xxv)

Gilroy's focus on historical representation in Hollywood demonstrates just how slippery our common understanding of English history is and can be. Learning about Britain's history through the filmic lens of heroic conflict frames it as a glorious era and shields us from the more unpleasant truths, including that without our American allies we would most likely have been defeated. By refusing to reckon with England's brutal history both within the UK and throughout the British Empire, politicians and citizens alike can remain fervently and unapologetically patriotic, and they absolve themselves from the duty of understanding the grievances of other people and nations. In this way, nostalgia in its modern form is not only a manipulative political device—it is also a cruel one that shrugs off the responsibility of helping those who feel disenfranchised, instead blaming forces outside of England's direct control. As with most things, the education that young people, and indeed adults, receive about the British Empire shapes how they are likely to view its decline. Resting on an imaginary pedestal of moral righteousness for banning slavery without considering how its aftershocks continue to affect the black British population is a masterclass in gaslighting and erasing history. It also explains how individuals like Nigel Farage are able to frame English nationalism as simultaneously white, virtuous, and still destined to be 'in control' — of itself at least, if it cannot be in control of others.

The obsession with control which I have discussed at length in relation to xenophobia is another distinct feature of contemporary Englishness, and the final one I will cover in this chapter. Throughout the Brexit campaign, the Leave campaign sought to persuade the population that British — meaning in this case English — culture and identity was in jeopardy because decision-making in Brussels sought to wash it out entirely. The liberal international project of the EU does of course mean answering to laws written outside the UK, but more than that it offers a new closeness (which is ideological but often perceived as geographical) between European countries that many feel entails stripping each nation of their individuality and creating one large, monolithic region. Of course, this is not only a European phenomenon, but a global one. Ironically, the British Empire played a central role in initiating the process of globalization, and yet there is deep dissatisfaction with its effects on the home nation. For a country that, God-like, sought to make others in its image, England has a hard time acknowledging that it has little about it that is unlike anywhere else.

There is a palpable sense that the cultural integrity of the nation is being lost at the hands of both supranational organizations and global corporations — a concern that predates the Brexit referendum campaign. In his book *Real England: The Battle Against the Bland* published in 2008, Paul Kingsnorth laments the 'totalitarian' (Kingsnorth 5) nature of the massive Bluewater shopping centre in Kent, suggesting that it represents the mass homogenization of English high streets—the crushing weight of capitalism that is literally levelling parts of the countryside to make way for new consumerist attractions. As the snowballing effects of globalization significantly change the English landscape, many seek affirmation of England's distinctiveness despite belonging to a global system, which the Leave campaign offered during the Brexit referendum.

Though each of the explanations for the resurgence of an English nationalism I have covered are convincing on their own, together they are deeply confusing, seemingly trying to work from two opposite perspectives: that of the dominator, and that of the dominated. In his book *Heroic Failure: Brexit and the Politics of Pain*, Fintan O'Toole straightforwardly explains how English nationalism is at its core an enigmatic project: working irreconcilably for both forms of modern nationalism. He suggests that the impulses and logic of contemporary English nationalism can only be explained by 'self-pity'. He writes:

Crudely, passionate nationalism has taken two agnostic forms. There is an imperial nationalism and an anti-imperial nationalism; one sets out to dominate the world, the other to throw off such dominance. The incoherence of the new English nationalism that lies behind Brexit is that it wants to be both simultaneously. On the one hand, Brexit is fuelled by fantasies of 'Empire 2.0', a reconstructed global mercantilist trading empire in which the old white colonies will be reconnected to the mother country. On the other, it is an insurgency and therefore needs to imagine that it is a revolt against intolerable oppression. It therefore requires both a sense of superiority and a sense of grievance. Self-pity is the only emotion that can bring them together. (O'Toole 3)

Here, O'Toole sums up what most have found nearly impossible to understand about English nationalism, and more broadly, a collective English identity. Englishness is problematic and troubling not because there is necessarily a total absence of identity—though the existing identity is not based on anything particularly convincing—but because it attempts to piece together two opposing impulses: dominance and liberation. England's privileged position within the UK remains intact, but the Brexit campaign convinced people that it was in jeopardy, and that England simultaneously needed to be liberated from the perceived domination of the EU. Although the contraction of power and the rise of new nationalist voices have certainly provided modern English identity with its fodder, the enigma of Englishness still cannot be pinned down, in part because England has managed to indulge itself in defeatism and exceptionalism simultaneously.

Chapter Two

The UK, the EU, and the Rise of Insurgent Nationalisms

England's position in relation to the rest of the world has historically shaped the nation's understanding of itself, and, as described in chapter one, as England's power has diminished, so has its national self-image. However, in order to understand the transformations that have destabilized and reshaped what it means to be English, it is vital to delve deeper into England's rocky relationships, both with its neighbours on the Continent, embodied through its relationship with the European Union, and with its neighbours within the United Kingdom. In this chapter, I will provide further context for how the UK arrived in its current situation, seek to explain the historical background that will inform much of the discussion in part two, and also set the scene for many of the literary texts covered in the second part of the book. I will explore the UK's relationship with the EU since Margaret Thatcher's prime ministerial term, devolution of power under Tony Blair, and David Cameron's role in holding a referendum that has changed the future of the UK. I will also look at the referendum campaign itself, to better understand not only why Leave captured the English vote, but how, and to demonstrate how powerfully divisive the Brexit referendum became over the course of 2 years—powerful enough to inspire a literary movement.

* * *

'A Stranger in Europe': The UK's Quest for Dominance in an Organization of Equals

As mentioned briefly in the previous chapter, the UK's

membership of the EU formally began in 1973 when it joined the EEC, which became known as the European Community (EC) in 1993. UK entry occurred just over 2 decades after the formation of the original ECSC in 1952, of which it was never a part, but a formal relationship between the UK and the six founding members was already developing over that time. When the UK originally declined to join the six founding members of the ECSC and EEC, the decision was made based on the idea that the UK approached politics differently from this newly forming community. Harold Macmillan, the Conservative UK prime minister from 1957–1963, wrote in his diary that it was the 'British "functional" versus the Continental "federal" approach' (Wall 1). There was also widespread consensus that the economy in the UK was strong enough that it didn't need assistance from a union of this sort, and so it remained adamantly out of the group. Stephen Wall suggests that it was only 'After the debacle of Suez in 1956' when 'our self-image of great power status could no longer be indulged' (Wall 2), and when the new EEC emerged with the Treaty of Rome in 1957, that the UK began to shift its attitude towards the supranational organization. Despite attempts to join the EEC throughout the 1960s, Britain was forced to pay for its ambivalence at the conception of the ECSC with two vetoes by France on EEC entry. It took until 1973 for the UK to gain ascension into the EEC bloc, and despite the political excitement of this new partnership, there was also a widespread view, spearheaded by the opposition leader at the time, Hugh Gaitskell, that Macmillan's decision to join 'was playing fast and loose with "a thousand years of history", a charge that resonates in Britain to this day' (Wall 3). Gaitskell's view that the UK was historically incompatible with the EU alludes to a deep-rooted concern that shifted into the foreground during the Brexit referendum: that the UK never belonged in a community of nations like the EU—one of power-sharing and interdependence. After all, the UK has always felt itself to be, as Arthur Aughey would say, exceptional.

After what Stephen Wall refers to as a 'brief honeymoon' (Wall 3), serious negotiations with the EEC began with the UK at the bargaining table. The UK was almost immediately wary of discussion surrounding major treaty changes, but their first major dissent emerged over the issue of the UK's financial contribution to the EC budget. The foundations of the agreement over financial contributions were already in place before the UK joined in 1973, which made it very difficult for it to influence proceedings. In 1969, the six original members had 'transformed EC financing into what is still known as the "own resources" system whereby the EC was funded by a mixture of levies and duties on imports into the Community' (Wall 4). British diplomat Sir Con O'Neill took immediate issue with the own resources system, suggesting that 'the levies we should pay on agricultural imports would be far higher than those paid by any other member', and that 'There was bound to be an equally profound bias against us on the expenditure side' (O'Neill qtd. in Wall 4). This was exacerbated by issues surrounding the Common Agricultural Policy instituted in 1962, which made it so that over half of the entire EEC budget was being directed into agriculture that was benefiting primarily French farmers at an additional cost to the UK. O'Neill's frustration at the apparent inequity of this arrangement even drove him to claim that France's veto of UK entry into the EU had been precisely so that France could develop financial terms 'favourable to her before Britain was in a position, as an EC member, to influence the outcome' (Wall 4). It was in this spirit of suspicion, and with this immediate conjecture that the UK would bear an unequal financial burden, that Britain's relationship with the EEC began.

As mentioned briefly in chapter one, the UK joined the EEC primarily because it offered them a strong economic opportunity. As Douglas Webber writes, 'the rationale advanced for [UK] accession was overwhelmingly economic—that membership would be good for the British economy and therefore for Britons' living standards. In contrast, the *political* case for European integration—that it promoted political stability and peace— was rarely made, leaving its EU membership vulnerable to a political backlash if its economic benefits failed to materialize' (Webber 184). At such an early stage it was of course unlikely that the UK economy would boom as a result of joining the EEC, but the lack of immediate results was initially worrying to those already unconvinced by this union. The turbulent beginning to the UK's relationship with the EEC caused much anxiety within British politics, and under Harold Wilson's Labour government in 1975, a referendum was held on EEC membership. It is notable that this first referendum was held under a Labour government; at this time most Euroscepticism came from the left-wing of British politics, while the Conservatives remained strong proponents of the EEC. The aim of the referendum was to gauge the public's support for EEC membership at a time when there was still widespread uncertainty about the project. The public voted overwhelmingly 'Yes' to remain a member of the EEC, the only exceptions being Shetland county and the Western Isles (Nelsson). England, among the four constituent parts of the UK, showed the most widespread support for remaining in the EEC, with the percentage of 'Yes' standing at between 60– 80 per cent across every constituency (*The Guardian*, 'How the regions voted in the referendum'). A *Guardian* report written in 1975 by Ian Aitken on the results of the referendum opened with: 'The champagne corks of the pro-Marketeers were still popping last night as Mr Wilson returned to Downing Street' (Aitken). Aitken suggests that the referendum was 'a unique and historic triumph for a Prime Minister who had secured the backing of the country over the heads of a majority in his own party. He celebrated it with a brief statement declaring the formal end of the 14-year controversy over Europe and calling on the anti-Marketeers to join wholeheartedly in working inside

Europe to solve the economic crisis' (Aitken). While Wilson's declaration of a 'formal end' to European controversy certainly seems premature, it is true that the overwhelming 'Yes' vote indicated that the UK, and England in particular, was united in its enthusiastic support for an ongoing partnership with Europe.

Despite the overwhelming result of the 1975 referendum vote and the UK's support of the EEC, the economic strain of membership began to take its toll in the late 1970s. When Margaret Thatcher became prime minister in 1979, 'budgetary inequity was becoming more pronounced. Britain was one of the poorer member states in terms of relative prosperity, but the second largest net contributor to the EC budget after West Germany, by far the Community's richest member' (Wall 5). Thatcher publicly dedicated herself to seeking a better deal for the UK, an undertaking that prime minister David Cameron would pick up 40 years later. At the Dublin European Council in 1979, after a series of proposals were made to alleviate the UK's financial burden, Thatcher made her infamous 'I want my money back' demand when she proclaimed that 'a series of ad hoc fixes would not be the answer', and told the press: 'I am only talking about our money, no one else's' (Thatcher qtd. in Wall 6). Thatcher's comment caused much anger among other members of the EEC who felt that Britain was already making self-serving demands on what was now an entire community's resources, and who worried that, should Britain get its way, they would ultimately lose out. Indeed, Thatcher's comment was an indication that the UK remained concerned exclusively with national self-interest from the outset and was never truly committed to establishing a federal political partnership with its European neighbours. However, the reaction of other members to Thatcher's demands also indicates that this suspicion worked both ways, and Europe has also always been wary of the UK, perhaps frustrated by demands that challenged the intention and direction of the EEC. Thatcher's demands—and their success—bolstered a British scepticism and resistance to the EEC that never completely dissipated; it may even have been the memory of Thatcher's economic negotiation that allowed the Leave campaign nearly 40 years later to so successfully mobilize support based on (false) claims about the profligate UK contribution to the EU budget.

The feud over the British contribution to the EEC budget continued over several years and intensified again in 1982 when Britain invoked the Luxembourg Compromise to challenge agricultural price fixing and further protect the UK economy while ensuring that UK contributions to the budget did not rise. The invocation was a failure and the UK's requests were rejected by other member states, which was met with more anger on the British side. The media reaction was more understanding of other members' behaviour: 'The Times saw the whole incident as "a gesture of exasperation at what our partners perceive as impossibly selfish and obstructive behaviour on Britain's part"' (Wall 14). The resistance with which both Britain and other member states engaged in these negotiations drove many more in the UK to doubt the entire project of the EEC. In 1983, foreign secretary Geoffrey Howe suggested that 'people are coming to see the Community as at best irrelevant and at worst obstructive to Europe's fundamental challenge to halt decline in its international competitiveness, to restore sustainable growth and to generate new employment' (Howe qtd. in Wall 28). Certainly, there was major concern that the project was running counter to Britain's national instinct to protect its own economy, and therefore that their membership within the organization was destined to fail.

As tensions over budget contribution continued to rise, the UK government did remain committed to the liberal international project that the EEC represented and continued to push for a successful compromise that would benefit the individual nation and be satisfactory for all other members. There were even marked attempts on the British side to push for a single-market European community that motioned towards the vision of the EU that first inspired the ECSC. Having said this, the priority was still the UK economy and what would most benefit the individual nation. Thatcher's government spent most of the 1980s fending off treaty changes and entirely new treaties that would have truly begun the process of creating a 'United States of Europe', blocking the path to an 'ever closer union' that went beyond linked economies.

Thatcher's sharpest derision of the EEC came in 1988, when at a commencement speech held at the College of Europe in Bruges, she said: 'We have not successfully rolled back the frontiers of the state in Britain, only to see them re-imposed at a European level with a European super-state exercising a new dominance from Brussels' (Thatcher qtd. in Wall 80). Thatcher overtly warns against a loss of control at the hands of the EU and expresses a clear concern that it could *be controlled* by forces outside of itself—a notion that was greatly unsettling to a nation so used to controlling others. This very fear of rule from Brussels also emerged as a key campaigning point of Leave throughout its Brexit campaign, demonstrating that the source of this sentiment dates back much further than many care to believe. Indeed, Douglas Webber ultimately roots today's continued Euroscepticism in Thatcher's prime ministerial term, suggesting that 'she played a key role in this period planting the seeds of Euroscepticism that would grow during the next 25 years to the point where this movement not only overwhelmed and destroyed the prime ministerships of her two Conservative successors, Major and Cameron, but also brought the UK to the brink of Brexit' (Webber 188). If this is true, then the foundations of the Brexit referendum were formed almost 40 years before the referendum vote happened.

A decade on in 1997, the UK government under Tony Blair made the controversial decision not to join the euro in the 'first wave' in 1999. The impression was, at first, that the UK would join later, once it had been assured that the move would benefit the UK economy and to allow a smoother transition into something as yet unknown. That process was analysed over the next few years through a series of tests, but even as preparations were made, by 2005 the British economy was performing much better than the eurozone economies, and the potential for success in a referendum on the euro was extremely low (Wall 171). As we know, the UK never relinquished its own currency—pound sterling—in favour of the euro, and this decision remains one of the starkest indicators that Britain saw itself as exceptional within the EU.

Blair furthered this message through his attempts to assert the British perspective on the Iraq War. While many other EU members remained strongly sceptical or vehemently opposed to military action in Iraq, Blair followed US president George W. Bush into combat. The decision to eschew the euro coupled with Blair's attitudes towards Iraq yet again emphasize how British interests and action have, for decades, been divergent from Europe's. Stephen Wall, a now-retired British diplomat who served as Britain's ambassador to Portugal and is also a former ambassador to the EU, describes Britain as 'A Stranger in Europe' in the title of his book, suggesting both that Britain was an imposter in the bloc from the outset, and that its relationship with the EU throughout its membership was fraught with difference. Certainly, the exceptionalism with which Thatcher and Blair conducted their politics with the EU shows marked attempts to protect British interests while performing dedication to European interests as a whole. The UK's focus on the economic benefits of the EEC meant that whenever the economic gain began to look weaker, the UK drew back and retreated into Euroscepticism. However, even though most of the UK's grievances with the EU were initially based on the economy, there was also a clear power dynamic threatening the relationship between the two. The struggle for pre-eminence and the UK's focus on individualism also points out a key aspect of Englishness: the apparent belief in their superiority over other countries. Evidently, such a belief precludes an ability to thrive in a system that places them on an equal level to others. It was perhaps for this reason that David Cameron's Thatcher-like promise to renegotiate the terms of EU membership for the UK in 2015 resonated particularly strongly in England. While his tactics paid off when he was re-elected, ultimately, his decision to call a referendum, assuming he did so hoping to echo Wilson's 'Yes' success in 1975, turned out to be a serious miscalculation.

* * *

Threats to a 'United' United Kingdom: Insurgent Nationalisms and Englishness

The English pursuit of dominance within the European project mirrors the Anglo-centric axis of power that has existed within the territorial UK for centuries. England's dominance has been established over centuries of oppressing its UK neighbours, and while there are more challenges than ever to that power, Anglo-centrism is so deeply ingrained in English society, and in the imagination of many outside the UK, that it cannot be overcome without serious upheaval. Just as whiteness in Britain is considered the 'norm' and blackness it's racial opposite, Englishness is the norm in the UK, while Scottishness, Irishness, and Welshness are peripheral regions and identities that are often depicted as existing in addition. At the time of writing, the Times' news app has specific sections for Scotland, Wales, and Ireland, but none for England; it is seemingly a given that when we read the first page of news it most likely relates to either issues that affect the entire UK, the world, or exclusively English affairs. Another, more cultural, example of Anglo-centrism is that when you meet an American and they exclaim over your 'British' accent, they mean your English accent. Scottish, Welsh, and Irish accents do not elicit the same response; they are seen as separate despite ostensibly being other examples of British accents. Of course, there is actually no such thing as a British accent because it changes so drastically depending on which nation (even region) of the UK you are in.

Alongside the issue of imbalanced governmental power, Anglo-centric subliminal messaging such as the example above has driven the recent insurgent nationalisms in Scotland, Wales, and Ireland that threaten to break up the UK. Calls for political or total independence in Scotland, Wales, and Ireland have been a central point of conflict and negotiation in Parliament for the last 50 years. During Tony Blair's prime ministerial term from 1997–2007, he attempted to quell this growing threat by offering a plan for political devolution throughout the UK. Blair intended to appease the growing desire for political autonomy in Scotland, Northern Ireland, and Wales that was being fuelled by nationalist political parties in each nation: Sinn Féin in Ireland, the Scottish National Party (SNP) in Scotland, and Plaid Cymru in Wales, and to secure the ongoing union of the UK. However, the plan carried out by Westminster ended up being a flawed attempt at power-sharing and has only led to even louder calls for independence. This conflict has only been exacerbated since the Brexit vote, in which voting patterns across the UK were starkly different across border lines. For the sake of concision about what is in reality a vastly complex set of relationships, this section will cover the insurgence of Scottish, Welsh, and Irish nationalism specifically in the last century, though it will focus primarily on the years since UK entry into the EEC (1973) and on the implications of Tony Blair's devolution promises since 1997.

Irish nationalism has been among the most fervent nationalisms in the UK over the last century, and has constituted a genuine threat to English people, and indeed Irish people, for almost all of that time. The Irish nationalist ambition is, in Arthur Aughey's words, 'to bring about the end of partition in Ireland' (Aughey, *Nationalism, Devolution* 129) meaning to reunite Northern Ireland with the Republic of Ireland. Since the Act of Union in 1801 that first officially bonded Ireland with the Kingdom of Great Britain, Tim Coogan suggests there has been 'a constitutional movement for the repeal of the Union and for Home Rule' (Coogan 4). This movement has been spearheaded by two groups in particular: the first is the Irish political party Sinn Féin (whose name means 'we ourselves' though it is often spoken as 'ourselves alone'), and the Irish Republican Army, commonly known as the IRA. While Sinn Féin were the parliamentary negotiators of the Home Rule movement, the IRA, an extremist organization with no elected political power, also affected policy-making through acts of terrorism — arguably even more so.

In fact, it was the actions of the IRA, not of Sinn Féin, that brought Irish nationalism to the forefront of the UK's mind, as its violent attacks on England in particular caused widespread fear and unrest. The IRA was founded in 1858 by James Stephens and Thomas Clarke Luby, following the suppression of an earlier revolutionary group (Coogan 11–12), and since 1903 it has undertaken several violent campaigns against both England and Northern Ireland. The first in England was the 'Dynamite campaign': 'a series of dynamitings carried out by young Irishmen throughout England for approximately two years beginning in 1903'. This was then followed by a bombing campaign in 1939 (Coogan 14–15). In 1969, what became known as 'the Troubles' officially began — a 3-decades-long conflict between nationalists and unionists spearheaded by the IRA. In July of 1972, the IRA bombed Belfast killing nine people and injuring 130, known as 'Bloody Friday' (*Boston Herald* 'What was the IRA?'), and in 1974 it bombed two pubs in Birmingham — one of which is recounted in Jonathan Coe's *The Rotters' Club*, which I will explore in the next chapter. Various ceasefires occurred during this period while the British government negotiated with the IRA, but it was not until 1998 and the 'Good Friday Agreement' (otherwise known as the Belfast Agreement) that the Troubles ended, and IRA violence finally ceased. In 2005, the IRA officially disbanded, but the legacy and trauma of its operations still linger in the relationship between Northern Ireland and the Republic of Ireland, and between Ireland and England. Evidently, the force of Irish nationalism has threatened England and Englishness for almost 100 years.

In Scotland, the nationalist movement has been around for centuries, and has sought to throw off English dominance since as early as the 1700s, most notably during the Jacobite rebellion and the Battle of Culloden in 1746. Today, Scottish nationalism strives for political devolution and, more recently, independence from the UK, and this movement has gathered both legitimacy and support extremely quickly since 1997 after Tony Blair made an election promise to introduce new plans for political devolution in all UK territories. Even before this point, Scottish attempts at devolution were supported by a majority of the population; a referendum in 1978 asking Scots to accept or reject the terms of The Scotland Act—a devolution bill—was successful by a 51.6 per cent majority (*BBC* 'The 1979 Referendums'). Later, while Blair put forth more plans for devolution, the desire for political autonomy within the UK slowly started to shift into a desire for independence from it altogether. The push for independence was led primarily by SNP leader Alex Salmond, who had significant support among voters who were distrustful of Blair after his decision to support George W. Bush in Iraq, and who was therefore able to take control of the Scottish Parliament in Holyrood, Edinburgh. While in power, Salmond laid the groundwork for a Scottish referendum on complete independence from the UK—a sign to Westminster and to England that devolution was not enough. The referendum was eventually held in 2014, 7 years after Blair left office, but the former prime minister continued to be involved in the debate despite his absence from government. Blair's tactics for dissuading Scots from voting in favour of independence focused (perhaps unsurprisingly) on the economic toll of that outcome. According to James Foley and Pete Ramand, 'Blair warned that independence would cost every Scottish family £5,000, an alarmist slice of fantasy arithmetic dreamed up by Whitehall officials' (Foley and Ramand 1). Blair's approach (alongside other campaigns carried out in support of UK unity) worked, and Scotland voted 'No' to independence, forcing Salmond out of office. This strategy was echoed by David Cameron in the lead-up to the Brexit referendum in 2016, when he warned that leaving the EU would cost the UK insurmountable amounts of money and plunge it into a recession. It's possible to speculate that Cameron's emphasis on economic scaremongering during the Brexit 'Remain' campaign was a result of the success of the economic perspective in Scotland in 2014, though if that is the case, the assumed similarity between the questions (and populations) at hand was sorely misjudged. According to Foley and Ramand, the Scottish independence referendum was Blair's doing: 'his major legacy was handing Scottish nationalists an indefinite right to govern Holyrood. Just as Thatcher's policies had produced devolution, so Blair's transformation of Labour produced 2014, perhaps the biggest threat to British statehood for generations' (Foley and Ramand 1). The symmetry cast here between Thatcher and Blair suggests a continuity between two prime ministers who, from across party lines, are both partially responsible for bringing the UK to the point of dissolution.

Turning finally to Wales; Welsh nationalism is arguably the most muted form of nationalism in the UK. Wales has been politically incorporated into England since the Laws in Wales Acts (1535, 1542), which extended England's legal systems and institutions across Wales. The long-standing political relationship between the two means that Welsh nationalism takes on a less violent, less urgent tone than Irish and Scottish nationalisms. Aside from simply being used to being incorporated into England, Wales is also culturally more similar to England—demonstrated most recently by its shared 'Leave' vote in the Brexit referendum. Until very recently, the vast majority of Welsh citizens have displayed an overt resistance to both devolution and independence. In his book *Nationalism, Devolution and the Challenge to the United Kingdom State*, Arthur Aughey writes that in 1973, the Royal Commission on the Constitution 'found that many of its witnesses thought Wales should continue to have a strong voice at Westminster. Equally, it found a deep anxiety that national identity was eroding because of policies which paid insufficient regard to Wales' (Aughey, *Nationalism, Devolution* 146). In 1979, after a bill on devolution in Wales was put forth by the UK government, Wales held a referendum, offering the opportunity to act on these anxieties. However, despite widespread concern that Welsh national identity was 'eroding', 'All eight counties in Wales voted no and by substantial margins' (Aughey, *Nationalism, Devolution* 146). According to Aughey, the results of the 1979 referendum suggested that the Welsh 'lacked confidence in each other' (Aughey, *Nationalism, Devolution* 147) and in their ability to govern themselves.

When Tony Blair's New Labour government reopened the discussion on devolution in 1997, there was a striking shift in Welsh attitudes towards embracing the opportunity to self-govern. Jonathan Bradbury suggests there were three reasons for this shift:

First, devolution offered itself as one way of realizing New Labour's concern for autonomy and responsibility within communities...Second, devolution was now more in tune with Welsh Labour sentiment...the Labour Party, perhaps even despite itself, had become a vehicle of local patriotism... Third, the Thatcherite programme of privatisation shifted the focus of Welsh politics from a concern to maintain an economy reliant on nationalised industries towards a need to attract inward investment...the imperative was to market Wales properly as an attractive nation/region within the European Union. (Bradbury qtd. in Aughey *Nationalism, Devolution* 147)

In Bradbury's analysis, Welsh nationalism was re-invigorated in the 1980s and 1990s during Margaret Thatcher, John Major, and Tony Blair's prime ministerial terms, and occurred in response to both growing alignment between Labour Party priorities in Wales and England, as well as the desire to become a more unique and distinctive country within the EU. While the nationalist movement did gain widespread support throughout Wales, unlike in Ireland and Scotland, it was 'more comfortable with the notion of devolution within the context of the UK' (Servini), and most of the population felt no strong desire to separate from the UK entirely. Devolution precipitated a resurgence and reinvigoration of Welsh nationalist sentiment that complicated the stability of the UK even more.

Ultimately, while devolution offered Northern Ireland, Scotland, and Wales greater opportunity to self-govern, anger surrounding the perpetual Anglo-centrism in the British government continues to fuel nationalist movements that seek total independence, and as a result, the dissolution of the UK. Foley and Ramand suggest that the intensity with which Scotland in particular—but I would argue also Ireland and Wales—have been seeking to assert their own identities, comes down to discontentment with the way that British politics is carried out, and the way that its power is portrayed. They write: 'British politics relies on an imaginary sense of power and purpose; but the reality often intrudes, exposing the shabbiness of Westminster's ambitions. When facts trespass on prevailing assumption, a crisis results; and UK politics faces crises on many fronts' (Foley and Ramand 16). Just as Aughey writes about English 'exceptionalism', here Foley and Ramand suggest that this exceptional idea is cast over Britain as a whole. However, they also remind us that the fractures within the UK paint a different picture; the three periphery nationalisms resemble each other closely in terms of their nationalist aspirations, while England remains an anomaly. While Irish, Scottish, and Welsh nationalisms seek to affirm their right to rule themselves, English nationalism seeks to maintain its right to rule them. Foley and Ramand go on to suggest that 'for the most powerful states, nationalism affirms their right to rule' (Foley and Ramand 17). It is this distinction that explains the nationalist projects in all four corners of the UK—the centre struggles to retain its power while the periphery seeks to escape from under it, and it is the threat of a disunited kingdom that explains, in large part, why discussions surrounding Englishness have been re-invigorated with such vigour over the last 2 decades since Tony Blair's devolution plans began.

* * *

David Cameron and the Brexit Referendum of 2016

The combined result of the UK's fraught relationship with the EU and the impact of devolution on the rise of insurgent nationalisms within the UK provides a convincing, though no doubt simplified, explanation for how Brexit came to be. Indeed, it was not until David Cameron promised a referendum vote on membership of the EU in the Conservative Party manifesto in April 2015 that the opportunity to turn these underlying feelings into action truly arose. At the time, the promise of holding a referendum was glossed over by the media, appearing last in a *BBC News* list of 'Key Messages' ('Election 2015: Conservative manifesto at-a-glance') and next to last in a *Guardian* article that also offered a summary of the manifesto (Perraudin). Despite the referendum being a key element of his political platform, Cameron spoke little of it throughout his campaign. Rather, he used this promise to quietly draw in voters, and members of his own party, who had always been sceptical of the EU. Pauline Schnapper writes that during Cameron's 2015 re-election campaign, Europe was 'The Elephant in the Room' in an essay of the same title. She predicted that debates about Europe would dominate the political discussion in the lead-up to a referendum, and argues that the inclusion of a referendum in Cameron's manifesto was the result of a 10-year attempt to 'please the growing number of Eurosceptics in his party'. Schnapper goes on to recount his previous attempts to do so:

> When the Lisbon treaty was signed by the Brown government in 2007, he had demanded a referendum and when this proposal was turned down, William Hague, the shadow Foreign Secretary, promised 'not to let matters rest there', although what he meant by this exactly was never clarified. Indeed, Cameron abandoned the pledge when the Lisbon treaty was ratified by all other member states, much to the dismay of his radical Eurosceptic backbenchers. He was therefore already on the defensive when he pledged in the 2010 manifesto to introduce a bill in Parliament which would require any new transfer of power to Brussels to be subject to a referendum. The party would also campaign for a repatriation of powers to the national level in three areas: the Charter of Fundamental Rights, criminal justice and social legislation. (Schnapper 2)

Schnapper argues here that Cameron's decision to offer an EU referendum was a politically motivated attempt to unite the Conservative Party around his leadership after several failed attempts to appease those who belonged to the Eurosceptic wing during his first prime ministerial term. She suggests that Cameron's re-election promise was driven less by a genuine desire to unite the UK and affirm its membership to a liberal international organization that he believed in, and more by a desire to maintain his position, though of course he and most of the country never imagined that such a referendum would ever end the way that it did.

Indeed, Schnapper's analysis raises serious questions; although the offer of an EU referendum may have made political sense for Cameron as leader of a party with a Eurosceptic wing, what is not so easily explained is how he could justify putting the future of the country on the line for a predominantly self-serving purpose. In the wake of Brexit and even now, Cameron is continuously and harshly criticized for so willingly offering a vote and giving voice to a wing of his party that he did not belong to—a voice that resonated with England far more strongly than Cameron and his cabinet anticipated. In the abstract of her essay, Pauline Schnapper goes further than to say that Cameron was unprepared, suggesting that 'it was not in the *interest* of either the Conservatives, Labour or the Liberal Democrats to make much use of the issue', which essentially meant they were 'leaving it to [UKIP] and, to a certain extent the SNP' (Schnapper 1, emphasis mine) to control the conversation. As Schnapper suggests, Cameron's decision not to discuss Europe and an EU referendum at length in the lead-up to the 2015 general election left a gaping hole that was filled by UKIP, a party that exists for the sole purpose of removing the UK from the EU, providing them with an unparalleled opportunity to assert their version of British (English) nationalism. Yet even with this unprecedented platform to promote their political agenda, those who most vehemently rallied for Brexit—notably Nigel Farage, the leader of UKIP, and Boris Johnson, who became the Conservative prime minister in July 2019, seemed to have no solid plans for what would happen if the vote delivered a Leave majority.

Although the platform that UKIP was handed during the Brexit referendum campaign was indeed unprecedented, the party has been a steadily growing force in British politics since its inception in 1993. The party's primary — and arguably only — political message lies in its opposition to the Maastricht treaty, and its desire to take the UK out of the EU. Even before there was an opportunity to make this happen, UKIP's popularity was on the rise. A *BBC News* article written by Alex Hunt in 2014 titled 'UKIP: The story of the UK Independence Party's rise' suggests that leader Nigel Farage 'seems to have struck a chord with disenchanted voters' (Hunt). He writes that by 2013, 'UKIP, rather than Westminster's official Labour opposition, seemed to have become the party of choice for the anti-government vote and the anti-politics vote' (Hunt). Since there was no impending referendum in 2014 to explain the trend towards UKIP votes, the reasons for UKIP's growing popularity at this stage was likely more closely tied to anti-establishment sentiment and a feeling of disenfranchisement that had been spreading since the 2008 economic crash. This is an especially convincing explanation given that after the 2008 crash, UKIP membership soared from 14,630 in 2008 to 32,447 in 2013 (Hunt).

The link between UKIP votes and the struggling economy is in fact reflected in UKIP's logo, which depicts the name of the party as the strike through the symbol for the British pound — the monetary symbol a promise of greater wealth and prosperity. Other logos include the word 'UKIP' appearing to the left of a lion roaring — a symbol that appears strikingly similar to the lion that represents Premier League football. The imagery used by UKIP began to catch the eye of voters who were frustrated with the narrow political sphere dominated by the Conservatives, Labour, and to an extent the Liberal Democrats, which for many represented the maintenance of a status quo that did not serve them.

Despite this gradual surge in popularity, UKIP never truly

held any political power in Westminster. They have only ever held two elected seats in Westminster (both won at by-elections in 2014), and none at all since 2017. Having said this, they have had better representation in the European Parliament as Members of European Parliament (MEPs), holding 24 out of 73 UK seats in 2014, beating both the Conservatives and Labour (TLDR News). When David Cameron was re-elected in 2015 and preparations for an EU referendum began, UKIP was able to fully mobilize, offering the first legitimate opportunity to not only protest the EU, but to take the UK out of it.

UKIP channelled frustration with the UK government towards Brussels and the EU, arguing that current problems stemmed from the UK's membership in a supranational organization. As I briefly covered in the previous chapter, under Farage's leadership, the party achieved this in a few ways. Firstly, Farage teamed up with the former Mayor of London Boris Johnson (Conservative) to spearhead the Leave campaign, which lent political legitimacy to him where he had previously had no stable power. In 2010 the Conservative Party pledge promised to reduce immigration to the tens of thousands, but in 2015, the migration level was recorded at 330,000 by the Office for National Statistics. Although the UK was never part of the Schengen area—the zone that allows the free movement of people across national borders in Europe—EU citizens were able to live and work in the UK, just as UK residents could live and work in any other member country. The UK had also been one of the only EU countries to accept Eastern European immigrants after many of the former-Communist countries joined the EU in 2004, which was the largest wave of immigration in its recent history (Warrell) and this raised questions surrounding how that surge would impact UK wages and employment prospects. Farage used concerns about lack of employment and the strain on social services such as the NHS and education to suggest that voting Leave would be a sure way to prevent such high levels of immigration from happening again—by 'Taking Back Control' of UK borders. He also claimed that Turkey was joining the EU (Stewart and Mason) (even though this was untrue) to incite fear over another immigration wave—now especially targeted towards the Middle East, inciting more xenophobia and, more specifically, Islamophobia as well. Further reinforcing the idea that the EU was draining the UK of its ability to care for its own people, the Leave campaign plastered the side of a red bus with the slogan 'We send the EU £350 million a week...let's fund our NHS instead' (see Appendix, Figure 2). Although this figure has since been contested for accuracy, the bus was a key focus of the campaign, garnering widespread media attention and inspiring many to be optimistic about the possibilities for life outside of the EU. During this intense and concentrated period of campaigning for Leave, quiet, latent Eurosceptics began to more firmly position themselves against the EU, and many more were newly convinced that the UK would be better off without it. While Cameron remained primarily silent or on the defensive, UKIP aided by Johnson, slowly but surely took control of the conversation on Brexit.

Over the course of the campaign, the political atmosphere throughout Britain started to become more toxic and threatening. As stakes rose, which side of the referendum one supported became not only a point of political difference, but of personal difference, and the UK became increasingly polarized. While the starkest indicator of the polarization felt among citizens is the 41 per cent increase in reported hate crimes after the Brexit referendum was held ('Race and religious hate crimes rose 41% after EU vote'), during the campaign itself there were also clear signs of an emerging divide. On June 16, 2016, exactly one week before the referendum was held, Yorkshire MP Jo Cox was brutally murdered by a man named Thomas Mair, a white supremacist and Nazi sympathizer. Cox was targeted for her support of the campaign to remain in the EU, and the attack was carried out as she was on her way to a public library to hold a surgery[1] for her constituents. Mair shot her before dragging her into the street where he repeatedly stabbed her and a 77-year-old man who attempted to intervene (Cobain, Parveen, and Taylor). According to eyewitnesses, as he carried out the murder Mair muttered: 'Britain first, keep Britain independent, Britain will always come first', before finally yelling 'This is for Britain' (Cobain, Parveen, and Taylor). This sickening act of terror revealed the way that the EU referendum had incited far-right extremism—not only empowering Eurosceptics, but also racist, white-supremacist factions and individuals across the UK. That the attack took place in Yorkshire—a Brexit hotspot—also demonstrates that the divide was felt most strongly in Leave epicentres. Indeed, England and Wales, where Leave won the majority, saw the sharpest increase in hate crimes post-Brexit referendum as opposed to Scotland and Northern Ireland who voted to remain ('Brexit "major influence" in racism and hate crime rise'). The polarizing effects of the EU referendum campaign empowered far-right movements that had lain simmering just under the radar and unleashed a torrent of hatred and violence from which the UK has yet to recover. Having won the battle to control the rhetoric surrounding Brexit, the Leave campaign's success was consolidated by a 52 per cent Leave vote on June 23, 2016.

* * *

Post-Referendum Britain: Uncertainty Looms

In my own personal experience, the aftershock of the referendum was tangible in the atmosphere of England in late June 2016. I felt a sense of overwhelming silence and reflection on what had just happened, which was then consequently overwhelmed by a seething sense of disappointment, then anger, and confusion on both sides. The unpreparedness of the government to tackle a successful Leave vote was a potent indication that there were two divergent understandings of Englishness—one portrayed by Cameron and his confidence in the UK's progressive attitude towards international institutions, and the other portrayed by Nigel Farage and his Eurosceptic, isolationist, and xenophobic rhetoric. Cameron, and indeed most of the UK's politicians and people, was unable to recognize the strength of the latter's resonance in England, suggesting that Brexit revealed features of Englishness that had laid dormant—features which many people had never fully confronted.

Given the difference in voting across the UK, the Brexit vote has also reignited debates surrounding Scottish independence in particular, while the debacle over how the border between Northern Ireland and the Republic of Ireland would be affected by Brexit has led to a greater resurgence of Irish nationalist sentiment as well. Although Wales also voted to leave the EU by a slim majority, independence debates are unsurprisingly having ripple effects there too, as the prospect of the disintegration of the UK seems to become an increasing possibility. SNP Leader and First Minister of Scotland Nicola Sturgeon has already requested another Scottish independence referendum, claiming that Brexit provides new grounds for independence that the Scottish people should have the opportunity to vote on. Prime Minister Boris Johnson has rejected that request, suggesting that the recent 2014 referendum renders it unnecessary. Of course, there is also the possibility that Johnson denied Sturgeon's request because he fears that she was right and, this time, Scotland might actually vote 'Yes'.

After David Cameron officially gave notice of his resignation— the exact response to a Leave vote he had previously claimed he would never give—the situation became even more complicated. Theresa May replaced Cameron as prime minister on July 19, 2016, promising to deliver Brexit under 'strong and stable leadership' despite having been on the side of Remain in the lead-up to the referendum. Luke McGee of CNN suggests that May was able to become prime minister because: 'She backed Remain, but her track record in the Home Office meant she was tough enough to stand up to the EU. She was the best candidate to unite two sides of the Conservative Party that voted for different things' (McGee). Indeed, although May's message was intended to provide composure to the Brexit proceedings, she was ultimately unable to live up to these expectations. In June 2017, less than a year after entering office, May called for a snap election to increase her parliamentary majority, which would allow her to push through her Brexit plans with ease (McGee). However, instead of gaining a larger majority, May lost her majority altogether, creating even greater challenges for securing the Brexit she wanted. Creating a confidence and supply agreement with the Northern Irish Democratic Unionist Party, May was able to 'prop up her minority government', and she continued to negotiate with the EU, during which time her negotiating position weakened (McGee). When an agreement was reached between May and the EU, her proposal was put to the House of Commons three times. Each time, it was rejected, leading to a state of political deadlock. Meanwhile, as May continued to push for her deal to be passed, the EU allowed the official date for Brexit to be pushed back multiple times to allow the prime minister time to unite her parliament. This not only created an atmosphere of frustration within the government, but across the UK as well. While many remained vehemently opposed to Brexit going forward at all, voters from both sides became gradually more frustrated, exhaustedly waiting for something to actually happen. Suddenly, the uncertainty of how and when Brexit might happen, for many, seemed worse than the prospect of it happening. In her final push to pass a deal, May told her party that if they backed her deal, she would resign as prime minister, allowing someone else to carry her work forward. Even though May had lost the confidence of her party and her cabinet, even this did not work, and May resigned in July 2019 without delivering Brexit.

The UK now has yet another new prime minister, Boris Johnson, a key figure of the Leave campaign from the outset. Although he is often derided for his scruffy appearance and remains severely unpopular among many Remainers, he has managed to successfully deliver a Brexit deal—the first Conservative leader in 4 years to live up to his own promise to 'Get Brexit Done'. Johnson entered office through a Conservative leadership contest, i.e., he was not voted in by the general public. Although he managed to secure a Brexit deal in October 2019, like May, Johnson's deal was rejected by Parliament, and he also triggered a general election in an attempt to prevent further deadlock and ensure that the UK left the EU by January 2020. The general election took place on December 12, 2019, and it proved to be one of the most remarkable votes in recent British political history. The Conservative Party under Johnson won 365 seats—47 more than they previously had ('UK results: Conservatives win majority'). Almost the entirety of England voted blue, i.e., Conservative, with the notable exception of London. These results were extraordinary because many constituencies which are historically red—i.e., who have consistently voted Labour for decades—switched to support Johnson, suggesting either that Brexit had become essentially the only policy that constituents were interested in, or that they were voting against a Labour government with Jeremy Corbyn at the helm. London remained the exception; many Londoners voted Labour, perhaps because Jeremy Corbyn promised to offer the chance for another referendum—a promise that may have proven difficult to keep. The rest of the UK was split; Scotland voted overwhelmingly for the SNP—an indication that the Scots are more interested than ever in independence, while Northern Ireland was split between Sinn Féin and the Democratic Unionist Party (DUP). Wales, too, was split between the Conservatives and Plaid Cymru—the Welsh national party. Though the general election results consolidated Johnson's position as PM and allowed him to successfully deliver Brexit in January 2020, they also suggest an even greater political divide is emerging throughout the UK along national lines—one that may see the union break apart for good.

The 5 years since the promise of a Brexit referendum have been filled with uncertainty and chaos. The shocking events that both led up to and proceeded the 2016 referendum have driven the people of the UK to re-evaluate their own identities and relationships to the world, as well as their relationship to their, for now, united kingdom. England, with its majority Leave vote, has revealed that its identity is steeped in a desire for and belief in its power and control, and that it feels aggrieved in a European organization of equals. To many, Englishness now appears to stand in opposition to the direction the world is heading in—towards increasing interconnectedness. Yet, it is also apparent that this identity is not felt unanimously, and that for many English people, Brexit has been a horrifying ordeal. In the literary world, England's struggle for identity has been a theme for decades—centuries even—but the unique and concentrated upheaval of Brexit has inspired a new literary movement that is essential for understanding how that identity continues to be shaped today. In part 2 of this book, I will move on to discuss both literature published before the 2016 referendum and the 'BrexLit' published afterwards, in order to demonstrate how literature contends with the remarkable problem of Englishness.

* * *

Endnote

1 In British politics, a 'surgery' is a 'session at which a Member of Parliament, local councilor, etc., is available to be consulted locally by his constituents, usually on regular occasions' (*OED*).

PART TWO

Chapter Three

Pre-Brexit Referendum Literature: Problematizing Englishness

As the poem that begins this book—*The True-Born Englishman* by Daniel Defoe—demonstrates, literature has often functioned as a means of understanding and responding to polemical debates surrounding English nationalism, and as a medium through which to reflect on the nature of English identity. In his book *Literary Englands*, David Gervais suggests that 'In our time "Englishness" has become a theme for speculation rather than dogma; twentieth-century writers have found it an elusive and ambivalent concept' (Gervais iii). Indeed, in post-referendum Britain as new theories and ideas surrounding Englishness emerge, an abundance of literary material has been published that considers both the reasons for and the implications of the Brexit referendum—a literary movement the *Financial Times* dubbed 'BrexLit'. These literary texts, alongside several published before the Brexit referendum, provide useful insights into the condition of Englishness as experienced in the immediate lived moment. The speed with which most BrexLit novels were published also attests to this. These are not just works of fiction; they are documents of history.

One cannot understand David Cameron's call for a referendum and the outcome in 2016 without considering the historical tensions between Britain and the EU, nor can we understand the marked difference between how the English voted compared with their UK neighbours without understanding the rise of insurgent nationalisms and their historical precedent. In the same way, one cannot understand BrexLit without first understanding the literary stage onto which it walks post-referendum in 2016. Of course, literature that grapples with Englishness pre-Brexit is incredibly extensive, and I could not hope to deal with all of it comprehensively. I have chosen to consider three works that best represent the pursuit and formation of an English identity at the turn of the twenty-first century. They are as follows in the order they appear in the chapter: *England, England*, a novel by Julian Barnes, *The Rotters' Club*, a novel by Jonathan Coe, and *Jerusalem*, a play by Jez Butterworth. These texts are all renowned for their representations of modern-day England and Britain and provide vital insight into how Englishness is portrayed in literary texts in the 2 decades leading up to the Brexit referendum. The contemporary nature of the works is deliberate and intends to provide relevant context for discussions surrounding Englishness today. They will each serve to ground the forthcoming BrexLit conversation and demonstrate how the referendum altered—or didn't alter—portrayals of Englishness in literature.

* * *

Julian Barnes' *England, England*: Creating England's 'Tourist Mecca'

Julian Barnes' *England, England* was published in 1998, 18 years prior to the Brexit referendum, but this novel is extremely valuable, and almost prophetic, in its engagement with Englishness, isolationism, and the invocation of history and myths as a tool of manipulation, making it central to the BrexLit discussion. In Barnes' own words, *England, England* is 'about the idea of England, authenticity and the search for truth, the invention of tradition, and the way in which we forget our own past' (Barnes, *Conversations* 27). Certainly, the novel explores how English identity and ideas about England are formed. Whether intentional or not, Barnes achieves this in a manner that can be explained by Jean Baudrillard's theory of simulation, which is laid out in his theoretical text *Simulation and Simulacra.* Throughout *England, England,* the protagonists Sir Jack Pitman and Martha Cochrane, along with their colleagues, realize a collective vision of building a new and improved England on the Isle of Wight, which incorporates only the 'best', most quintessential symbols associated with England and Englishness: a theme park that they call 'England, England'. The name of the theme park simply being a repetition conveys a newness yet retains the original connotations of the land that it is based upon. By creating this theme park, they simulate that original land — which comes to be known as 'Old England' — but as Barnes describes and Baudrillard's theory will explain, the 'fake' England produces the same symptoms of nationalism as the 'real' one and therefore the difference between the theme park and what it intends to simulate becomes murky. Over the course of the novel, the island becomes a destination for tourists to experience England as they believe and *want* it to be, and England, England slowly becomes indistinguishable from the real thing. Though the beliefs and desires that it satisfies are steeped in fiction and myth, by the end of the novel, the simulation that recreates England, which is based on myth and falsehood, 'threatens the difference between the "true" and the "false", the "real" and the "imaginary"' (Baudrillard 4). That is to say one finds it difficult if not impossible to discern what is real and what is simulated — what Baudrillard refers to as a consequence of the 'hyperreal' (4) world that we live in (which I will return to later). In this way, despite its overt disruption of historical accuracy and the incorporation of fiction into the island, England, England cannot be easily labelled as a pretence. The theme park both satisfies desirable beliefs about what England and Englishness looks like while simultaneously challenging the difference between the 'real' England and the theme park version. All of this offers Barnes a unique opportunity to examine how English identity is formed, how tradition is invented, and how a nation, and the world, can be fooled into forgetting its 'true' past.

Before considering the text itself, it is vital to understand the context in which this novel was published. As discussed in part one, contemporary English nationalism has been forcefully activated in response to the threat of insurgent nationalisms within the UK and the retraction of England's global significance and power. When Barnes was writing *England, England*, Scotland had just had a successful referendum vote on devolution, meaning that for the first time since 1707, there would be a Scottish parliament that could make decisions away from Westminster (albeit only in areas not specifically reserved to Westminster). The vote sent a message to England that Scotland remained a distinct entity—in other words, it reminded people that Scottish nationalism still exists, and that it continues to push back against an Anglo-centric British government. In his recent book *English Nationalism: A Short History,* Jeremy Black suggests that it is the very rise of insurgent nationalisms around the UK—in Northern Ireland, Wales, and Scotland—that 'precipitated, and, in part, forced upon England' (Black 2) the need to define their own national identity. Given that Barnes' novel depicts an Englishness that firmly rejects its UK neighbours and appeals to instinctual touchstones of English identity that are often based on myth, *England, England* can also be read as a direct reaction to the phenomenon Black describes. Barnes' response is to satirize the inclination to define Englishness in isolation from its United Kingdom neighbours, and to deeply criticize the supposedly desirable form of Englishness that England, England represents. Yet, as mentioned above, while this satire reveals how identity can be constructed based on falsehood and myth, the simulation of England, England has more menacing implications when the simulation becomes indistinguishable from the truth.

Sir Jack's decision to build England, England in the form of a theme park crucially informs our reading of how it achieves both popularity and legitimacy in the world of the novel. The theme park is an attempt to simulate reality within a space that is, by definition, thematic and fantastical in its representation. To explain his theory of the simulacrum, Jean Baudrillard draws on the real-world example of Disneyland, which is also, of course, a theme park. He writes: 'It is first of all a play of illusions and phantasms: the Pirates, the Frontier, the Future World, etc. This imaginary world is supposed to ensure the success of the operation. But what attracts the crowds the most is without a doubt the social microcosm, the religious, miniaturized pleasure of real America, of its constraints and joys' (10). What Baudrillard means is not that Disneyland attempts to reconstruct American society accurately within its walls. Rather, he suggests that the theme park conceals 'a simulation of the third order' (10), and that it becomes a microcosm of joy which we are supposed to believe reflects the whole. Baudrillard goes on:

> Disneyland exists in order to hide that it is the 'real' country, all of 'real' America that is Disneyland (a bit like prisons are there to hide that it is the social in its entirety, in its banal omnipresence, that is carceral). Disneyland is presented as imaginary in order to make us believe that the rest is real, whereas all of Los Angeles and the America that surrounds it are no longer real but belong to the hyperreal order and to the order of simulation. (10)

What Baudrillard says, in essence, is that the society we live in is 'hyperreal', which is to say that we are no longer able to distinguish reality from simulation in the every day. He argues that Disneyland (among other places and events that take place in our world) is something that we affirm is 'imaginary' so that we can also affirm that the world we live in—i.e. the spaces anywhere outside of Disneyland, are indeed real and concrete. This layered approach to reading the world reinforces the threat of being unable to distinguish between the 'real' and the 'false'. In the case of England, England, Sir Jack and his colleagues dream up an imaginary version of England in order to satisfy their audience. However, by the end of the novel people are no longer able to distinguish between the theme park and 'Old England', which is the original or the 'real' thing that England, England attempts to simulate. In this way, *England, England* tracks Baudrillard's theory of simulation and simulacra in order to demonstrate not only the appeal and process of building a concrete and appealing version of Englishness, but also the flailing grasp on reality that we have as a society.

From the outset of *England, England*, one of the pillars of English nationalism is defined as knowledge of England's history and the retention of a definitive collective memory. However, both memory and history are regarded as unreliable and therefore untrustworthy. The novel opens with Martha Cochrane, the female protagonist of the book, being asked: 'What's your first memory?' (Barnes 3). She replies: 'I don't remember', (3) for the very simple reason that, to Martha, all memories are lies. She defines memory as 'a memory now of a memory a bit earlier of a memory before that of a memory way back when' (3), making it impossible to actually remember the first memory itself because each version is layered with the memory of remembering. Knowing that it is in all likelihood a lie, Martha sets the scene of her first memory: putting together a Counties of England jigsaw, which she describes as looking like 'a bulgy old lady sitting on a beach with her legs stretched out' (4). She goes on to make a retrospective quip on her inaccurate puzzle attempts: 'you know what children are like with jigsaws, they just pick up any old piece and try to force it into a hole, so she probably picked up Lancashire and made it behave like Cornwall' (4). The forcefulness of this image—as if Martha is trying to make a square fit into a circle—indicates a strenuous attempt to unite England geographically. As Peter Childs points out, the image of a young child jamming a puzzle piece depicting a specific part of England into the wrong place 'becomes not just a metaphor for the forcing of memory but a metonym for part two of the book, in which pieces of England are assembled and forced into place to provide a potted toytown version of the country' (Childs 110). Indeed, when Martha suggests that she probably made Lancashire '*behave* like Cornwall', she indicates a performativity that becomes essential to the functioning of England, England later in the novel, when various geographical places are squashed together into a simulation that behaves like a cohesive whole. This scene also ironically depicts one of the key figureheads of the England, England project—a project about revitalizing and affirming English identity and nationalism—unable to geographically identify areas of her own country. Although Martha is young in this scene, this contributes to an immediate sense of scepticism about whether Martha and her colleagues are really qualified for the undertaking of recreating England and leads them to question the entire project's legitimacy later in the novel. Having said this, we come to find out that the purpose of England, England is not to create an accurate representation of England in the first place, which makes Martha and her colleagues actually rather suitable for their roles and makes the project's eventual success all the more jarring.

Martha's jigsaw also allows us immediate insight into how she perceives England as part of the greater UK conglomerate. She remembers that 'she would usually work her way round the coastline—Cornwall, Devon, Somerset, Monmouthshire, Glamorgan, Carmarthen, Pembrokeshire (because England included Wales—that was the bulgy old lady's stomach)—all the way back to Devon, and then fill in the rest, leaving the messy Midlands till last' (Barnes 5). The dismissive suggestion that 'England included Wales' is notable, because although English courts have included Wales since 1536, Wales is not a part of England in any other sense. It is a part of the United Kingdom, but not England. Furthermore, Wales becomes 'the bulgy old lady's stomach', which evokes the idea that England (the old lady) has swallowed Wales whole—as though England is literally able to consume other countries. There is a distinct sense of English dominance in this image, and it suggests that even though Martha is very young, she has already been conditioned into an Anglo-centric view of the UK. Furthermore, that England is an 'old lady' here signals towards England's long history and, in a respect-your-elders type of way, suggests that England commands more respect and importance than its neighbours—not least because its neighbour is here depicted as a morsel of food.

In Martha's puzzle scene, we find the first instance of Anglo-centric thinking in the novel, but this trope continues throughout the book, primarily because the project of England, England is isolationist and Anglo-centric in itself. However, the creators of the project not only centre England in their plans, but they actively seek to erase all things associated with Wales, Scotland, and Northern Ireland; they all only appear very rarely and always negatively. Indeed, when it comes to creating the blueprint for England, England, the group of entrepreneurs feels that its UK neighbours must be eradicated from the picture altogether in order to preserve England and Englishness. In part two, the 'Gastronomic Sub-Committee' (93) for England, England is discussing which foods should be on menus across the island, and they laud the inclusion of traditionally English foods while rejecting others for their non-English associations. On the list is 'Yorkshire pudding, Lancashire hotpot...Chelsea buns, Cumberland sausages...muffins, crumpets...and parkin', but 'The Sub-Committee banned porridge for its Scottish associations' and 'Welsh rarebit, Scotch eggs, and Irish strew were not even discussed' (93–94). In this passage, it becomes starkly clear that this project deliberately eradicates any trace of its neighbours' culture, creating a microcosmic vacuum filled with what is tenuously asserted as English culture. These strides towards complete isolationism are made even more apparent when Sir Jack decides to base England, England on the Isle of Wight, which is 'twenty-three miles in length, thirteen across at its widest point. One hundred and fifty-five square miles' (76) total. Compared with the actual size of England, which is over 50,300 square miles, the Isle of Wight is miniscule, but Sir Jack, the entrepreneur and self-proclaimed genius at the helm of the project, asserts that it is 'perfect for our purposes. A location dying for makeover and upgrade' (79). Ironically, the Isle of Wight is a colossal downgrade from Old England in terms of size and capacity, and on top of this, everything is designed to look like it used to at some point in the past—the exact opposite of what we would expect from a 'makeover and upgrade'. However, the fact that Sir Jack describes it as such suggests that he is tapping into what English people see as the idealized version of their country; he is appealing to the underlying hallmarks of English nationalism, which includes nostalgia for a great past, imagines that England is exceptional, and decides that when another place is built in its image, it is 'upgraded' somehow. In a sense, the overtaking of the Isle of Wight to build England, England is a microcosmic example of colonialism, which in the novel appears to be extremely gratifying to Sir Jack and his team, as well as to the theme park's visitors.

In another sense, the 'upgrade' Sir Jack seeks is achieved through his simulation of the real because he distorts reality by creating a visual manifestation of misguided ideas about what quintessential England looks like. As Baudrillard suggests, when it comes to ideas of Empire and national (Western) supremacy, 'Our entire linear and accumulative culture collapses if we cannot stockpile the past in plain view' (Baudrillard 8), so 'We require a visible past, a visible continuum, a visible myth of origin, which reassures us about our end' (9). The simulation of England,

England does exactly this, but it warps that 'visible past' into one that is non-confronting to those who believe England to be glorious and wish it to remain a prominent global superpower. As they attempt to erase Scotland, Wales, and Northern Ireland from the picture, Sir Jack and his team simultaneously make visible a version of history that is deliberately inaccurate, as they seek to revive mystical and mythical associations with England and inspire connection to the version of Englishness that people *want*. In a sense, the history they portray already exists in people's minds, but England, England, the simulation, becomes the visible manifestation of those desires.

To be sure, Sir Jack is entirely unconcerned with the accuracy of his project, just as long as it will satisfy the romanticized version of England that his visitors desire. He hires Dr Max as the team's 'Official Historian' — the word 'official' being deeply ironic given the fact that the history he is hired to deliver is totally unofficial. Dr Max is described paradoxically as a man who 'Considered himself cultured, aware, intelligent, well-informed. No educational or professional connection with History, as requested' (83). Though Dr Max seems utterly unqualified for the role of an official historian, his personal idea of himself as 'cultured, aware, intelligent' and 'well-informed' make him perfect for what Sir Jack is looking for — someone who *feels* like they know English culture, and can therefore replicate that feeling to satisfy the ignorance and desires of visitors. Indeed, it is not in the job description of the Official Historian that he should be precise. Another member of the team, Jeff, sums up Dr Max's actual role in a conversation with him:

'You are our Official Historian. You are responsible, how can I put it, for our history. Do you follow?'
'Clear as a b-ell, so far, my dear Jeff.'
'Right. Well, the point of *our* history — and I stress the our — will be to make guests, those buying what is for the

moment referred to as Quality Leisure, *feel better.*'

'Better. Ah, the old e-thical questions, what a snake-pit they are. Better. Meaning?'

'Less ignorant.'

'Precisely. That's why I was a-ppointed, I assume.'

'Max, you missed the verb.'

'Which one?'

'Feel. We want them to *feel* less ignorant. Whether they *are* or not is quite another matter, even outside our jurisdiction.' (73)

In this pivotal dialogue, we discover that in this novel, history is not used as a tool of information, but rather of deception—the idea that one is learning about a nation's past is the cornerstone of England, England's marketing strategy, but it is not its end goal. The emphasis on 'feel' implies that England, England is designed to deceive its visitors in its performance of England and Englishness—it purposefully corrupts history to create an emotive space where people can imagine themselves to be culturally immersed, but where they are actually being culturally brainwashed. Yet, that brainwashing is achieved by simply invoking traditional and folkloric versions of Englishness that are continuously asserted through myths and stereotypes, and are therefore both extremely gratifying for the visitors and deeply concerning for the reader. What they believe to be real manifests itself in the simulacrum, and the simulacrum in turn reinforces and recreates the symptoms of nationalism and Englishness that inspire it. Later, as Dr Max writes a historical report for the island, the narrator offers the reader a disheartening conclusion: 'that patriotism's most eager bedfellow was ignorance, not knowledge' (85). Jeff's earlier assertion that England, England is designed to fight feelings of ignorance rather than ignorance itself is ultimately exposed as a strategy to bolster patriotism while erasing all traces of the dark, unpleasant truths of England's history.

It is not until deeper into the novel that the reader becomes aware of which aspects of Englishness Sir Jack and his team believe the island should display; in other words, which mixture of truth and myth they believe will most satisfy its visitors' desired vision of Englishness. To inform their decision-making, Jeff creates a survey where 'twenty-five countries had been asked to list six characteristics, virtues or quintessences which the word England suggested to them' (86). The reader is reassured that those who took the survey 'were not being asked to free-associate; there was no pressure of time on the respondents, no preselected multiple choice', and that 'Citizens of the world therefore told Sir Jack in an unprejudiced way what in their view the Fifty Quintessences of Englishness were' (86). Jeff's survey and Sir Jack's instructions invite people from around the world—notably not from England—to define the country based on their personal perceptions of it. Their question is designed to bring to mind the most stereotypical and uncomplicated perceptions of England, and this is evident in the results of the survey: At the top of the list sits the '1. Royal Family', followed by '2. Big Ben/Houses of Parliament and 3. Manchester United Football Club' (86). Further down, we find 'Robin Hood and His Merrie Men' and 'Phlegm/Stiff Upper Lip' (86). Robin Hood's appearance in this list is notable, primarily because he is a legendary character, but also because he is a heroic one. Of course, for England, England this is the perfect subject: one that makes visitors feel a sense of English superiority and escapism simultaneously. That England, England is constructed based on the results of this list demonstrates that its ultimate project is to generate a pseudo-history that displays the most comfortable and attractive notions of Englishness, and that it relies on an extremely limited and romanticized vision of England. Furthermore, the resulting list of 'quintessences' is absent of any actual 'characteristics' or 'virtues' as was originally requested—

which comically implies that no virtues immediately spring to mind.

History and myth are, according to Baudrillard, used as a means of pacifying the world during 'a violent and contemporary period of history' (Baudrillard 31). It is the 'resurrections' of myth that invite hope and give people respite during an otherwise turbulent period, and Baudrillard argues it 'finds refuge in cinema' (31). Cinema is simply performance by another name, and is a label that can certainly be used to describe England, England. While Baudrillard distinguishes between history and legend—where the former is legitimate, and the latter is not—he also suggests that both are warped in order to satisfy our modern ideals. He calls this 'posthumous liberalization' (31). Given the blatant disregard for the accuracy of history throughout England, England, the incorporation of legends such as Robin Hood is of little consequence to how similar or dissimilar the resurrections of both are on the island. However, Baudrillard's focus on why and how they are used— in order to satisfy the imagination during a time of unrest or fragility, is vital. If England, England is an island that intends to reinforce Englishness in a manner that will legitimize the illegitimate beliefs of a noble past and satisfy desirable yet false notions, then it is also an attempt to solidify an identity, and indeed a nation, that otherwise holds no firm ground. Indeed, given the context of Scottish independence movements at the time of publication, the creation of England, England is a blatant attempt to reinforce traditions and ideas that might otherwise be dismantled.

Such reinforcement does not attempt to embellish or perfect aspects of English society that are overtly troubling either. The simulacrum does not attempt to fix what it sees, only to smooth the edges and satisfy what we wish was real without reflection. Barnes invites particular attention to the ironic way that Sir Jack's list of quintessences is labelled as 'unprejudiced'.

There is, in fact, blatant prejudice throughout the entire list—specifically racial prejudice. What people come up with when they think of England is a monolithic, and noticeably white interpretation of what England looks like. There is no mention of the ethnic diversity of England, or its embrace of a globalized world. Oppositely, all of the people listed are both powerful and white: 'Shakespeare', 'Winston Churchill', 'Francis Drake', 'Queen Victoria' (Barnes 87), and the quintessences are all associated with the upper-class, highly-educated strata of English society: 'Oxford/Cambridge', 'Harrods', 'flagellation/public schools' (87). Even the legends and fairy tales that are listed as associated with England, such as 'Robin Hood' and 'Alice in Wonderland' (87), betray a distinct lack of ethnic and socioeconomic diversity. There is a clear acknowledgement that England is a place of prosperity and power, and one that is dominated by white, bourgeoisie citizens and leaders. As the man most directly contributing to the endurance of these associations, Dr Max becomes another link in the chain, adding himself to the long list of white men that have the power to write England's history. He is 'Caucasian, middle-class, of English stock though unable to trace his ancestry beyond three generations. Mother's origin Welsh borders, father's North Midlands...Spoke one language. Married, no children' (82–83). Although this passage indicates that he is 'unable to trace his ancestry', it seems more likely that he is unwilling, for fear of finding out that—horror!—he is not 100 per cent 'English stock', which as I mentioned in chapter one, likely means white. The racially imbalanced perspective of English history is not news to anyone, but the effect that it has on the way that not only the English, but the entire world perceives England has far-reaching consequences, which are put on display here during the process of development for England, England.

England, England is certainly also a venture that intentionally marginalizes the voices of those traditionally underserved by

English society, and its placement on a small island becomes an opportunity to reduce the number of people that have access to it—to be more selective about who those people are. One way that the island excludes people, and disproportionately people of colour (though this is never explicitly mentioned as a side effect), is by making it a pre-requisite of entering the island to have a good credit rating (184). Because wealth is accumulated more easily by white people (especially white men), England, England is not only isolationist, but also racist and xenophobic—a disturbing precedent to set in their development of a supposedly untarnished and improved version of England. Later in the novel, it becomes clear that this tone is carried forward by those living on England, England when one of the island's new employees, Johnson, has complaints filed against him for his 'racist remarks about many of the Visitors' countries of origin' (214). Disturbingly, UKIP's mantra of 'Take Back Control' and its spread of propaganda that depicted long lines of refugees during the Brexit referendum achieved exactly the same goal as Sir Jack's credit rating—it made people fear and sneer the other, creating a prejudiced, and more importantly inaccurate, depiction of what English people look like. It also unleashed a similar torrent of racial abuse that has yet to abate. Unfortunately, just like in England, England, that depiction had an undeniable appeal, and drew support from those who share this vision of what England should look like. In this instance, the simulacrum does not greatly alter or smooth over the truth; in fact, it is indistinguishable from the original entity that it intends to reflect—that this is designed to be wish-fulfilling and is perhaps the only somewhat accurate depiction of England is deeply disturbing.

The consequences of the credit rating also pose questions about capitalism and the role of the free market in this novel. England is far older than capitalism, but the development of England, England as a profit-making venture is an immediate indication that capitalism is a central component of the nation-building process on the island, and Barnes suggests that the greedy preoccupations of the market-driven endeavour to create England, England thwart the proper functioning of democracy. In turn, this leads to the corruption of morality on the island. The idea of a flailing democracy becomes evident during the 'two sets of negotiations' (127) held at the outset of the (re-)building process on the island. The narrator notes that 'The public was admitted and all proper democratic procedures followed: which meant, as Sir Jack privately observed, that tokenism, special interests, and minority groupings ran the show, the lawyers made a bundle, and you spent your time on all fours with your arsehole getting sunburnt' (127). Sir Jack's comical internal observations suggest that democracy functions in a distinctly un-democratic manner, and he satirizes its ability to operate in a capitalist world. Tokenism and special interest imply that the market-driven preoccupations of government lead to internal corruption, while Sir Jack's sneering note that 'minority groupings ran the show' seems to betray a distaste for the protection of minority groups, since it is an exaggerated statement about how influential minorities are able to be in the democratic process. Furthermore, the final phrase of this sentence invokes an image of someone doubled over, or perhaps even begging, demonstrating in physical terms the ways that capitalism exerts unquestionable control over political and legal proceedings. The breakdown of democracy and decency on England, England is elaborated on later in the novel, when Martha reflects:

> In some parts of the world they'd already be facing multi-million-dollar suits for sexual harassment, racial abuse, breach of contract in failing to make the client laugh, and God knows what else. Thankfully, Island law — in other words, executive decision — recognized no specific contract between

Visitors and Pitco; instead, reasonable complaints were dealt with on an ad hoc basis, usually involving financial compensation in exchange for silence. (218)

Martha's rumination demonstrates the extent to which a project based on profit and patriotism can bring a democracy into ruin and allow shallow corporate interests to become more important than the people they serve. Barnes satirically (yet morosely) demonstrates here that when England is created in the image of what people want it to be, it leads to moral ruin and the breakdown of laws upholding basic rights, even implying that the island has become a dictatorship. He seems to send a clear message to the reader that what results from Sir Jack's recreation of England is an extremely bleak vision of what Englishness stands for.

The strategy of the team of entrepreneurs who create England, England—from the survey on the quintessences of Englishness to the belief in the power of ignorance—is ultimately extremely successful. In part three of the novel, a reporter writes an article about the island titled: 'A Tourist Mecca Set in a Silver Sea' (181), giving the impression that England, England has become a destination akin to a religious pilgrimage. She writes approvingly of Sir Jack:

It was also his original stroke of lateral thinking which brought together in a single hundred-and-fifty-five-square-mile zone everything the Visitor might want to see of what we used to think of as England. In our time-strapped age, surely it makes sense to be able to visit Stonehenge and Anne Hathaway's Cottage in the same morning, take in a 'ploughman's lunch' atop the White Cliffs of Dover, before passing a leisurely afternoon at the Harrod's emporium inside the Tower of London. (183)

Tellingly, the reporter suggests that the island contains 'everything the visitor might want to see of what we *used* to think of as England' (italics mine), suggesting that the project has successfully rewritten a new, more popular and more satisfying history. This also suggests that the simulacrum has indeed blurred the line between the real and the imagined—it is no longer easy for people to distinguish whether the truth can be found in Old England or in England, England. The geographical proximity of the attractions on the island are also a key selling point here, which demonstrates the appeal of convenience over true cultural immersion—another market-driven preoccupation. England, England provides its visitors with an opportunity to essentially skim read the supposed 'best' parts of England and provides an experience that will simply validate their existing beliefs rather than challenge them.

As the article above indicates, just as England, England's corrupt version of history has replaced the true version of events, England, England also replaces Old England altogether. By the end of the novel, the narrative depicts Old England as in decline, and it is eventually forced to rebrand itself as simply 'Anglia'. Unsympathetic to the downward trajectory of the mother nation they claim to love, the island puts out an official statement, that reads:

Old England had progressively shed power, territory, wealth, influence, and population. Old England was to be compared disadvantageously to some backward province of Portugal or Turkey. Old England had cut its own throat and was lying in the gutter beneath a spectral gas-light, its only function as a dissuasive example to others. FROM DOWAGER TO DOWN-AND-OUT, a Times headline had sneeringly put it. Old England had lost its history, and therefore—since memory is identity—had lost all sense of itself. (259)

This passage unashamedly asserts that England's identity is rooted in its exceptionalism, and that Old England's loss of power has occurred in a manner akin to a suicide. As I outlined in part one, England's rejection of globalization and multilateral institutions is deeply ironic given that it had a hand in creating this very world order, and here we find an acknowledgement of shame at this irony. Indeed, the 'shedd[ing] of power, territory, wealth, influence and population' refers scathingly to the collapse of the British Empire, while the suggestion that it represents a 'dissuasive example to others' laments the breakdown of the global relevance of a once-prosperous nation. On top of this, the comparison of Old England to a 'backward province of Portugal or Turkey' arrogantly displays, once again, England's belief in its own superiority and exceptionalism. The idea that 'Old England had lost its history' and therefore 'all sense of itself' suggests that England, England has effectively stripped Old England of its historical veracity, creating a new, marketable version of Englishness that keeps visitors both entertained and ignorant, and satisfies a fraudulent yet apparently ubiquitous vision of the nation. Unlike Disneyland, England, England does not become a fantastical distraction to assure the concreteness of our supposed reality; instead, Barnes demonstrates how quickly the 'real' world can be lost to a simulacrum, to the point where the simulation becomes more real than what it intends to simulate, and in this way reveals the difficulty in determining what reality actually looks like.

The final description of the decaying Old English nation nudges the reader towards a sense of disappointment and loss, and portrays England, England as a power-hungry, corrupt, and neglectful place. Ultimately, the island is about convenience, money, and the appeal of a version of Englishness that is romanticized and steeped in myth. Despite this, it overtakes Old England in terms of relevance and power. Such is the disturbing conclusion of Barnes' alternative world: people are driven not by a desire to truly understand England, but to idealize it; people are driven not to protect English history, but to recast it through rose-tinted glasses. By inviting us to consider how a simulation can appear more real than what it originally simulated, Barnes asks the reader to consider the boundaries between the real and the imagined, and to think critically about how Englishness is recreated and performed in order to maintain the illusion that the reality we believe in is true. Ultimately, *England, England* unveils the pretences under which English identity is constructed and reinforced, and bleakly concludes that if the ideas about England that people envision were true, it would result in moral and social corruption and decay. In all of these ways, Barnes passionately rejects contemporary manifestations of Englishness, invites the reader to consider the dangers of English nationalism in its current form, and pushes us to question reality in true Baudrillard-fashion.

* * *

Jonathan Coe's *The Rotters' Club*: Conflict and Coming of Age

Set against the backdrop of industrial Birmingham in the 1970s, *The Rotters' Club* is both a bildungsroman and a fictional yet historically precise account of the political turbulence in England during this decade. Published in 2001, the novel tracks the lives of Benjamin Trotter and his friends, as well as their families, as they deal with the troubles of adolescence, the struggles of class warfare, rampant racism, and the emerging threats of the IRA and sub-nationalisms within the United Kingdom to England and Englishness. Over the course of the novel, we are invited to imagine the backdrop against which identities are formed in England in the 1970s, and encouraged to understand the forces that, eventually, created the conditions for Brexit in 2016. Furthermore, *The Rotters' Club* is a valuable novel for this project as it is part of a trilogy that ends with a BrexLit novel, *Middle England*, in which Coe revives the same characters to explore how they engage with the political turmoil of the referendum. While I will explore *Middle England* in the next chapter, this section will focus on how *The Rotters' Club* depicts Englishness in the 1970s, and how we might use that to better understand Englishness in the age of Brexit.

From the outset, *The Rotters' Club* is written against the backdrop of class-based and racial tensions that lie bubbling under the surface of everyday life in Birmingham. One of the central characters in the novel is Bill Anderton, father of Benjamin's friend Doug Anderton, and a 'shop steward in the Longbridge underseal section' (Coe 14)—Longbridge plant is a motor vehicle factory. Alongside his day job, Bill is also a key leader in the labour union movement and remains firmly committed to his cause throughout the novel. While Bill's life is defined by the class struggle, many remain resistant to, or unpersuaded by, the fact that class warfare still exists in 1970s Britain. When Jack Forrest, the smug boss of Colin Trotter, who is in middle management at the Longbridge plant, invites both Colin and Bill to the pub for a drink, he announces the reason for the evening: '"You have something in common, you see." Jack regarded them both in turn, pleased with himself. "Don't you know what it is?" They shrugged. "You've both got kids at the same school"' (15). He goes on:

'Britain in the 1970s. The old distinctions just don't mean anything any more, do they? This is a country where a union man and a junior manager—soon to be senior, Colin, I'm sure—can send their sons to the same school and nobody thinks anything of it...What does that tell you about the class war? It's over. Truce. Armistice.' He clasped his pint of Brew and raised it solemnly. 'Equality of opportunity.' (16)

Jack's proud assertion that Britain has overcome the class war suggests something more than denial—there is an air of righteousness, and perhaps even a warning in his proclamation, as if to say: see, your sons have 'equality of opportunity', so you have nothing to complain about. Of course, Jack's is an extremely myopic view of what the class struggle looks like in the first place; there is certainly a desire for equality of opportunity, but labour unions also demand better pay, better working conditions, and raise a plethora of other issues that directly affect the workplace and workers' quality of life outside it. Recognizing his own difference of opinion, 'Bill said nothing: as far as he was concerned, the class war was alive and well and being waged with some ferocity at British Leyland, even in Ted Heath's egalitarian 1970s, but he couldn't rouse himself to argue the point' (16). Bill's resignation to silence suggests that while the issue remains untouched for now, it is stirring beneath the surface and threatens to spoil the illusion of an equal society for people like Jack—the same kind of stirring that caused a generation's worth of frustration with the EU to come to the boil during the Brexit referendum campaign in 2016.

Alongside an illicit affair with Miriam Newman, her disappearance and suspected murder, and an internal feud with right-wing colleague Roy Slater, Bill Anderton continues his efforts to support the labour movement at Leyland throughout the novel. Despite those efforts, ultimately the factory enters a phase of 'restructuring' (303) brought about by a delegate vote on the chairman of British Leyland's proposals to support the failing factory. The proposals involved cutting the workforce in half, leaving many unemployed and unable to support themselves and their families. Bill mourns this loss:

Twelve and a half thousand redundancies. A painful but necessary process. He pitied the management their twinges of conscience...and thought too about the weeks and months and maybe lifetimes of hardship and hopelessness that so many thousands of his men were going to face in the bitter, market-driven era to come...there had been plenty of days, good days, and not so long ago, when he truly believed that the struggle could be won; but the decade was old now and he was growing old with it, and he knew that those days would never come back. (304)

Bill's tragic acceptance of defeat and his reflections on the hardships ahead clearly demonstrate that these redundancies will have widespread, hard-hitting implications for workers. The story of the restructuring of Longbridge is grounded in reality, and with Coe's own fictional restructuring of the event in the world of the novel, the reader gains insight into the immediacy with which these jobs were taken away. The sharp loss of these workers' livelihoods is portrayed as a result of the market-driven era, and the struggles that people will face as a result imply that their grievances will lie with the market and, inevitably, the government that controls the economy. Indeed, the loss of income that Bill describes here is a familiar phenomenon that leads to disenfranchisement and a deep-seated resentment for the establishment. Given the economic indicators of voting Leave or Remain in 2016, Coe's portrayal of the situation at Longbridge Factory provides some insight into the economic backdrop against which English people are making political decisions. Birmingham did indeed vote Leave, albeit by a very small margin, and many testify that the primary driver of that decision was the economic situation in which many still find themselves ('EU Referendum: Birmingham votes Brexit by a whisker'). Indeed, where Bill reluctantly leaves the days of optimistic class struggle behind, it is possible to speculate that the Brexit referendum provided a long-overdue opportunity to make a statement about class and economic wellbeing—about how modern life in the EU (and in the West more generally) rewards some and strips others of their livelihoods. Those who are losing want to retreat to a past where they believe they had permanent job security and where their future is not dictated by what is often perceived as a foreign body.

Similarly, racism is simultaneously an uncomfortable yet blatant force that profoundly affects life in the novel, most notably at King Edward's School, the school that Benjamin Trotter and his classmates attend. Steve Richards, 'the only black pupil in their year: the only one in the entire school, in fact' (Coe 27), becomes the target of both subconscious and targeted racism, and his treatment demonstrates the severe overestimation of social equality and progress in the 1970s. In our first introduction to life at the school, Culpepper, the school's most notorious bully and an overt racist, begins to criticize one of their teachers:

> 'Fletcher's a dreadful old liberal softie. He wouldn't let anyone get away with impersonating a nigger.'
> 'You shouldn't use that word,' said Chase. 'You know you shouldn't.'
> 'What—nigger?' said Culpepper, enjoying the effect these two tiny syllables were having upon them. 'Why not? It's in the book. Harper Lee uses it herself.'
> 'You know that's different.'
> 'All right, then. Wog. Coon. Darkie.' (25)

Chase's discomfort indicates that Culpepper's racist language is taboo, but Culpepper's blasé willingness to continue to use offensive terms in spite of criticism also demonstrates that racism is still an entrenched social norm. Further reinforcing the pervasive nature of racism in this novel, the narrator tells us that from the moment Steve joins the school, 'the other ninety-five boys in his year called him "Rastus"' (27), an offensive nickname given to black men based on the caricature figure associated with the Cream of Wheat breakfast porridge company in the United States. Even Benjamin, who is generally outraged by Culpepper's actions and becomes a good friend of Steve later in the novel, sees little wrong with the nickname when challenged by his friend Claire. Claire is revealing which boy at school *'everybody's* crazy about' (93):

> 'Benjamin waited for her to elaborate, but apparently it was too obvious to need spelling out. In the end he hazarded a guess. 'Is it Culpepper?'
>
> 'Culpepper! Give me a break. He's Mister Repulsive.'
>
> 'OK then: who?'
>
> 'Richards, of course.'
>
> Benjamin was dumbfounded. 'You mean Rastus?'
>
> Claire gasped, and almost choked on a crisp. 'You don't call him that, do you?'
>
> 'Why not?'
>
> 'It's so...insulting.'
>
> 'No it's not. It's a joke.'
>
> 'You can't call him Rastus just because he's black. How would you like it if nobody ever called you by your real name?'
>
> 'Nobody does. Not at school, anyway. They call me Bent.'
> (93–94)

In this dialogue, we see Benjamin struggle to understand the fundamental difference between the joking nickname given to him and the racist nickname assigned to Steve, and we witness an important learning moment for him. After this conversation, Benjamin becomes slightly more attuned to the problematic nature of Steve's treatment by other boys at the school, though his progress is somewhat slow. This scene harkens back to Akala's book *Natives: Race and Class in the Ruins of Empire*, when he writes that there is 'A Very British Racism' that quietly acknowledges and then ignores or outright denies instances and systems of racial prejudice. Claire bucks this trend, but we see in Benjamin's confusion the product of a country that rarely faces up to its injustices. Through the eyes of this young boy, the reader begins to witness the process of understanding and confronting the forms of racism that often go unacknowledged in every day English life.

Perhaps unsurprisingly, not all the boys in the novel are as willing to learn as Benjamin, and Steve's treatment gets progressively more violent at the hands of Culpepper in particular over the course of the novel. Benjamin recounts an incidence of Culpepper's malicious feelings towards Steve to his sister Lois, telling her that while playing rugby, there was 'some sort of tackle' (169) between Steve and Culpepper:

> and the next thing you know Culpepper's down on the ground screaming in agony—and I mean literally screaming—and it turns out he's broken his arm. Well, Richards is very contrite, as you might expect, and very upset about it, actually, because he's a gentle sort of bloke and doesn't like to hurt anybody, but now Culpepper's going around telling people that he did it on purpose. Which is rubbish, anyone'll tell you that. The fact is that he just hates Richards and he'll do anything he can to make life hard for him. He's hated him ever since he first came to the school, some people say it's because he's black but I don't think that's the reason, I think he just hates him because he's a better athlete than he is, a better sportsman, better at everything really. (169)

As he recounts the event, Benjamin roots Culpepper's frustration solely in jealousy, again demonstrating a naïve lack of recognition that his accusation is grounded in his racist attitudes towards Steve. Mirroring Jack Forrest, Benjamin's quick dismissal of the notion that Culpepper would spread lies based on the colour of

Steve's skin implies once again that even as racist acts continue to happen with frequency, society is resistant to seeing them for what they are, instead making excuses that paint a picture of moral and social progress that has not really occurred.

Having said this, there is some truth in Benjamin's perception of the root of Culpepper's hatred; it becomes clear that Steve is indeed the superior athlete, and that Culpepper *is* consumed with jealousy about this, going to some extreme lengths to try and out-compete Steve. On the school sports day, Steve is unable to find his St Christopher's medal—a good luck token that has obvious sentimental meaning to him—and he 'openly accused Culpepper of stealing' (253), fully aware of Culpepper's vendetta against him. The reader is encouraged to believe Steve's accusation, and to feel delight when, despite Culpepper's effort to play mind games, Steve wins sports day. However, this victory is Steve's last, as it drives Culpepper to make his final sabotage attempt, this time with far graver consequences. Sat waiting to take their final physics exam, it is strongly speculated that Culpepper slipped a drug into Steve's drink, distracting him first by returning the St Christopher's medal which he had supposedly 'discovered...while rooting around in Mr Nuttall's lost property box' (317), and then serving him a spiked tea. This time, Culpepper's efforts are far more effective, and Steve does poorly in his exams, causing him to lose his place at Cambridge and ultimately setting him on a far lower path than he was capable. Reflecting on this misfortune later, and on his own relationship with Steve, Benjamin muses:

> why have we not invited Steve?, is it because his future seems so uncertain, after what happened last year, and I just cannot envisage where he is going to be in forty years' time, or is there another reason, a nastier reason, for excluding Steve from my little fantasy, you can never tell, these things go very deep, and when Cicely and I went to visit him the other

day there was certainly an element of hostility, I thought, of bitterness, even though he didn't hold me to blame personally, a gulf had opened up between us, a little gulf, if there can be such a thing...(378)

The undertones of subconscious racism in Benjamin's internal monologue open up serious questions about how black people in England at this time are excluded from opportunities and social life by both systemic and malevolent forces. The suggestion that 'these things go very deep' suggests that subconsciously entrenched racism remains firmly rooted in Benjamin's mind, even though he is able to somewhat recognize it, and consequently demonstrates that racial tension remains an everyday fact of life in England. Steve's treatment throughout the novel and his uncertain situation at the end all serve to direct the reader's empathy towards him, while Culpepper embodies the rampant racism in society, and Benjamin embodies society's unwillingness to confront people like Culpepper for what they are.

As class and race threaten the stability of people's lives on the ground level, an arguably even greater threat is ever present: the Irish Republican Army (IRA). The IRA was originally founded as the Irish Republican Brotherhood on St Patrick's Day in 1858 by James Stephens and Thomas Clarke Luby, following the suppression of an earlier revolutionary group (Coogan 11–12). The IRA's political platform was grounded in the Home Rule movement—a movement that gained momentum after the Act of Union in 1800 that incorporated Ireland into the Kingdom of Great Britain and provided Ireland with seats in the UK Parliament in Westminster. Despite this political incorporation, which theoretically empowers Ireland to affect UK affairs, Tim Coogan suggests that absorption into Westminster actually disempowered Ireland to make its own laws: 'Ireland could no longer legislate for herself under the British crown, and the hundred or so members that she sent to Westminster were able to make very little impression on an assembly of 670 when it came to matters affecting Irish interests' (Coogan 4). There were two attempts to pass bills on Home Rule by prime minister William E. Gladstone in 1885 and 1893, but both were blocked by the House of Lords (Coogan 8). Taking matters into its own hands, the IRA operated as a terrorist organization throughout the twentieth century, attacking primarily England and Northern Ireland in bouts of violent bombing campaigns, several of which took place during the 1970s. The targeted attacks on England, as opposed to on Scotland and Wales, are a manifestation of the anger directed towards England by its neighbours, and make clear that England is seen as the cause of Ireland's modern struggles for political independence.

The first mention of the IRA in *The Rotters' Club* comes when Bill Anderton finds a leaflet circulating around members of his charity committee. The leaflet reads:

IRA BASTARDS KILLED 12 PEOPLE
ON MANCHESTER BUS YESTERDAY
REFUSE TO WORK WITH
IRISH BASTARD MURDERERS[.] (Coe 37)

The leaflet serves both to highlight the kind of rhetoric that surrounds not only the IRA, but Irish people at large, as it reads like a xenophobic attack itself towards all Irish people, even though Northern Ireland is part of the UK. It also serves to remind the reader that these attacks are happening in several cities throughout England. The brief mention of IRA bombings here serves as foreboding for a later bombing that profoundly affects the characters of the novel. The event happens when Benjamin's sister, Lois, and her boyfriend, Malcolm, are spending the evening together at a local tavern, for a 'special occasion' (103). As they sit, Malcolm begins a profession of love that he never gets to finish:

> Malcolm fingered the leather box in his jacket pocket. He had
> not meant to ask her so early, but it was no use: he couldn't
> contain himself.
>
> 'Look, love, you know what I think about you, don't you?'
>
> Lois didn't answer. She just looked back at him, her eyes
> starting to brim over.
>
> 'I love you,' said Malcolm. 'I'm crazy about you.' He took
> a long breath, an enormous breath. 'I've got to say something
> to you. I've got to ask you something.' He grasped her hand,
> and squeezed it tightly. As if he would never let go. 'Do you
> know what it is?'
>
> Of course she knew. And of course, Malcolm knew what
> the answer would be. They understood each other perfectly,
> at that moment. They were as close to each other, and as
> close to happiness, as it is possible for two people to be. So
> Malcolm never did ask the question.
>
> Then, at 8.20 precisely, the timing device set off the
> trigger, the battery pack sent power running through the
> cables, and thirty pounds of gelignite exploded on the far
> side of the pub.
>
> And that was how it all ended, for the chick and the hairy
> guy. (104)

We later discover that the 'thirty pounds of gelignite' was planted
by the IRA, and that Malcolm is taken victim in an extremely
violent way; after the bombing happened, when Lois came to,
she found herself on the ground holding Malcolm's head—only
his head—in her hands (312). The space dedicated to this scene
in the narrative is intended to both deeply disturb and evoke
pathos in the reader; it paints a vivid and chilling picture of the
human experience of terrorism, and invites us to imagine what
it might feel like for Lois to have the hope of a lifelong future

with someone ripped away because of something entirely out of her and Malcolm's control. The effect of this bombing on the lives of Lois and Benjamin will last through until the final book in the trilogy, well into adulthood. Immediately after the event Lois is taken to a mental asylum, unable to so much as speak for a long time after the incident. Even when she returns home, 'Loud noises still scared her, and she could not tolerate violent films on the television' (272). Lois' trauma is frequently returned to throughout the novel as a reminder of the IRA's nationalist mission, and through our horror and sympathy also serves to place the reader in an Anglo-centric frame of mind that views the IRA as a malevolent force.

Benjamin holds a deep-seated resentment for the IRA after it destroys the life of his sister, but he never reflects upon these emotions until he is confronted with a man who oppositely supports the IRA movement. The confrontation occurs in Wales, after Benjamin has gone to find the girl he loves, Cicely. It is the first time that Benjamin has found himself somewhere in the UK that is not Birmingham—that is not *England*—and his geographical relocation in the novel provides an opportunity for Benjamin to learn about a perspective on England that he has never been exposed to before. Cicely is staying with her uncle, who, it turns out, is a Welsh nationalist. Benjamin is alarmed by this revelation: 'He had heard about the Welsh nationalists on the news. They burned people's holiday cottages down' (348). As Cicely describes the extent of her uncle's affiliation with the Welsh nationalist movement, she reveals: 'He's always giving quotes about it to the English newspapers and getting into all sorts of trouble. He supports the IRA as well' (348). Benjamin's response is one of shock, anger, and most of all, confusion:

Benjamin's eyes widened even further. For years, ever since the pub bombings, or even before the pub bombings, he had heard nothing—whether from his family, his friends,

the teachers at school, the politicians on the television—
nothing but vilification and contempt being poured on
the IRA. He had heard them being called everything from
child-murderers to lunatics and psychopaths. It had simply
never occurred to him before that there might be another
way of looking at it...And yet this man supported the IRA!
The people who had killed Malcolm and caused Lois such
dreadful suffering. How could that possibly be? Was the
world even *more* complicated than he had imagined—weren't
there even *any* arguments with only one side to them? How
on earth did people like Doug keep hold of their certainties,
their clearly defined, confidently held political positions, in
a world like this? (348)

In this baptism of fire, Benjamin struggles to reconcile issues
of place and perspective, for the first time realizing that
there could be reasons for supporting the attacks against his
sister and other English people across the country that he has
never considered. His most profound confusion is that he has
never heard anything except 'vilification and contempt' from
news outlets and television platforms in Birmingham, which
points again to the Anglo-centrism of national media, and the
hegemony of the English perspective in controlling how people
perceive issues affecting their fellow Brits. The scene in Wales
offers an opportunity for the Anglo-centric view, to which both
the reader and Benjamin are accustomed, to be de-centred,
and gives voice to the conflicting perspective. While Benjamin
cannot truly shake his resentment of the IRA for what it does
to Lois, nor is the reader encouraged to empathise with their
methods, in this moment he does realize that there is more than
one way to look at the issue, and that for other people across the
UK, Malcolm and Lois' lives were merely collateral damage in a
project of national self-determination.

Cicely's uncle goes on to elaborate on his political position towards English-Welsh relations to Benjamin. Referring to him as 'Englishman' (350) in a jeering manner, he explains his discontent with England and the English people:

> 'Personally, I don't like the English...Do you know why?' Without waiting for an answer, he went on: 'I'll tell you, then: the Welsh have hated the English for as long as anyone can remember, and they'll carry on hating them until the English leave them alone and stop interfering in their affairs. They've hated them ever since the thirteenth century, when Edward the First invaded Wales and his armies slaughtered the women and children and Llewellyn the Second was slaughtered too and laws were passed which banned Welsh people from holding positions of authority...' (350)

Cicely's uncle's explanation is grounded in the lingering grievances surrounding the historical relationship between England and Wales that continue to simmer, and he articulately explains the problematic nature of England's continued insistence on controlling Wales politically. The lack of punctuation as he goes deeper into his speech speeds up his dialogue and makes his explanation appear more frantic and extensive. His monologue is an indication to the reader—and of course to Benjamin—that sub-nationalisms within the UK are gaining ground, and that whether they are Welsh, Irish, or Scottish, they are all united in their anger at the English, and understandably so (for if English people resent being 'controlled' by Brussels for 50 years, imagine that resentment building over centuries). While we have already seen the personal devastation of the IRA's nationalist attacks, Benjamin's experience in Wales draws the reader's attention to the bigger picture, and reveals that there is an even greater threat at large: one that threatens England and Englishness, as well as the unity of the UK as a whole. It is by exploring political groups like the IRA and characters like Cicely's uncle that Coe reveals the underbelly of a disunited kingdom built on distrust and conflicting desires to assert unique political identities. The major difference for England as opposed to Wales, Ireland, and Scotland, is that their political identity *is* the control of its neighbours' affairs. So, as much as England retaining its identity threatens the identities of the Welsh, Irish, and Scottish people, the demands of the Welsh, Irish, and Scottish people also threaten the identity of the English. It is this tension that Jeremy Black suggests creates the desire to shape and fortify English identity—a project that we see take place in *England, England*—and a version that retains its dominance and exceptionalism.

The Rotters' Club examines the struggles of class, race, and sub-nationalisms to provide the reader with many valuable insights into the landscape of Englishness in 1970s Britain. While the novel is ultimately fictional, it draws from history with a keen eye to expose what it might really have felt like to grow up during this era of uncertainty and political tumult. The centrality of Birmingham and Benjamin's intense struggle to understand the anti-English perspective also helps explain why many in England increasingly felt that their identity was threatened by external forces, and thus sought to assert a version of Englishness that was cohesive, superior, and retreats slowly yet deeply into isolationism. Throughout the novel, Englishness is continuously characterized by racism, classism, and Anglo-centric understandings of the United Kingdom, ultimately depicting a fractured and uncertain sense of self. As the protagonist of the novel, Benjamin best encapsulates this uncertainty; while he learns to appreciate the perspective of others throughout the novel, he also remains deeply confused about what to think—who to believe, and how to have strong and unchanging convictions. Benjamin becomes the lens through which the reader sees an Englishness that is unwittingly blinkered and unable to confront any uncomfortable or unpleasant narratives about the history of their nation's pre-eminence. The revival of Benjamin and many of his friends and family in the final book of Coe's trilogy, *Middle England*, continues to provide insight into how the experience of Englishness is threatened, asserted, and reinforced, which I will explore in chapter four of this book.

* * *

Jez Butterworth's *Jerusalem*: Defending England Against the World it Shaped

In 2009, Jez Butterworth's play *Jerusalem* became an overnight sensation. It received widespread critical acclaim and became immensely popular for its seductive representation of Englishness. Dominic Cavendish of *The Telegraph* encapsulates the critical reception of the play by suggesting that *Jerusalem* is a 'state-of-the-nation drama with an incendiary difference. It speaks about a nation that has almost forgotten it is a nation' (Cavendish). Indeed, *Jerusalem* is a play that attempts to perform and re-forge Englishness through a mystical revival of the enchanted forests of England, an appeal to the English soil, and a distinct rejection of the laws that govern that land, symbolized by the Kennet and Avon council that protagonist Johnny 'Rooster' Byron fervently defies. Throughout the play, the land is intimately linked with the identity of the characters, and thus with Englishness—a romantic relationship that Wendell Berry encapsulates in the statement: 'If you don't know where you are, you don't know who you are' (Berry qtd. in Kingsnorth 1), written in his book of essays titled *The Gift of the Good Land*. Furthermore, the world of *Jerusalem* inspires the belief that there is something more magical in the rural— the 'real'—England than the version to which we have become accustomed: the cookie-cutter housing estates, chain restaurants, and global capitalist projects that increasingly dominate the landscape. Through Johnny Byron and his friends' rejection of globalization, the free market, and the English law, Butterworth seeks to revive a lost mysticism—a lost love—of England. And yet, to argue that *Jerusalem* is a 'state-of-the-nation' play is misleading. *Jerusalem* is not a representation of the England we are confronted with today, but rather a representation of an England, and an Englishness, that the nation, perhaps even the world, *desires*.

Jerusalem is set on April 23, which is St George's Day in England, traditionally understood as England's national day. St George is the patron saint of England despite having been born in Cappadocia, a region in central Turkey. He was a soldier in life but became a martyr in death for refusing to renounce his faith as a Christian man. Upon his death, St George acquired his own written legend in bishop Jacobus de Varagine's *The Golden Legend*, in which he slays a dragon and rescues a princess. Although the same tale has been associated with other patron saints as well, the legend remains associated almost exclusively with St George. Immediately grounded in the context of both national celebration and magical tales, the curtain opens on a supernatural landscape. The stage directions of the Prologue read: '*A curtain with the faded Cross of St George. A proscenium adorned with cherubs and woodland scenes. Dragons. Maidens. Devils. Half-and-half creatures…A fifteen-year-old girl*, PHAEDRA, *dressed as a fairy, appears on the apron. She curtsies to the boxes and sings, unaccompanied*' (Butterworth 5). The stage direction that the cross of St George is 'faded' is immediately notable; its worn appearance suggests both that this is a long-held tradition—that this flag is a symbol that reaches deep into England's history—and also implies that the meaning of the celebration is becoming less clear over time. In other words, the faded flag connotes that there is no clear definition of who the English are as a people on its national day, but it is a tradition that withstands nonetheless. Phaedra proceeds to sing the song after which the play is titled:

'Jerusalem'. The song's lyrics are from William Blake's poem: 'And did those feet in ancient time' — a poem inspired by the folklore that Jesus visited England as a young man. 'Jerusalem', like the cross of St George, is an appeal to the nation, as it is often considered a patriotic song and is even regarded as England's unofficial national anthem. Both the cross of St George and Phaedra's singing are direct appeals to the nation and the national consciousness, designed to immediately invite the audience into a carefully curated version of Englishness.

The central protagonist of the play is Johnny 'Rooster' Byron, who in the words of Ben Brantley is 'a boastful wreck of a man held together by drugs and drink, existing as a 24-hour party guy in a squalid mobile home in the English countryside' (Brantley). Johnny's primary engagement throughout the play is a face-off with the English law, as the Kennet and Avon council attempts to forcibly remove him from his mobile home, which is illegally located on land that does not belong to him. Johnny's entrance onto the stage occurs as Linda Fawcett, 'Senior Communication Officer' of the council, and her male colleague Parsons, request an audience with him: 'FAWCETT: Mr Byron? Mr John Byron? Johnny Byron? (*Knocks.*) John Rooster Byron...Mr Byron? (*She knocks.*) Mr Byron? Would you care to step outside for a moment?' (Butterworth 7). Fawcett's address wavers between formality and casual greeting, before returning to formality, and Johnny's silence demonstrates that that formal address, authority, and the law are all meaningless to him. Fawcett's stiff, official language continues as Parsons records her outside the home: 'Linda Fawcett, Kennet and Avon Senior Community Liaison Officer. 9 a.m., 23rd April. Serving notice F-17003 in contravention of the Public Health Act of 1878, and the Pollution Control and Local Government Order 1974' (7). As Fawcett states the laws that Johnny is breaking, a '*Loud barking can be heard from inside*' (7), which eventually becomes '*Plaintive howling*' (8), and the audience discovers that it is coming not from an animal, but from Johnny himself. Fawcett patronizes Johnny by remarking: 'Very funny, Mr Byron. Extremely amusing' (8), as though rebuking a child for making light of a serious situation. He is not dissuaded, and *'A hatch opens on the top of the mobile home. A head appears, wearing a Second World War helmet and goggles, with loudhailer, like out of the top of a tank. Barking'* (8). When Fawcett and Parsons leave the stage, he continues to frustrate their purpose by parodying their legal jargon:

> JOHNNY. Testing. Testing, one two. This is Rooster Byron's dog, Shep, informing Kennet and Avon council to go fuck itself. Woof woof!...
>
> Hear ye, hear ye. With the power invested in me by Rooster Johnny Byron—who can't be here on account of the fact he's in Barbados this week with Kate Moss—I, his faithful hound Shep, hereby instruct Kennet and Avon to tell Bren Glewstone, and Ros Taylor, and her twat son, and all those sorry cunts on the New Estate, Rooster Byron ain't going nowhere. Happy St George's Day. Now kiss my beggar arse, you Puritans! (9)

Johnny's bizarre actions immediately mark him as a defiant, lawless creature, and his monologue completely undermines the legitimacy of attempts by the council to enforce the law. Johnny's cursing is also a starkly uncensored contrast to the polite formality of Fawcett's tone on the recording device, and for the audience, is extremely comical. Moreover, in this very first appearance, Johnny immediately becomes the embodiment of modern frustrations with the forces that seek to control our movement and our lives. Johnny's defiance taps into the disillusionment with the law that many in the audience likely feel. He acts in ways they wish they could—is rebellious, and free, and he actually gets away with it. For this reason, his character becomes instantly likeable.

Johnny is equally popular, particularly with young people, within the world of the play, and his friends deeply admire him for his defiance of the law and his protection of the land. The action on stage revolves solely around Johnny's mobile home, with characters constantly moving into and through his space. Some come for drugs and parties, others to say hello or goodbye as friends, and still others seem to simply gravitate towards the space regardless of whether they are particularly fond of him. Patrick Healy describes Johnny as 'a kind of Pied Piper, drawing the young and the old into his clearing—in part for his drugs, but also because he is a romanticised embodiment of the William Blake poem' (Healy). Here, Healy points out that Johnny's rejection of modernity—the 'dark Satanic Mills' of Blake's poem—and embrace of 'Englands green & pleasant Land' marks him as the defender of the kind of England and Englishness that Blake's poem describes, and he becomes a Christ-like figure himself. Healy's argument becomes even more convincing in a scene involving Lee, a character who has a one-way ticket to Australia the following day and spends his last 24 hours almost exclusively in Johnny's company. Lee suggests that Johnny's home stands on a 'ley line...lines of ancient energy, stretching across the landscape. Linking ancient sites...This is holy land' (Butterworth 72). Ley lines refer to a concept developed in ancient Europe that draws a series of lines across the Earth connecting historical structures and landmarks, supposedly demarcating 'earth energies', and in this way they are a natural component of the land ('The ley of the land'). That Lee roots Johnny's home on 'holy', 'ancient' land, and on the path of natural energy that connects historical landmarks further reinforces the notion that Johnny is seen as a figure who is entwined with nature, and specifically with the English soil. As Johnny fiercely protects his home, his visitors and his audience are both entranced and inspired by his venture to protect his plot of land, and the audience begins to perceive it as a noble and heroic endeavour.

Mark Rylance, who played the character of Johnny in both the London and New York productions of *Jerusalem*, advances our understanding of Johnny further in an interview with Andrew Marr. Rylance suggests that Johnny is, 'providing a certain kind of wildness for the young people that's not totally destructive at all. A certain kind of rite into adulthood…And something crazy not to do with corporate efficiency or any of the news… it's something to do with the land I guess and people's true nature' (Rylance). Like Healy, Rylance pays attention both to the characterization of Johnny as a drug-dealing party animal, but also as a man who becomes inseparable from English soil. The mention of 'corporate efficiency' returns us to the Kennet and Avon council, whose plans for the development of a New Estate epitomize the homogenization of the English landscape to fit the global capitalist mould. Johnny's defiance of the bulldozing council depicts him as the ultimate defender of English land, and this appeals to an underlying sense that a connection to the earth is becoming increasingly difficult in our modern reality. Paul Kingsnorth wrote an entire book titled *Real England: The Battle Against the Bland* on this very idea: how the homogenization of England is disrupting English people's connection to their land. He first states the reasons for his frustration. He writes:

> England matters to me. Not because I am a 'patriot' in the old-fashioned sense of the word. Not because I think it's better than everywhere else. Not because I don't like foreigners or have a visceral desperation to win the World Cup. Simply because it is my country. It is the place I was born and grew up in and it is the place I belong. I know its landscapes and its history, and feel connected to both. (Kingsnorth 12–13)

Then, Kingsnorth goes on to state exactly the problem that he has observed:

> I discovered that the real England is being eroded by three
> forces, which are meshing together to form a uniquely
> destructive whole: a powerful alliance of big business and
> big government; an unspoken, twenty-first-century class
> conflict, in which every nook and cranny is being made
> safe for the wealthy urban bourgeoisie; and a very English
> reluctance to discuss who we are as a nation or to stand
> up for our places, our national character and our cultural
> landscape. (Kingsnorth 13)

Kingsnorth's passage is powerful in its suggestion first that
there is such a thing as a 'real England' and that what we see
in England today is *not* real—i.e., it's global, it's corporate,
it has lost its uniqueness. He suggests that Englishness is
reluctant to recognize its own peculiarities, and that England's
unwillingness to defend itself is causing it to be destroyed. Of
course, no one is a stauncher defender of the English soil on
which he stands than Johnny, and perhaps it is for this exact
reason that he, and the play *Jerusalem*, had such a profound
effect on audiences. There is something invigorating about his
defiance perhaps because the (English) audience, whose daily
lives already operate within the context of a globalized world,
are reminded of the exceptional nature of the English land.
Johnny becomes the mouthpiece for a feature of Englishness
that people seem to be missing but cannot easily express—one
that looks to the land as a grounding force and a place to attach
a feeling of shared home. He displays a reverence to the land
that inspires reflection on its beauty, and effortlessly convinces
the audience that Englishness lies in a connection to nature and
the land, which they too should fight to protect.

Kingsnorth's book also points us towards notions of
England's uniqueness within the world, and his desire to

reject the effects of globalization and modernization imply an embrace of isolationism and a sinking into a past associated with glory and power. As mentioned previously, Johnny's home is the centre of the play—we never leave his space and the land that is being fought for. With our eyes trained so firmly on the mobile home, the audience develops a myopic vision of what England looks like—one that is also shared among the characters. Johnny's circle—his community—is isolated by virtue of being situated in the woods away from the man-made society that surrounds it. Furthermore, the only character who expresses any desire to leave is Lee, and his friends are unable to understand his wishes. Johnny does no more than to remark: 'I shouldn't worry, boy. You'll be back next year' (Butterworth 21), implying that Lee won't be able to stay away from England for too long. Davey spends more time expressing his opinion on the matter:

DAVEY. Rather you than me, mate. I've never seen the point of other countries. I leave Wiltshire, my ears pop. Seriously. I'm on my bike, pedalling along, see a sign says 'Welcome to Berkshire', I turn straight round. I don't like to go east of Wootton Bassett. Suddenly its Reading, then London, then before you know where you are you're in France, and then there's just countries popping up all over. What's that about? I can't help it if I like it here. I can't help it if I'm happy. (24)

Davey's quip, 'I've never seen the point of other countries,' reveals a belief that there is no need for any place other than England; he indirectly betrays his extreme Anglo-centrism with the notion that everything else is simply 'other', and takes up space in a world that belongs to England. The image of Davey's ears popping when he leaves Wiltshire also suggests a literal change in the atmosphere and indicates that his body is either unaccustomed or unprepared to exist in an atmosphere that is not the one which he currently inhabits. Furthermore, the proximity he describes to Reading, London, France, and the rest of continental Europe demonstrates a sense that everything is moving closer together—narrowing in a way that feels like an ever-encroaching threat.

However, the depiction of Englishness that *Jerusalem* provides to its audience here is incredibly ironic. To suggest that the characters' pushback against a globalized world is a noble instinct inherent to the English character ignores the fact that it was Britain who created such a world in the first place. At its height, the British Empire controlled approximately a quarter of the land on Earth (Taylor), and Britain has invaded a staggering 90 per cent of the world's nations (Seymour), demonstrating its historical mission to make the world in its image. While globalization and empire are two distinct projects—the former seeking to pull the world into a closer but mutual relationship and the latter seeking to dominate the world—they are similarly poised to homogenize culturally disparate places. Therefore, in *Jerusalem*, globalization is threatening because it takes a step towards a united world that is *not* dominated by England; it implies that England will undergo the same changes to accommodate cultures from the rest of the world that it forced upon others not so long ago. Despite the difference between globalization and empire, England has played a role in both, which makes pushing back against a close-knit world almost *anti*-English, and therefore seems to be an incredibly ironic impulse in the world of the play.

Regardless, Davey continues to lament the loss of the local and the encroachment of more distant places by recapping a story that he saw on the local news about an old woman who was kicked to death: 'I'm at home, on me own, watching, getting that upset, tearing up, the lot, before I realise it's some old biddy from Wales. Some Welsh nonsense. Good luck to 'em. I ain't never even fucking been there and I never fucking will'

(Butterworth 60). Here, Davey makes an even clearer statement about locality—one that suggests he cannot feel empathy for anyone outside his immediate vicinity. Others begin to pile in on Davey's frustration:

DAVEY. You want to gas yourself in your garage in Gloucester, be my guest. How could I possibly care less?

TANYA. Show me a good house fire in Salisbury. Now *that's* tragic.

LEE. Way I see it, for local news to make *any* sense, you've got to have at least a *chance* of shagging the weather girl. (60)

Davey and Tanya display a distinct insensitivity to issues that lie outside of their immediate geographical vicinity, even though the events they describe should invite sympathy even from afar. Lee even suggests that news covering more distant places is nonsensical. The myopic narrowness of these characters' perspectives betrays the isolationism of their community, and reiterates their firm stance against the forces of globalization. Butterworth surely remains aware of the absurdity of his characters' convictions, and perhaps directs the audience to acknowledge the moral dangers of retreating inwards in this way. However, that Johnny and his friends are paragons of Englishness suggests that the audience did not see this scene as problematic, but rather as a comedic exchange that encapsulates feelings that people are often unable or unwilling to express.

Certainly, Davey's lament for the loss of local news is not entirely unfounded. Local news platforms are indeed beginning to disappear as they are outcompeted by larger regional and global news sources, which serve to further blend the world into one and eradicate the uniqueness of one's small place in that world. Davey's rejection of such erasure demonstrates his desire to remain insulated in his community—a desire shared by the other characters in the play—and this invites the audience to imagine the allure of feeling that one's place in the world matters in its own right, as opposed to being simply a fragment of a greater global whole. Furthermore, Davey goes on to quip that the local news is too busy 'merging with BBC Belgium' (60) to notice local events. Here, rather than commenting on his frustration with news expanding to cover European events, Davey targets Belgium, the country where the EU is based, indicating a Eurosceptic viewpoint. Of course, it would make sense for Davey and his fellow community members to be sceptical of the EU's liberal project in light of their rejection of global connection and cooperation, and this dialogue suggests that at least in the world of the play, the EU is perceived as being partly responsible for the loss of a local English identity—one rooted in the soil that Johnny and his friends so fervently seek to protect. Davey and Tanya's dialogue in this scene affirms the fact that grievances with the European project were felt long before the referendum was announced in 2015, and provides some precedence for the notion that Brexit was a response to the belief held by many English people that belonging to Europe meant a loss of identity—one that they hoped to reclaim upon exit.

Isolationism and the rejection of globalization aside, Johnny appeals to the English collective psyche as a man who represents, and is connected to, the mystical version of 'Englands green & pleasant Land'. Over the course of the play, he and other characters talk about him as though he himself is a mystical being—one that defies not only the legal, but even the natural laws that bind humans. The first instance of this occurs when Ginger tells the story of when Johnny was a daredevil at the Flintock Fair: 'He was a daredevil. Used to jump buses on a trials bike. All over Wiltshire. Dorset. The Downs. He jumped the lot. Buses, tanks. Horseboxes. Jumped an aqueduct once. He was gonna jump Stonehenge but the council put a stop to it' (31). He goes on: 'Broke every bone in his body. Broke his back in Swindon. Both arms in Calne. His legs in Devizes. His neck in Newbury. Then, at the Flintock Fair, 1981, he died' (31). Lee aptly describes the audience's likely reaction to the news that Johnny once died: 'Bollocks' (31), but Ginger remains adamant: 'I was there. I saw it with my own eyes' (31). To further surprise, Ginger recounts Johnny's return to life: 'They pronounce him stone dead...Paperwork, everything...suddenly everyone turns round and he's gone. He's vanished. There's just a blanket with nothing under it. They follow this trail of blood across the field, past the whirler-swirler, into the beer tent, up to the bar, where he's stood there finishing a pint of Tally-Ho' (32). The description Ginger gives of Johnny's revival is reminiscent of Jesus' resurrection, particularly given the sudden disappearance of the dead body. Given this parallel between Johnny and Jesus, alongside the fact that the play is titled after Blake's poem about Jesus' mythological visit to England, Johnny can be regarded as a Christ-like figure for England—a divine protector of sorts. However, while Jesus' resurrection is temporary until he returns to Heaven, Johnny remains Earth-bound. Johnny's resurrection and perpetual grounding in place might indicate to the audience that he is a different type of religious figure—one who seems Christ-like, but who is not sent by a divine power that does not exist on the earthly plane. Instead, Johnny is commanded by nature and the land—his duty is to the English soil, not to the world as a whole. So, while Jesus is a universal figure of redemption for Christians everywhere, Johnny becomes a figure of redemption and protection for English people alone. He is the answer to the desire for a uniquely English messiah that Blake's poem captures.

While Johnny is portrayed as being mystical himself, he also claims to have born witness to many supernatural events. His first tale is that he 'once met a giant that built Stonehenge' (57). Incorporating giants into the world of the play connects *Jerusalem* to the English medieval literary canon, and feeds into what Jeffrey Cohen calls the 'cultural function of the giant' in English literature: 'to serve as a powerful expounder of dominant contemporary myths, from how the world was formed and where linguistic difference originates to why stone ruins dot the British countryside, and what comprises heroic male identity' (Cohen 1). Indeed, Johnny's claim that the giant he encountered 'built Stonehenge' stems directly from the medieval notion that giants are the only explanation for such a site to exist in the first place, and to suggest that he met a giant at all implies that he is a heroic figure. Later, Johnny is asked where this meeting occurred, to which he replies: 'Just off the A14 outside Upavon. About half a mile from the Little Chef' (Butterworth 57). The absurd juxtaposition between the plainness of this location and the supernatural sighting of a giant is sincerely amusing, and serves to integrate the mystical into everyday England in a way that irresistibly links the medieval world to our modern one, inviting the audience to believe that despite the blandness of the A14, such wonders as seeing a giant are still possible. The allure of such mysticism over the bland every day that an English audience is accustomed to is extremely powerful, and offers them new possibilities for imagining the nation of which they are a part—one that is far more exciting, vibrant, and fundamentally and distinctively *English*.

Johnny's encounters with the supernatural do not end with giants. Later, in a conversation with Phaedra, who is described throughout the play as a 'fairy', Johnny reveals more of what he has witnessed in the forest surrounding his home:

JOHNNY. I've seen a lot of strange things in this wood. (*Beat.*) I seen a plague of frogs. Of bees. Of bats. I seen a rainbow hit the earth and set fire to the ground. I seen the air go still and all sound stop and a golden stag clear this clearing. Fourteen-point antlers of solid gold. I heard an oak tree cry. I've heard beech sing hymns. I seen a man they buried in the churchyard Friday sitting under a beech eating an apple on Saturday morning. (102)

Johnny's tales paint a picture of the enchanted forests of England in a similarly alluring way to the depiction of giants roaming around A roads. The 'plague of frogs'—the second plague of Egypt in the Bible's Book of Exodus—like Blake's poem, locates religious and divine events on English soil, while the crying oak tree and singing beech denote a natural world that can feel and do things beyond what we are capable of understanding. For an English audience, all of this imagery revives the notion that there is a magic indigenous to the English land, and provides yet another moment of escape from the blandness of everyday life. Sparking the imagination of the audience in this way invites them to take more pride in being connected with the enchanted English land. Like *England, England, Jerusalem* seeks to satisfy its audience's latent desires.

While the allure of mysticism in the play can be read as an opportunity for escapism, Laura Barton of *The Guardian* actually suggests that there is an impulse while watching *Jerusalem* to believe Johnny—to take him at his word and believe in his assertions that England is an enchanted place. She writes: 'And for all the outlandishness of his tales, there lingers the unshakeable, unsettling feeling that maybe it isn't all bombast and bluster. Maybe there truly were giants and bullets and fairies and dragons. Perhaps, in all the fable and folklore, and in the fire and fathom of those eyes, Rooster might just be telling the truth of this land' (Barton). Here, Barton provides insight into why *Jerusalem* received such critical acclaim in its short run on stage; namely, because it inspires feelings of reverence towards the history of English land that are absent from any formal or informed understanding of what it means to be English. Once again, Johnny's performance is able to persuade the audience that England's land is magical; perhaps rather than allowing them to escape from blandness, Butterworth is encouraging them to view it in a new way. Where globalization seeks to make everywhere look the same as everywhere else, and where the mundane boredom of chain restaurants plagues the local landscape, the play asks the audience to envision an England that maintains its mystical roots, and inspires them to protect it from the globalizing forces that threaten to destroy its exceptional nature.

While many are, like Barton, deeply enamoured by *Jerusalem's* depiction of the supernatural and by Johnny, the Christ-like protector of Englishness, the invigoration the audience feels from his tales is also absurd. Johnny's success as protector of his patch of land is fairly long-lasting throughout the play despite being under siege from the very first scene with the visit from the Kennet and Avon council. However, even though we never see him evicted from his home, which gives him a sense of permanence in the land, Butterworth never makes it clear either way whether Johnny will win this fight. We can assume that he won't, considering that he is literally surrounded by council members ready to forcibly remove him from the site at the close of the curtain. The lack of a firm victory for Johnny indicates that he—and if he is the embodiment of Englishness, then consequently, Englishness—are incompatible with modernity and will ultimately be crushed by the forces they push back against. There is no smugness in this conclusion— on the contrary, it is a sad one, but nonetheless, the mysticism that surrounds Johnny's life ultimately comes across as a drug-hazed delusion and perhaps even a naïve belief that England can exist separately from the rest of the global capitalist modern world—a world that it helped to create.

Jerusalem is a play that appeals to a nation without a firm identity. It draws on folklore and mythology, and harps on modern frustrations with legal enforcement and global expansion to inspire a newly invigorated sense of Englishness rooted in land that is at its core mystical, divine, and permanent. It is, in Ben Brantley's words, 'a mythic England that may never have been but that everyone, on some level, longs for' (Brantley). The allure of the play is that it provides the audience with an English national identity that is worth fighting for — one rooted in defying the law and protecting the land as Johnny does. Indeed, the English land feels worthy of such fervent preservation against modern capitalist forces as we watch Johnny's spirited defence of his home, Davey's lament for the loss of the local, and as we imagine giants reaching down to lay the stones of Stonehenge. However, the play is brimming with a love of Englishness that is based on fiction, and illogically positions England in opposition to the capitalist world that it enabled through British colonial pursuits and membership of global supranational organizations. Although Butterworth is certainly aware of the limits of his characters, and despite the fact that many areas of post-Brexit England today likely find the type of patriotism it displays objectionable, the appeal of *Jerusalem*'s assertion of a firm, unique, and magical identity might explain why the political strategy of the Leave campaign worked in 2016. Politicians campaigning for Leave were able to exploit the English desire to identify itself as special by making vague promises about restoring the UK to its former glory, and using xenophobia to suggest that Leaving would offer a chance to protect the land from foreigners — to push back against an interconnected world. *Jerusalem* pre-emptively struck the exact same chord with its English audience as the promise of Brexit struck in its people 7 years later.

Chapter Four

BrexLit: Preserving the Present to Change the Future

Here's an old story so new that it's still in the middle of happening,
writing itself right now with no knowledge of where or how it'll
end.
Ali Smith

The texts that I have covered to this point have allowed the reader to gain an understanding of how Englishness has been portrayed in literature leading up to the Brexit referendum. These texts will continue to provide comparative significance in this chapter, which will focus specifically on BrexLit — works published post-Brexit referendum. These works will appear in chronological order: *The Book of Baruch by the Gnostic Justin*, a volume of poetry published posthumously by Geoffrey Hill (2019), *Autumn* by Ali Smith (2016), *Perfidious Albion* by Sam Byers (2017), *Middle England* by Jonathan Coe (2018), and *The Cockroach* by Ian McEwan (2019). These works all consider the seismic shifts that caused the Brexit referendum, or that occurred afterwards, and each allows us new insights into the problem of Englishness and where it might be headed next.

Before analysing these texts, it is vital to note that historically, literature is often written to glorify events that are in reality devastating failures. As Fintan O'Toole points out in his book named after this phenomenon — *Heroic Failure* — English literature follows suit, epitomized by Alfred Tennyson's poem 'The Charge of the Light Brigade', which commemorates one of the most brutal and unnecessary massacres of Englishmen in a war, and yet has become a rallying cry for English patriotism. O'Toole uses George Orwell's words to describe this phenomenon: 'English literature, like other literatures, is full of battle-poems, but it is worth noticing that the ones that have won for themselves a kind of popularity are always a tale of disasters and retreat. There is no popular poem about Trafalgar or Waterloo, for instance...The most stirring battle-poem in English is all about a brigade of cavalry which charged in the wrong direction' (Orwell qtd. in O'Toole 82). With this in mind, BrexLit can be seen as both an iteration of and a break away from this literary tradition. While much of the popular literature that has been produced in response to the 2016 referendum is indeed rooted in what appears to be the devastating failure of Brexit, it does not offer any glorification of the event. O'Toole argues that this is because England has ceased to be confident about its own superiority, meaning that turning failure into 'a statement of strength' (O'Toole 84) has become difficult at best and impossible at worst. Perhaps it is not that England lacks confidence, but that Brexit provides no room to conceal failure as success. Instead of glorifying Brexit itself, many BrexLit authors focus on visualizing new and better versions of Englishness— ones that will allow England to move forward from Brexit and remain part of an interconnected world.

* * *

Geoffrey Hill's *The Book of Baruch by the Gnostic Justin*: Dying Man, Dying Nation

Geoffrey Hill is a renowned English poet, best known for his 1971 volume of poems titled *Mercian Hymns*. *The Book of Baruch by the Gnostic Justin* is Hill's final volume of poetry, and it was published posthumously in 2019. Hill died just one week after the Brexit referendum in 2016, and *The Book of Baruch by the Gnostic Justin* is filled with his final reflections on the state of Englishness in the lead-up to, and just following, the referendum. Despite the fact that this is not the first published example of

BrexLit, it was the first to be finished—albeit finishing was not really Hill's decision. Although the volume is a series of separate poems, they flow from and between each other, and all share an almost identical form, separated only by numbered breaks. Indeed, the poems are each preceded by a number in the order that they appear in the book, which suggests that one should read this volume chronologically, almost like an epic poem. Regardless of how the text is read, Hill's final volume is a weighty grappling with England; Hill described the poems as 'odes' (Hill 3), and in his review of the book, David Wheatley of *The Guardian* suggests that the poems address a 'nation out-of-kilter' (Wheatley). As Wheatley writes: 'There is scarcely one of the 271 sections in this book that does not assail the reader with the force of a vatic last judgment' (Wheatley). Certainly, Hill wrote these poems as a dying man in a dying England, and, while Hill's speaker only *represents* himself, one feels that his final volume is a divination for the country that he leaves behind.

The form of *The Book of Baruch by the Gnostic Justin* is consistent with much of Hill's earlier work. He frequently uses assonance, consonance, and internal rhyme as opposed to end rhyme, generating a distinct rhythm and heightening the unity of the lines. Hill's uses of assonance and consonance not only link the sounds of words with each other, which enhances the reading experience, but also reinforce a shared meaning between the words, offering an even greater sense of accord within the lines of the poems. The poems also all follow the form of free verse, and are laid out like prose, often with multiple sentences making up a single line within the poem. Free verse does not follow a set meter or rigid rhyme scheme— though as mentioned it does make use of internal rhyme—but rather reflects natural speech patterns, and is better able to encapsulate complex ideas and the meandering trail of thought. Although free verse has been the primary form of poetry since the twentieth century, and therefore was not Hill's creation, this form is apt for the religious and prophetic associations of his volume. Indeed, in the book of Psalms, prose poetry is used as a way of communicating a religious or prophetic message. Furthermore, Hill's attempts to grapple with English identity would appear far more straightforward if he adhered to a set meter and rhyme scheme; the use of free verse reflects the sinuous attempts to locate and pin down what Englishness means. The volume's contention with Brexit further emphasizes this; in the turbulent period that defined the Brexit referendum debate, Hill uses poetry to mirror this turbulence through free verse—a somewhat chaotic, yet cohesive attempt to reconcile meaning.

Before considering the poems themselves, it is imperative to understand how the title of the volume relates to them and their overarching message. There are two Books of Baruch, each with a vexed position in relation to the religious canon. The first is a book in the Apocrypha—one of the books of the Old Testament that not all Christians accept as legitimate (Hogan). In the second and third centuries, Christian beliefs were extremely diverse; many recounted episodes of Jesus' life and spoke of angels that are not mentioned in the Bible that we have today. In an attempt to standardize these various beliefs and create a cohesive religion, multiple councils were formed to decide which beliefs should be suppressed and which should be promoted as the true word of God, and 'Heresiologists—heresy hunters of a bygone age who busied themselves exposing people judged dangerous to the Christian masses—fulminated against what they maintained was the falsehood of the gnostics' (*The Gnostic Bible* 2). The result was that the monotheist belief—that Jesus was not eternal and does not participate in the same substance as God—was suppressed and condemned as the heterodoxy, while the trinitarian position—that endorsed the holy trinity of the Father, Son, and the Holy Spirit—became the new orthodox position (*The Gnostic Bible* 11). Among those whose ideas were rejected were the Gnostics, who 'provided innovative and oftentimes disturbing interpretations of the creation stories they read' (*The Gnostic Bible* 2), and their gospels were cast out and hidden for centuries—that is, until they were discovered in 1945 in a cave in Egypt (Pagels). The second Book of Baruch—a gospel written by the Gnostic Justin—was not found among these Gnostic gospels, but we know of its existence from the writings of Hippolytus, who wrote disdainfully of the Gnostics in Book 5 of his work: *Refutation of All Heresies*. Hill's decision to title his work *The Book of Baruch by the Gnostic Justin* indicates that he is aligning his poetry with a suppressed text—one that conveys a belief that is contrary to the orthodox manner of understanding. He is also identifying with a gnostic—a heretic—writer, which intimates a belief that his work might be suppressed by others, or if not suppressed, at the very least rejected. It may also predict that it could be lost for good—relegated to the dust of history; after all, he knew he would not be around to see that the work was published. The cover art of Hill's book of poems reinforces this idea. Taken from William Blake's painting *America: A Prophecy*, it shows an old, haggard man with a walking stick entering the mouth of a cave himself—easily read as Hill entering the world of the dead, but more importantly, entering the same kind of space in which the Gnostic gospels were hidden for hundreds of years.

Hill's sense of connection to the Gnostics becomes more apparent throughout the poems themselves, and foregrounds the volume's political position. In poem 59, the speaker defines his terms: 'By gnosis I mean both what it ought to have been and what it is, to tell truth' (Hill 26). The speaker's emphasis on truth here falls directly in opposition with how the orthodoxy viewed the Gnostics—as heretics and liars—and rather suggests that gnosis is a pursuit of truth and knowledge. The notion that the Gnostics were those who told the truth is, in itself, heretical.

Yet, this idea is reinforced in poem 70, when the speaker speculates: 'Almost always the wrong people are admired, rewarded, and sedulously guarded; it is how things are wired and starred' (32). Again, these lines reverse the narrative of truth between the orthodoxy and the Gnostics, suggesting that the council members who chose which beliefs became the official canon were the 'wrong people' and consequently that the Gnostics were right. In this way, the poem offers emancipation from the label of heretic ascribed to the Gnostics, and casts doubt on the ways that narratives and 'truths' are formed and consolidated. Furthermore, the line 'it is how things are wired and starred' suggests that the power structure that allows the wrong people to remain on top is 'wired' into society. The word 'starred', though, can also be used to mean fractured: 'To make a radiating crack or fracture in (a surface of glass, ice, etc.)' (*OED*), which suggests that the ingrained system that keeps the 'wrong people' in power is also what will cause it to fall apart. The word 'starred' used in this sense also connects to a line in a later poem depicting a cracked mirror (Hill 92), indicating that the splintering of reflective surfaces is used throughout the volume to represent a contorted vision of power and identity in England. Certainly, the musings in these poems, while they appear to be reflections on an ancient Greek council's judgments, might also be read as reflections on the UK government, and the Conservative government in control at the time Hill was writing. Such a reading becomes even more convincing upon completing the book, when the reader has been more exposed to the poet's own political tendencies, which will be discussed later in this section.

While Hill does reflect on the Gnostics as a way of understanding frames of power and truth, he also demonstrates a personal attachment to the idea of gnosis that does not necessarily relate to the Gnostics themselves. Several times throughout the volume, the same line repeats: 'what I love and admire is true gnosis; everything that I hate is not' (38), and in poem 81 he follows this repeated phrase with the line: 'Of my thesis this is the ghost-score' (38). The speaker suggests that they may not be following an objective standard for gnosis throughout, but rather that knowledge to them is a subjective endeavour. However, this poem also returns to the notion of the vatic—the word Wheatley uses to describe the effect of Hill's poems ('a vatic last judgement'). Using this word likens Hill as a poet to Old Testament prophets—a key romantic turn—and forces us to consider the role of the prophet. Prophets deliver divine, universal truths that often appear in contrast with mankind's common certainties, which leads people to reject them. In this way, the indication towards subjectivity in the line 'what *I* love and admire is true gnosis' may be intended to insinuate that the speaker, under divine supervision, is the only one who can truly distinguish the truth, rather than suggesting a personal bias that prevents them from reaching it. Furthermore, in poem 90, the speaker describes how they read and relate to *The Book of Baruch*: '*The Book of Baruch* is easy going, compliant with my disproportionate ideal, surviving surreal mismanagement with humour and style; collapsible for ease of stowing' (41). This poem links Hill's identification with the Gnostics and his own political position, which lies in opposition to the system of power in place in the UK. The phrase 'surreal mismanagement' reinforces Wheatley's sense that Hill was writing about 'a nation out-of-kilter' (Wheatley), and more blatantly criticizes those currently in power. The word 'surreal' on its own also suggests something about the atmosphere of England—that there is something bizarre about what is happening in this country. That the poet reacts with 'humour and style' suggests a somewhat therapeutic approach to dealing with the strangeness of the present. As opposed to a barrage of politically disillusioned poems intended to overwhelm the reader with dread, Hill elects to imbue his work with wit and enjoyment as a means of healing.

Many of the early poems in the volume focus specifically on the capital city, London, and its ability to withstand attack. One of the longer verses in poem 36 recounts the devastation of the London Blitz during World War II, and begins:

> Like much else rebuilt out of brick dust, ash, and silt of soot; a holocaust in that word's true cast: a multiplex burnt offering, residue of scorched hollows, roast flesh, hallows torched, when the City went up.
>
> Roman and Saxon roused from half-houseled sleep where they had housed. (Hill 15)

These lines depict a scene of total ruin; the word 'holocaust' is used for its original definition, as opposed to the twentieth-century associations we attach to it. One *OED* definition of 'holocaust' reads: 'Complete consumption by fire, or that which is so consumed; complete destruction, esp. of a large number of persons; a great slaughter or massacre' (*OED*). The deadly image of 'complete consumption by fire' depicts total ruin, and forms an image of London utterly destroyed after the Blitz. The reference to the roused Roman and Saxon further emphasizes the notion of ruin; Roman ruins lie scattered throughout London — the remnants of buildings once destroyed by the Saxon Boudica in a devastating and flattening attack on the city. These lines could be read as suggesting that the ruin of the Blitz revealed more ruins that lay undiscovered throughout London, but they could also simply be read as references to the city's history of destruction. If the latter interpretation holds, Hill is indicating something remarkable about London and its ability to endure attack. Indeed, Matt Brown of *Londonist* suggests that after the Saxons destroyed London, 'a bigger and stronger city rose in its place' (Brown), the poet's suggestion that the Blitz raised sleeping Romans and Saxons may imply that though the Blitz destroyed London, it also reinforced it and made it stronger.

Throughout the rest of poem 36, the speaker considers all of the religious buildings that were gutted in the Blitz: 'St Andrew Holborn...St Mary Abchurch...St Mary-le-Bow...St Margaret Pattens...St Andrew Undershaft' (Hill 15). Apart from St Andrew Undershaft, all of these churches are known as the 'Wren churches' (Downes), as they were rebuilt after the Great Fire of London in 1666 by architect Christopher Wren, whose most famous project is St Paul's Cathedral, which he also designed to replace the rubble of the old St Paul's left by the fire (Downes). Just as Wren's churches were rebuilt in the aftermath of a fire in 1666, so were his churches rebuilt again in the aftermath of the Blitz in the 1940s. Hill expands on the reconstruction that was necessary to preserve them after the Blitz in poem 50. He writes: 'The beauty of the restored Wren churches should be a matter of record, indeed of gratitude; or, failing that, of duty' (Hill 23). These three words: record, gratitude, and duty, all imbue a sense of patriotism to the rebuilding process, as though we owe something not only to history and the record of the past for the benefit of the future, but to the capital city itself — the centre of England and its power. Indeed, duty to one's country and land is a prominent nationalistic idea — one that was strongly reinforced in the two world wars of the twentieth century. The patriotic idea of restoring some of London's most architecturally significant buildings after they have come under attack reminds the reader of the capital's history of destruction and rejuvenation. Drawing on Wren's churches in particular goes even further, painting a picture of the city as palimpsest, where traces of the past remain even though they have been obliterated. The repetition of fire and destruction — by the Saxons, by the Great Fire of London, and by the Blitz — suggest that though the country's foundation may be destroyed, it can be rebuilt, and will return stronger than before. In this way, these poems perhaps contain a more hopeful message for post-

Brexit England—that although leaving the EU might constitute a destructive act, as it has many times before, England will heal and emerge more resilient than ever.

Having said all this, and despite the patriotic zeal with which the poet relays the rebuilding of the Wren churches, Hill's volume as a whole rejects the idea of a 'romantic nationalism' (29), and ridicules those who find ways to reassert English exceptionalism. In poem 21, he writes: 'Royal Tudor satyr masks, with horns and tusks worn down to papier-mâché husks conserved, or not, at Hampton Court, are revelled-in by those who would maintain our nation's token place—even now, without grace—in the Divine Plan' (10). The consonance of this line is reflected not only in internal rhyme, but also in meaning. The masks and tusks turn to husks—a historical sequence of degradation. The material the poet describes has been worn down to papier mâché, suggesting an impermanence and fragility that undercuts the notion that these royal relics are eternal symbols of the 'nation's token place', or exceptional status. The speaker of the poems also inserts his own position on patriotism in poem 64: 'I am an old-fashioned patriot even though, long ago, I fell to praising the Easter Rising' (29), suggesting that his love for England has been challenged by feelings of camaraderie with the Irish rebels who led an armed insurrection in opposition to English rule in 1916. In other words, the speaker recognizes England's flaws as an oppressor, and that feeling appears to be held in contrast with a sense of patriotism.

In the next line of the same poem, Hill writes: 'Our fellow citizens, chiefly, make fools of us; not uncommonly at grand funerals and the unveiling of national memorials' (29). This line speaks to the act of reinforcing a national identity; through 'grand funerals' we feel a collective sense of mourning for an individual who presumably means something to England, while the 'unveiling of national memorials' similarly imbues the country with a collective sense of pride in English achievements of the past. Yet, the poet suggests that these acts 'make fools of us' — that they reveal an almost laughable impulse to swoon at the grandeur of the nation based on hollow displays of national honour and egotism. The final line of the poem reads:

There are fools enough to be made fools of, I grant you that.
Romantic nationalism (*supra*) is a kind of fate. (29)

Here, Hill depicts nationalism as foolish, while also suggesting that the impulse to form strong nationalisms is 'fated' in today's world — that it is necessary. Indeed, it is difficult to exist apart from one's national identity — the world is divided into nations and one's national identity dictates everything about how one is able to live. Yet, in poem 262, Hill relates the notion of fate and romantic nationalism to the patriotism of the year of the Blitz:

That there is strong correlation between character and fate is probably proven somewhere.
  If so, our nation in nineteen forty was a major exception to that rota (141)

The Blitz began in 1940, and the speaker suggests here that the 'foolish' romantic nationalism of today is distinct from the feeling of patriotism in that year. In this way, Hill is suggesting that something fundamental has changed about England and Englishness since the Second World War — perhaps pointing out that strong national pride during a time of destruction and war is far less foolish than romantic nationalism in a time of peace and prosperity. It seems that the romantic nationalism of today that Hill speaks of relates to the re-emergent rhetoric of British superiority, and the form of baseless yet fervent nationalism that proliferated during the Brexit campaign in 2016.

  Although Hill's poems read distinctly as though they hold the key to what Englishness means, in the latter part of the volume the poems fall into the same pattern as the pre-Brexit referendum texts of the previous chapter: into recognizing that there is no simple answer to the conundrum of identity in this nation. In the first line of poem 174, Hill writes: '"All the mirrors in England are broken" I've taken from *Jonathan Strange & Mr Norrell*. Possibly it is how we all feel' (92). Amidst the reference to the 2004 novel by Susanna Clarke, *Jonathan Strange & Mr Norrell*, which is about the revival of practical magic and is set during the Napoleonic Wars, this line generates several layered meanings. The first relates to the fact that in Roman times, people believed that mirrors contained the soul of the person looking into them, and if the mirror broke, it meant that the person's soul was damaged, hence 7 years of bad luck. From this, one might understand poem 174 to be a reflection (no pun intended) on the broken soul of England—on the evil that it has historically been capable of—and an omen for bad luck (which could be considered a kind of practical magic to punish wrong-doers). On this reading, the poet condemns what the nation stands for historically; rather than pride, there is a sense of disappointment in England. The image of a broken mirror also implies that England is unable to see itself clearly even when confronted with its reflection, and without that clear image of itself, it inevitably lacks a coherent identity. England's lack of firm identity is further emphasized in poem 182, in the line: 'The England of my fable an unstable floating island seldom in the same place' (99). The word 'fable' here suggests that there is a moral message about Englishness to be extracted from *The Book of Baruch*, while the untethered image of a floating island indicates a kind of placelessness—an uprootedness that leaves it without a foundation. Combined with the word 'unstable', these images once again point the reader towards a conception of an England that has been politically and physically uprooted, and that is being pushed along by the waves and tides of the world rather than charting its own course. In this way, there is also a distinct lack of agency in this image, and England loses not only its identity, but its control and power too.

Furthermore, as Hill is clearly grappling with Englishness, the use of the first-person narrative throughout might reveal how he actually feels about the current state of the nation. In the latter half of the book, the poems become more brazen, and the poet begins to reveal his outlook on contemporary and future events in England. In poem 186, the poet concisely expresses his allegiance to the Labour Party and his hope that they be elected at the next opportunity with the line: 'Corbyn must win' (102). He goes on in poem 194:

The radical politics are not an obstacle: a revival of archaic, anti-oligarchical zeal.

If the free spirit is unelectable, so be it.

Come the turn of the wheel it shall have my vote, posthumous or not. (107)

These lines blatantly reveal that Hill is discouraged by the 'oligarchical' country he sees before him, and disclose that he views 'radical [leftist] politics' as the only antidote. Collapsing the distinction between poet and speaker, he definitively states his beliefs and casts his ballot for Corbyn from beyond the grave. As the Brexit proceedings begin, the poet continues to relay his voting intentions and remark on the world around him. In poem 264, in a line separated on the page from the rest of the poem, Hill writes: 'Come June I shall vote 'Remain' though disquieted by what I know will even then, even if we win, squat in the high seats, acting as if benign albeit of covert reign' (142). Here, Hill acknowledges that even if Remain were to win, Euroscepticism would 'squat in the high seats', lying in wait for a future opportunity to realize its agenda, and he foretells that tensions will remain either way after the votes are cast.

Hill engages even more explicitly with the Brexit referendum in his final poems, becoming more and more direct—perhaps as he felt time was running out to say his piece. Poem 266, ostensibly written very close to his death and perhaps with a mind to the increased violence that accompanied the referendum debate, begins as follows:

> I look at the handsome intelligent face of Stephen Lawrence, and mourn; and at the coarse blebbed features of his murderers, and feel shame.
>   The virtues attributed to our nation are a Referendum scam, as with misinterpretation of *A Midsummer Night's Dream*, or 'Jerusalem' or the nuclear deterrent or Classic FM or the Heir Apparent. (143)

In the first line, Hill draws his mind to the face of Stephen Lawrence, a Black British teenager who was murdered in a racially-motivated attack in south-east London in 1993. As was outlined in chapter one, Lawrence's murder became one of the most infamous in British history after the botched police response let his killers roam free for almost 2 decades after the attack—and some still remain unpunished. Hill's shame implies a collective guilt that lies on the non-black English population who are complicit in a system that allows such tragedies to occur. The second line feels more urgent and angrier. The poem moves from the face of Stephen Lawrence, which evokes feelings of sympathy, anger, and guilt, to criticizing how the referendum erased history by framing England as virtuous despite its brutal, racist history. Hill also refers to Jez Butterworth's *Jerusalem*; it appears that he agrees with the reading I put forth in chapter three, in which I argue that *Jerusalem* is a performative representation of what people *want* England to look like—that it is romanticized and ahistorical, not to mention hypocritical in its attack of the global world that England helped to build (though perhaps purposefully so).

The final poem of the volume, poem 271, is a wonderfully crafted description of how Britain looks after the Brexit referendum in 2016, in the final week of Hill's life:

> The numbness after the shock of exit, big-bummed Britannia in her tracksuit; her phantom lap of honour; no other runner.
>
> July the dark month; the lime leaves turned matt. The newly-bloomed mallow will see us re-autumned before it falls fallow.
>
> Even so, the power of stout roses has risen watt by watt against the afterglow of each brief thunder-shower. (Hill 145)

The first words of this poem, 'The numbness after the shock of exit', gives the poem an almost lethargic feeling; the reader is forced to slow down, imagining the nation like a body paralyzed in shock—frozen, silent. The line 'big-bummed Britannia in her tracksuit' is extremely comical, using quintessentially English trackies to depict a nation on its arse. Hill continues to mock Brexit triumphalism as a 'phantom lap of honour', suggesting that Brexiteers are imagining themselves as having beaten something or someone, when really, they have only beaten themselves. The next line, 'July that dark month', brings to mind the cyclicality of the seasons, but where July ought to be one of the brightest months of the year, the vote has plunged it into darkness and decay—nature will be 're-autumned'. Yet, despite the morose (and darkly humorous) tone of this final poem, Hill ends on a note of national rebirth: 'the power of stout roses has risen watt by watt against the afterglow of each brief thunder-shower'. Roses, the flower often used as a symbol of Englishness, appear here as a symbol once again of rejuvenation. As Hill reminds us in his poems on the Blitz and the restoration of Wren's churches, with destruction comes the opportunity for rebirth and rejuvenation; the reassertion of this in these final lines ends the volume in an overwhelmingly positive and hopeful way.

Geoffrey Hill's *The Book of Baruch by the Gnostic Justin* is an extraordinary book of poetry that tracks a poet's final reflections on Englishness as he stares both death, and a dramatically changing nation, in the face. He sees poetry as an opportunity to contribute to the resurgence of the nation that he hopes for; in poem 200, Hill writes: 'Poem as urgent sperm bank for sunk re-emergent nation' (110). Indeed, in the final years of his life, Hill's poems become his children—his legacy—and his attempt to bring something into the world that can heal and rebuild a nation he believes is suffering a slow death by nationalism. Although Hill never lived to see the rest of the Brexit proceedings unfold, his poems can be read as a document of what Englishness, and the debates about Englishness, look like at this watershed historical moment. Hill dedicates much of his volume to recounting esteemed English writers, poets, and figures whom he admires or doesn't. He recounts English history as a way of understanding English identity, and he recognizes the difficulty of defining Englishness at a time when the answer seems murkier than ever before. Hill also likens all of his reflections to the work of a supposed heretic—a reminder to the reader that he intentionally writes the unconventional story, but also that it is his words that hold prophecy—that hold the truth. Despite its sombre reflections, Hill's final volume ends on a note of hope; when London is destroyed by fire, it always rises like a phoenix from the ashes. Although Brexit looms large as a force as destructive as fire, Hill reminds us that English roses will bloom once again. Without taking away from the pain that Brexit brought to many or ignoring the hatred that surfaced as a result of the referendum debate, Hill concludes that England can and will re-grow into a better nation as a result.

* * *

Ali Smith's *Autumn*: Time, Love, and Collage

Autumn by Ali Smith was published less than 4 months after the Brexit referendum in 2016 and is often referred to as the first BrexLit novel. Smith is a prolific Scottish author, playwright, academic, and journalist, and she has accrued a number of awards over her career, in addition to being shortlisted for the Man Booker Prize four times. Although she is from Inverness, she currently lives in Cambridge, England. *Autumn* is the first in Smith's latest series of novels, which make up a seasonal quartet. Each novel is named after a season of the year, but despite their apparent continuity, each has its own unique plot. As the titles suggest, time, and our experience of time, is the central theme that connects all four novels, and *Autumn* in particular grapples with time in marvellously complex and subtle ways. Ironically, *Autumn* is set primarily in the summer of 2016, in the midst of the Brexit referendum debate, vote, and aftermath. However, the novel is not dedicated to reminiscing directly about these events. The primary narrative of the novel follows old friends Elisabeth, who is 32 years old, and Daniel Gluck, who is 101 years old, unconscious, and on his death bed, through their relationship, past and present. The novel is organized achronologically, jumping seamlessly to different points in Elisabeth's and Daniel's lives. *Autumn* also operates in a strange limbo between life and death, as Daniel lies quietly dying, dreaming and slipping slowly but surely away from his connection to the living. Although autumn is a time of decay—and Smith is sure to link the experience of Brexit to that decay—like Geoffrey Hill, the novel offers a conception of time as a restorative, cyclical force. While division and political turmoil is rife throughout the book, so is friendship, art, and love. Ultimately, Smith allows the reader to imagine a world beyond Brexit, even as death—both of Daniel and of the nation as we know it—looms large.

Autumn begins with a riff on Charles Dickens' *A Tale of Two*

Cities—a historical novel set in both Paris and London during the French Revolution that pays close attention to the dichotomy between the two capital cities at a time of immense upheaval. Dickens' opening line reads:

> It was the best of times, it was the worst of times, it was the age of wisdom, it was the age of foolishness, it was the epoch of belief, it was the epoch of incredulity, it was the season of hope, it was the winter of despair, we had everything before us, we had nothing before us, we were all going direct to Heaven, we were all going direct the other way—in short, the period was so far like the present period, that some of its noisiest authorities insisted on its being received, for good or for evil, in the superlative degree of comparison only. (Dickens 1)

Opening his novel in this way, Dickens calls the reader's attention to the dichotomy between London and Paris during this time, and depicts a world in which 'the superlative degree of comparison' becomes the orienting force. Dickens' call to associate this atmosphere with 'the present period' feels timeless, as though it could also connect to our present moment in the age of Brexit, yet in this instance, the opposition is not between nations, but within one. Ali Smith uses her own version of Dickens' opening line; much shorter, but no less impactful, Smith writes: 'It was the worst of times, it was the worst of times' (Smith 3). By imitating Dickens, Smith immediately indicates that she is writing about a period of division, yet she offers us no actual contrast between supposed sides. Smith continues: 'Again. That's the thing about things. They fall apart, always have, always will, it's in their nature' (3). Smith's use of the word 'Again' to refer to the very first line of her novel is the first example of her complex handling of time; the reader has no background for when 'the worst of times' might have happened before, since the book has only just begun. Yet, Smith makes a statement about how things fall apart: 'always have, always will', which offers a simple yet profound explanation of the cyclicality of life and time. While the immediate notion that things always fall apart appears like an image of hopelessness, Smith subtly weaves this idea throughout the rest of the novel in a way that actually casts it as an image of hope.

Smith continues to introduce the reader to her simple yet simultaneously complex framework of time in the first chapter of the novel with a dream sequence in which Daniel, who lies unconscious in a care home, believes he has passed over into death. In this sequence, Daniel hovers between life and death, and between earthly time and a timeless place. Like any dream, his visions cast the images we see in life onto an unfamiliar backdrop—one that often uncomfortably reveals those things that we try the hardest to repress. The sentence that begins the sequence goes: 'So an old old man washes up on a shore' (3). Without going further, this image of a body washing up on shore immediately casts the reader's mind to the reel of news stories about migrants' bodies appearing on European beaches. The most well-known instance of this occurred in September 2015, when a young Syrian boy was found face-down on a Turkish beach after a failed attempt to sail to Greece (Helena Smith). Of course, in this case it is an old body that turns up, but the image is nevertheless topical and sets a disturbing precedent. The narrative goes on: 'He looks like a punctured football with its stitching split, the leather kind that people kicked a hundred years ago. The sea's been rough' (3). The leathery image of the old man's skin paired with its likeness to a punctured football suggests a kind of deflation and violence that are grotesque and upsetting. However, our concerns for this body are temporarily alleviated as it seems to be reanimated in the form of Daniel Gluck: 'Daniel sits up on the sand and the stones ¶ — is this it? really? this? is death?' (4). Looking down at his naked body,

Daniel 'sees that his body's still the old body, the ruined knees' (4). Wandering around the beach he has found himself on, Daniel sees a girl and attempts to hide his naked body from her, retreating to a forest where he discovers that he can sew leaves together to form a jacket (9). When he emerges from the woods, the landscape has changed:

> But the sea? Silent, like sea in a dream.
>
> The girl? No sign. The ring of dancers round her? Gone. On the shore, though, there's a washed-up body. He goes to look. Is it his own?
>
> No. It is a dead person.
>
> Just along from this dead person, there is another dead person. Beyond it, another, and another.
>
> He looks along the shore at the dark line of the tide-dumped dead...
>
> Further up the beach there are more people. These people are human, like the ones on the shore, but these are alive. They're under parasols. They are holidaying up the shore from the dead. (12)

Daniel 'looks from the death to the life, then back to the death again' (13), bearing witness to this shocking and stark representation of life and death existing in the same place. The living either ignorant of or unbothered by the trail of dead bodies littering the beach they are tanning on. For the reader, what seemed to transform into a harmless, enchanted vision of what death looks and feels like returns to a distressing and familiar reminder of the refugee crisis, and we are confronted with the uncomfortable reality that life and death are happening simultaneously—that one space can be a respite for some, and a tragedy for others. Daniel comes to realize that he is in his imagination, and that 'it will not last, the dream' (13), but even as the reader is pulled back into a more quotidian world, our preconceived notions about time, space, life, and death begin to disintegrate.

As with the surrealism of the first chapter, the novel as a whole follows an unconventional form. Structurally, the book is divided into chapters of varying length. As Sarah Lyall of the *New York Times* notes in her review:

Chronology skips forward and backward and sideways, moving slowly and then quickly. 'A minute ago it was June,' the author says. 'Now the weather is September.' Smith's writing is fearless and nonlinear, exploring the connectivity of things: between the living and the dead, the past and the present, art and life. She conveys time almost as if it is happening all at once, like Picasso trying to record an image from every angle simultaneously. (Lyall)

As Lyall notes, time in *Autumn* does not operate on a straight line; it is a loop, or many loops, that overlap and interweave with each other and create a three-dimensional and angular imagining of the world that betrays our natural predilection to a sequential narrative. At the start of each chapter, there is a time-phrase to locate us in a specific moment. For example, one chapter opens: 'It is a Wednesday, just past midsummer' (Smith 15), another opens: 'It is just over a week since the vote' (53), and still another—which Lyall refers to above—opens: 'A minute ago it was June. Now the weather is September' (85). Tellingly, most (though not all) of the lines that open a chapter do not mention a specific year. In the cases quoted above, they mention either the day of the week, a unit of clock-time, or a month—all things that are constantly repeating themselves—contributing towards a reading of time as cyclical and repetitive.

Furthermore, in chapter thirteen, whether Smith means to say that between June and September, 3 months have gone by in what *felt* like a minute, or whether she is noting how fluctuations in temperature confuse our understandings of what time of year it is, she draws a distinction between how time actually works, and the experience of it. In her review of *Autumn*, Joanna Kavenna spends some time considering this contradiction: 'This question—of the nature of time itself, and the nature of our experience of time—is ancient and baroque. We conduct our lives with reference to an agreed symbolical system, clock-time, and yet there is also the wholly subjective experience of time—which the philosopher Henri Bergson called *la durée* or duration. As in: time flies when you're having fun' (Kavenna). Indeed, Smith draws on this exact idea of *la durée* in *Autumn* when she describes how one day on a walk with Daniel, Elisabeth remarks: 'Time flies,' to which Daniel responds: 'Well, yes. It can do, Daniel said. Literally. Watch this,' and he 'took his watch off his wrist and threw it into the water' (Smith 76). This marvellous visualization of time literally flying—a watch soaring through the air—is one that is both obvious and unexpected, and the reader continues to engage with time in this novel in a completely new and unconventional way. As Smith draws our attention to these two alternate ways of thinking about how time operates, and as the chapters dart back and forth between the past and present, the reader is invited to re-evaluate their own relationship to time in the current moment. It is as though there is nothing anchoring us to the present alone—our past and present exist, like the living and the dead on the beach, simultaneously. Furthermore, as Kavenna asks: 'If time demolishes all things, then does the febrile, forlorn present matter anyway?' (Kavenna). On this reading, *Autumn*'s stance on the Brexit vote might be read as one of indifference: 'things. They fall apart' (Smith 3), Smith writes. The UK joined the EU, the UK leaves the EU. What is made is always destined to disintegrate—like the cycle of the seasons that causes the leaves to fall.

Smith continues to explore time through the relationship

between our 32-year-old protagonist, Elisabeth, and her 101-year-old friend, Daniel Gluck. Their relationship is both confusing and heart-warming—it is an unconventional, loving friendship that crosses the boundaries of age, time, and space. The first time we see Elisabeth and Daniel interact, Elisabeth visits him in the nursing home. Yet, before we are privy to their actual interaction, there is a short chapter where Elisabeth speculates about what will happen when she sees him: 'The last three times Elisabeth's been, he's been asleep. He'll be asleep this time too, when she gets there. She'll sit on the chair next to the bed and get the book out of her bag...Daniel will be so asleep that he'll look like he's never going to wake up' (29). She goes on:

> If he were to wake, the first thing he'd do is he'd tell her some fact from whichever fruitful place in his brain he'd been down deep in [...]
>> Sounds serious, she'd say.
>> It was, he'd say. Nothing comic isn't serious [...]
>> What you reading? he'd say.
>> Elisabeth would hold it up.
>> Brave New World, she'd say.
>> Oh, that old thing, he'd say.
>> It's new to me, she'd say. (29–31)

Although the reader is immediately told: 'That moment of dialogue? Imagined' (33), the reader senses that Elisabeth knows Daniel so well that the words may as well have been exchanged. As we discover later, Daniel always asks Elisabeth what she's reading—it's his version of 'how are you?' That Smith picks *Brave New World* for Elisabeth to be reading in this moment is striking—as Daniel lies on the precipice of leaving the world, as the country teeters on the edge of a historic vote that will shift the direction of the nation, and as Elisabeth's life still unfurls ahead of her, a seemingly infinite string of new beginnings. Daniel's dismissive (or sarcastic and therefore reverent) remark 'Oh, that old thing' followed by Elisabeth's reply: 'It's new to me,' also feeds into Smith's conception of how time works and connects us all. Oldness and newness, like past and present, seem to each have a place on a linear plane, yet Smith challenges this by showing us how something can be old and new simultaneously. Once read this seems to be an obvious observation, but it undercuts the way we often order lives and things, offering a new framework for how we conceptualize the world and our time on it.

Their imagined dialogue continues as Elisabeth admires Daniel, 'as still as death in the bed. But still. He's still here' (35). Again, this line alone uses the word 'still' to place Daniel in an intermediary position between the states of life and death; he looks 'still', i.e., unmoving, as in death, but he is 'still', i.e., continues to be, alive. Curious about her own use of the word, Elisabeth looks up the word still 'just to see what'll come up' (35). After the last sentence she reads: '*People were still alive who knew the Wright Brothers*' (36), Daniel's voice once again emerges (though it doesn't):

Ah yes, Orville and Will, the two flighty boys who started it all, Daniel, lying there so still, says without saying. The boys who gave us the world in a day, and air warfare, and every bored and restless security queue in the world. But I will lay you a wager (he says/doesn't say) that they don't have the kind of *still* on that list which forms part of the word dis*till*ery. (36)

Here, Smith continues to explore something that both happens and doesn't happen at the same time, allowing us insight into a character who lies dying through the imagination of another. In this passage that Daniel both says and doesn't say, Smith explores the plethora of meanings associated with the word 'still', using language as yet another tool to demonstrate the interconnectedness of things. The same word can bring to mind quietness, motionlessness, endurance, and the word 'nevertheless' among more, forming a connective tissue between concepts and things that are otherwise not overtly linked to one another.

The power of this imagined dialogue is consolidated later in the novel as we leap back in time to a moment when Elisabeth is young, and she and Daniel are playing a storytelling game. Elisabeth makes up one character: 'A man with a gun' (118), and Daniel chooses the other: 'I choose a person who'd come in disguise as a tree' (118). Elisabeth is appalled:

A what? Elisabeth said. No way. You're supposed to say something like another man with another gun.

Why am I? Daniel said.

Because it's war, Elisabeth said.

I have some input into this story too, and I choose a person who's wearing a tree costume, Daniel said.

Why? Elisabeth said.

Ingenuity, Daniel said.

Ingenuity won't win your character this game, Elisabeth said. My character's got a gun [...]

Bullets are faster and stronger than tree costumes and will rip through and obliterate tree costumes, Elisabeth said.

Is that the kind of world you're going to make up? Daniel said.

There is no point in making up a world, Elisabeth said, when there's already a real world. There's just the world, and there's the truth about the world.

You mean, there's the truth, and there's the made-up version of it that we get told about the world, Daniel said.

No. The *world* exists. *Stories* are made up, Elisabeth said.

But no less true for that, Daniel said. (118–119)

In this dialogue, Daniel challenges Elisabeth's understanding of the truth, suggesting that even though something doesn't physically happen, it can still be real (just like when Elisabeth hears what Daniel would say as he lies unconscious, not saying a word). When Daniel offers his friend a bizarre character, he appears to break an unspoken rule of storytelling, and Elisabeth rejects it as too absurd even within the realm of the imagination. In this scene, Smith invites the reader to consider the truth of the 'real' world and the truth of worlds that exist in, say, novels like this one. The reader's impulse might be to initially side with Elisabeth as she refuses to suspend her disbelief, but Smith encourages us to see this scene through Daniel's eyes instead. She gives us a view of fiction not as a place of solely escapist fantasy, but as something that has real bearing on the world and, on some level, exists. Once again, she blurs the boundary between two things we often see as separate. Stories become truth just as truth becomes stories.

In the following chapter, the narrative conveys the rest of the story about the man with a gun and the man in a tree costume, and it becomes a metaphor for a world that we actually recognize. We whizz forward in time again: 'Time-lapse of a million billion flowers opening their heads, of a million billion flowers bowing, closing their heads again, of a million billion new flowers opening instead' (123); and we find that 'Elisabeth, sitting in Daniel's room in The Maltings Care Providers plc just short of twenty years later, doesn't remember anything of that day or that walk or the dialogue described in that last section' (123). However, the narrative offers us the story regardless: 'here, preserved, is the story Daniel actually told' (123). His story begins with the man dressed as a tree, asking: 'Sure you want war?' (124). The man with the gun, though he aims his weapon at the man dressed as a tree, says:

I'm a peaceable person...I don't want trouble. That's why

I carry this gun. And it's not like I have anything against people like you generally.

What do you mean, people like me? the person dressed as a tree said.

What I said. People dressed in stupid pantomime tree costumes, the man with the gun said.

But why? the person dressed as a tree said.

Think what it'd be like if everyone started wearing tree costumes, the man with the gun said. It'd be like living in a wood. And we don't live in a wood. This town's been a town since long before I was born. If it was good enough for my parents, and my grandparents and my great grandparents.

What about your own costume? the person dressed as a tree said.

(The man with the gun was wearing jeans, a T-shirt and a baseball cap.)

This isn't a costume, the man said. These are my clothes. (124–125)

The story ends with a brutal image of 'shot-dead pantomime characters' (126) piled-up on top of each other. When the man with the gun turns to finally shoot the man dressed as a tree:

the person dressed as a tree transforms before the gunman's eyes into a real tree, a giant tree, a magnificent golden ash tree towering high above waving its mesmerizing leaves.

No matter how hard the man with the gun shoots at this tree he can't kill it with bullets.

So he kicks its thick trunk. He decides he'll go and buy weedkiller to pour on its roots, or matches and petrol, to burn it down. He turns to go—and that's when he gets kicked in the head by the half of the pantomime horse it's slipped his mind to shoot.

He falls to the ground, dead himself on top of the

pantomime fallen. It's a surrealist vision of hell. (126−127)

The 'othering' of the man dressed as a tree in the line 'people like you generally' is extremely familiar, and the fact that the man dressed 'normally' is pointing a gun at the man dressed as a tree, and takes the pains to state that he doesn't have anything against him, actually translates that he does have a problem with this person—a big one. The gun betrays the man's perceived need for protection against a threat—one that in this story clearly doesn't exist. The pile of dead bodies—'the pantomime dead'—that results from this story is both comical and deeply disturbing. Daniel's story may just appear to be a messed up fairy-tale, but read against the backdrop of Brexit-Britain, it becomes uncomfortably reminiscent of disputes surrounding who, or which 'kind' of people belong in a place, and which do not. The person with the gun's assertion: 'Think what it'd be like if everyone started wearing tree costumes...It'd be like living in a wood. And we don't live in a wood. This town's been a town since long before I was born' (125) reveals that this man's concern is that the inclusion of others will endanger his way of life—a sentiment emboldened throughout the Brexit referendum campaign.

Although all of this language in the novel is comically cast towards a man dressed like a tree, the moral of the story is that one man's costume is another man's clothing, and it's easy to apply this fable to post-Brexit referendum Britain. In his article 'Feeling at Home: Some Reflections on Muslims in Europe', Bhikhu Parekh notes that an attack on multiculturalism in Europe is 'often a coded word for Muslims' (Parekh 51), and this scene can certainly be read as synonymous to the Islamophobia that courses throughout England. Muslim people who wear religious attire are visibly 'other', marked out by garb such as the hijab. For non-Muslim people, the clothing is unfamiliar, which is used to justify a notion of difference that is illogical. Just as the man wearing a tree costume is still a man (who happens to wear something different), people in their religious attire are still people (who happen to believe something different). When Daniel cleverly flips the conversation when he comments on the man with the gun's 'costume', Smith satirizes the notion that there is any difference between the men at all, and encourages the reader to see how illogical these fears truly are. Daniel's story is ultimately a metaphor for an English person swept up in the fear of someone who does not look or think like them, and since the reader is encouraged to take the side of the man dressed as a tree, it offers an alternative narrative to xenophobia and a new way of understanding our differences. (Smith's use of a metaphor here is also yet another example of using liminal space—in this case between what is said and what is meant.)

As this reading of Daniel's story suggests, although *Autumn* is often indirect in its approach to Brexit, the novel does take the time to closely consider the atmosphere in England at the time of the referendum. Smith's Dickensian refrain that begins the novel continues in a later section, which describes how the results of the referendum vote were received throughout England. In one short chapter, every line begins 'All across the country' (Smith 59–61), and highlights the binary opposition between the experience on either side of this debate:

All across the country, there was misery and rejoicing.

All across the country, what had happened whipped about by itself as if a live electric wire had snapped off a pylon in a storm and was whipping about in the air above the trees, the roofs, the traffic.

All across the country, people felt it was the wrong thing. All across the country, people felt it was the right thing. All across the country, people felt they'd really lost. All across the country, people felt they'd really won. All across the country, people felt like they'd done the right thing and other people had done the wrong thing. All across the country, people looked up Google: *what is EU?* All across the country, people looked up Google: *move to Scotland.* All across the country, people looked up Google: *Irish passport applications.* (59)

Notable here is how the references to Scotland and Ireland indicate that the 'country' Smith talks about is not the UK as a whole, but rather England on its own, with Wales either remaining complicit or absent. This chapter reveals the extreme polarization within England during the Brexit campaign and immediately post-referendum. While it displays a sharp dichotomy: 'people felt they'd really lost...people felt they'd really won', if we cast our minds back to the opening of the novel we are offered no dichotomy about the overall outcome: 'It was the worst of times, it was the worst of times' (1). This suggests that even for those who celebrated the results, the Brexit referendum was not a pleasant affair.

While the novel's assertion that this is 'the worst of times' for all could be read as Smith betraying her bias as an author, the novel also exposes instances of hatred which prove this point. In a chapter that precedes the 'All across the country' passage in the novel, but proceeds from it chronologically, we are told that: 'just over a week since the vote...Elisabeth passes a cottage not far from the bus stop whose front, from the door to across above the window, has been painted over with black paint and the words GO and HOME' (53). Elisabeth notices that, 'People either look down, look away or stare her out. People in the shops, when she buys some fruit, some ibuprofen and a newspaper for her mother, speak with a new kind of detachment' (53–54), and her mother 'tells her when she gets there that half the village isn't speaking to the other half of the village' (54). The rhetoric of 'go home' became a familiar refrain throughout the Brexit campaign, targeting not only immigrants, but also those members of British society who do not fit a white British archetype. Even those who had lived in England their entire lives were subjected to this kind of xenophobic attack. While the words and the atmosphere of this scene are recognizable, they are still unsettling to the reader, and the stark image of a village sliced in half demonstrates in visual terms the polarization that emerged in the wake of the vote. The division of the town becomes even more pronounced with the erection of an electrified fence 'slicing straight across a path Elisabeth's walked several times since her mother came to live here' (56). The fence prevents Elisabeth from taking her usual walking route, suggesting that a new limitation has been imposed on her movement, which stands in perfectly for the looming retraction of options to live elsewhere in the EU, and the constricting isolationism that Brexit produced. The fence is also a symbolic barrier between two opposing sides of the referendum debate; the fact that it would shock you if you were to try and get through it demonstrates both the inability and unwillingness to mix with those of differing beliefs, precluding opportunities for mutual understanding and further reinforcing division.

We learn of another xenophobic attack while Elisabeth sits at her mother's home and reflects on the journey she had to get there. She thinks 'most of all about the Spanish couple in the taxi queue at the station. [¶] They'd clearly just arrived here on holiday, their luggage round their feet. The people behind them in the queue shouted at them. What they shouted at them was to go home. [¶] This isn't Europe, they shouted. Go back to Europe' (130). The targeting of individuals clearly only visiting the UK as tourists demonstrates an alarming reflex to immediately reject anyone who is not quintessentially English, i.e., white and English-speaking. It demonstrates the extent to which xenophobic individuals have been emboldened and suggests that those speaking in such terms not only don't want people to settle in England, they don't even want people to visit. The repetition of 'go home' reminds us that these are not isolated instances—the words which would in 'normal' times be unacceptable are being used in chorus across the nation having been normalized by political figureheads and a national debate stage. Elisabeth recognizes this; she 'sensed that what was happening in that one passing incident was a fraction of something volcanic' (130). She then admits: 'This is what shame feels like' (130). Although Elisabeth was clearly only a witness to the incident, she feels shame nonetheless—a particularly pertinent example of how almost half the country, and likely more, since not everyone who voted for Brexit condoned carrying out these kinds of verbal attacks, is complicit in the actions of people using this language. Elisabeth's recollection of this event in the taxi queue is yet another example of how polarized the country has become.

The first encounter with Brexit-related physical violence in the novel appears when Elisabeth first visits Daniel in the home. In another dream sequence—this time in the mind of Elisabeth—they go on a walk together, and Elisabeth tells him about the murder of Jo Cox. She begins the conversation: 'Someone killed an MP, she tells Daniel's back as she struggles to keep up. A man shot her dead and came at her with a knife. Like shooting her wouldn't be enough' (38). Elisabeth's disgust at this act of violence is palpable and reminds the reader of the initial shock of Jo Cox's death. She continues: 'But it's old news now. Once it would have been a year's worth of news. But news right now is like a flock of speeded-up sheep running off the side of a cliff' (38). Elisabeth's comment that such a horrific act almost immediately became 'old news' once again bares the unprecedented amount of violence that has been unleashed. Indeed, the normalization of these instances of physical and verbal violence is one of the disturbing conclusions that *Autumn* draws.

However, Smith does not isolate this rise of violence and

right-wing nationalism in England alone. Zooming out from the English case, Smith dedicates the chapter immediately after the 'All across the country' passage to describing a mix-up involving a swastika banner being raised in Nice, France in 2015. The chapter relays how it was 'a film production unit filming an adaptation of a memoir, using the Palais to recreate the Hôtel Excelsior, where Alois Brunner, the SS officer, had had his office and living quarters after the Italians surrendered to the Allies' (63). The film unit had, without warning the locals, raised 'a long red banner with a swastika at the top of it' (63), and it incited a visceral reaction: 'Some people screamed. There was a flurry of shouting and pointing' (63). The local authorities ran a survey to ask: 'Were locals right to be angry about the banner: Yes or No?' (64), and of four thousand votes, 70 per cent said no (64). In this scene, we leap from the Brexit referendum to a display of 1940s fascism. That the majority of locals said there was no need for concern at the display of an enormous Nazi symbol is concerning in itself. Although later discovering that it was all for a film dulled their horror, the symbolic value of raising the flag at a time when right-wing nationalist and fascist groups were indeed resurfacing and gaining strength across Europe points towards a reading of this scene as a stark warning that the ideas and events that accompanied the Brexit referendum seem to be mirroring a very dark period of history. Furthermore, that this chapter appears right next to the chapter recounting the sharp polarization in England following the referendum is telling; Smith offers us a rather grim comparison. As we know, the novel is not ordered chronologically, but this sequence clues us into another way that Smith threads her novel together: by finding moments in time that resemble each other in some way, augmenting a framework of time that is based on simultaneity and repetition of history.

Post-referendum, many conclusions were drawn about why the nation voted so disparately and has had such strong and different reactions to the same question. Although the novel closely tracks many of these patterns—patterns of violence, patterns of polarization—one that it ignores is the explanation about a generational schism. In the aftermath of the Brexit referendum, most of the results coverage stated that the old voted to leave (presumably because they remembered the 'good old days'), while the young voted to remain (presumably because the EU was all they knew). However, rather than playing into this narrative, Smith creates a harmonious intergenerational relationship that is based on mutual respect, trust, and shared values, and that provides a platform for shared ideas and reciprocal learning. Despite their age difference, they become companions for each other and develop a genuine friendship that becomes more like a familial bond. For Elisabeth, it even feels like love: 'It isn't that kind of relationship, Elisabeth said. It isn't even the least bit physical. It never has been. But it's love. I can't pretend it isn't' (146). Given that novels historically emphasize sexual love, it is notable that Smith chose an atypical, non-sexual relationship to form the strongest bond in the novel. Elisabeth and Daniel's relationship is further proof that *Autumn* is purposefully flouting literary and social expectations; both the non-linear form of the novel and its central narrative of a nonconforming loving relationship legitimize new frameworks for understanding the world. The development of their cross-generational friendship defies conventional understandings of friendship and love, as well as how Brexit came to be.

Elisabeth and Daniel's relationship not only defies common understandings of friendship, but it also feeds into Smith's conception of time. Elisabeth and Daniel are undeniably from different generations—different times. However, if we imagine that time operates cyclically, then we can imagine it not as a line but as a wheel. While their lived experiences may have occurred at different points on the wheel, their large age difference might mean that there is actually very little space separating them. When Daniel and Elisabeth first meet, Elisabeth is only 8 years old and is new to the neighbourhood. Daniel's greeting immediately confounds her:

Very pleased to meet you...Finally.

How do you mean, finally? Elisabeth said. We only moved here six weeks ago.

The lifelong friends, he said. We sometimes wait a lifetime for them. (52)

Daniel's suggestion that one sometimes waits a lifetime for a lifelong friend seems contradictory—surely if you have already lived a lifetime you cannot newly meet a lifelong friend. However, his statement once again suggests that time is not operating linearly, but cyclically—as though, even though he is just meeting Elisabeth now, he has known her his whole life. Here is another example of the difference between time and the experience of time—the familiar feeling of meeting someone and remarking: 'It feels like I've known you my whole life,' though of course you haven't. Daniel's character makes this suggestion seem less clichéd and emotional, and more matter-of-fact, as though he knows something about time that the reader does not.

Smith also considers how other characters in the novel see their age difference as a problem. Elisabeth's mother is deeply concerned by their friendship, telling Elisabeth:

Unnatural.

Unhealthy.

You're not to.

I forbid it.

That's enough. (83)

However, Elisabeth defies these orders, and their relationship continues to flourish. Smith beautifully recycles Elisabeth's mother's words later in the novel, although this time reversing the situation so that Elisabeth uses them when speaking to her mother, who is falling in love with another woman:

> It is like magic has happened in my life, Elisabeth's mother whispers to Elisabeth when Zoe's left the room.
>
> Unnatural, Elisabeth says.
>
> Who'd have known, who'd have guessed, it'd be love, at this late stage, that'd see me through? Elisabeth's mother says.
>
> Unhealthy, Elisabeth says. I forbid it. You're not to.
>
> She gives her mother a hug and a kiss. (238)

In this moving scene, Smith demonstrates that, like Daniel, Elisabeth's mother finds her life partner later in life—she has been waiting forever but she has also had her the entire time. This passage illustrates that what may seem 'unnatural' and 'unhealthy' is often the most beautiful, and non-normative expressions of love form the strongest relationships in the novel. *Autumn* flouts expectations and once again offers the reader new ways of understanding the world that allows us to reframe it into a much more tolerant and far less assuming place.

Due to its label as a BrexLit novel from the outset, many have struggled to reconcile key parts of *Autumn* to the politics of Brexit. The most critical of such under-analysed moments is how Smith grapples with various different art forms, and Daniel becomes the mouthpiece through which she does so. Every time Daniel sees Elisabeth, the first thing he asks is: 'What you reading?' (68). The first time he asks, Elisabeth 'showed him her empty hands' (68), and he replies: 'Always be reading something, he said. Even when we're not physically reading. How else will we read the world? Think of it as a constant' (68). Daniel's emphasis on reading as a way of reading the world suggests several things: the first is that literature is a key tool that allows someone to become more perceptive of the world around them—to build stories, perhaps, out of the things that they see. The second is that literature contains information about the world we live in, so that we might better understand it. Towards the end of *Autumn*, one of the chapters begins with: 'Here's an old story so new that it's still in the middle of happening' (181)—an apt way to describe the novel itself, which is being published in response to, and in the midst of, Brexit.

If Smith is indicating that literature is a way of understanding the world, then she is also clueing the reader into why this novel is important, and how she intends for the reader to use it.

Daniel is not only partial to literature but also to visual art. One day, as they sit together on a bench after a walk, Elisabeth confides in Daniel that she is 'planning to go to college when I leave school...If I can afford it' (71). Without hesitation, Daniel replies: 'Oh, you don't want to go to college...You want to go to collage' (71). While Elisabeth asserts that Daniel is using the wrong word, Daniel disagrees: 'Collage is an institute of education where all the rules can be thrown into the air, and size and space and time and foreground and background all become relative, and because of these skills everything you think you know gets made into something new and strange' (71–72). Immediately, Daniel's description of collage appears to be a description of *Autumn*—it is a work that throws out the traditional narrative of storytelling and becomes a patchwork of scenes and moments that jump back and forth in time, a work where past, present, life, and death all intermingle. Daniel continues his speech by asking Elisabeth to close her eyes as he describes a piece of art—a collage—to her from memory. When Elisabeth asks where he saw it, Daniel replies: 'I saw it in the early 1960s...He said it as if a time could be a place' (75). Later in her life, Elisabeth discovers the actual painting in an art shop, and we discover that the painter was a female Pop artist named Pauline Boty (1938–1966). Boty is a largely forgotten female Pop artist, even though she was the only female painter in the British wing of the Pop Art movement and was also one of its founders. Elisabeth is studying art at the time, and she finds her discovery of Boty interesting, especially because her tutor had 'told her that categorically there had never been such a thing as a female British Pop artist, not one of any worth, which is why there were none recorded as more than footnotes in British Pop Art history' (150). Clearly, her tutor suffered a chronic lack of effort to look for one, or he would have found Boty, but Daniel, on the other hand, has her work etched into his brain.

The most striking aspect of Boty's works is that they are all collages, explaining (in part) Daniel's fascination with them — the other part being that we discover Daniel was once in love with Boty in his youth. The works by Boty that are described in *Autumn* are big and bold, and all of them express an elision between playfulness and seriousness. One painting, titled: 'Untitled (Sunflower Woman)' (see Appendix, Figure 3) is described by the narrator as:

> It was of a woman on a bright blue background. Her body was a collage of painted images. A man with a machine gun pointing at the person looking at the picture formed her chest. A factory formed her arm and shoulder.
>
> A sunflower filled her torso.
>
> An exploding airship made her crotch.
>
> An owl.
>
> Mountains.
>
> Coloured zigzags. (151–152)

Every layered image depicts a kind of explosion — most obviously in the gun and the exploding airship, but also in the sunflower, which is an explosion of colour and life. Notably, the image of a man with a gun is located at the woman's chest and throat where her voice is, while the sunflower is located at her abdominal area, which is associated with maternity and child-bearing. By making up a woman's body with these sometimes violent and explosive fragments, Boty represents both a reclaiming of the female body and an admission of its occupation by a confusing mixture of suppression and freedom. The juxtaposition of the grey images and the bold colours of the sunflower and the zigzags highlights this aesthetically as well. It is remarkable that the woman has a smiling face, despite the chaotic imagery displayed from the neck down. Although it is unclear whether the smile is genuine or contrived, one can read the painting as a depiction of the contrasting forces that define and pull apart the female body, as well as her resilience, or perhaps the social expectation that she remain smiling. Boty is clearly making a statement on how women are constructed in a man's world—'A Man's World' being a title she uses for some of her other paintings. Her unapologetic imagining of this feminist trope is daring, and Smith provides ample space in the novel to appreciate this.

In a review in *The Guardian*, Joanna Kavenna suggests that Boty is a presence in *Autumn* primarily as "a symbol of all those who are 'Ignored. Lost. Rediscovered years later. Then ignored. Lost. Rediscovered again years later. Then ignored. Lost. Rediscovered ad infinitum" ([Smith] 239),' and that the rebellion Boty's art expresses reflects the rebellious nature of the novel's characters (Kavenna). Indeed, Kavenna touches on the fact that Boty's artwork has frequently been buried and unappreciated in the years since Boty's premature death—yet another example of the cyclicality of time. In addition, Boty's work also seems to, in itself, reflect the form of *Autumn* as a whole, which indicates that Boty's collage aesthetic is a clue for how to read Smith. The patchwork of collage raises interesting questions about parts and wholes—do the individual images and chapters work together seamlessly and become part of a whole, or do they maintain their individuality? In a novel that is preoccupied with the polarizing Brexit referendum, the collage might function as a powerful artistic imagining of the polarized self and nation. Thinking back to the Sunflower Woman's smiling face, it might also depict how easily conflict can be disguised when you zoom out far enough. Collages also refuse to tell a simple story. Perhaps Smith chooses this form because there is no longer a simple story to be told—traditional narratives cannot capture the moment like they could before. Everything overlaps and interweaves—views, beliefs, time, and space.

Despite the many instances of violence and polarization that weave throughout the novel, *Autumn* is ultimately hopeful. The nasty spray-painted 'GO HOME' that we see earlier in the novel, originally written in black, is added to 'in varying bright colours, WE ARE ALREADY HOME THANK YOU', and someone has 'painted a tree next to it and a row of bright red flowers underneath it' (Smith 138.) Underneath these new murals, 'There are flowers, lots of real ones, in cellophane and paper, on the pavement outside the house, so it looks a bit like an accident has recently happened there' (Smith 138). The fact that the added lines proclaiming 'we are already home' are written in bright colours displays a hope and optimism that stands up against the threatening words 'GO HOME,' and although the image of flowers on the ground is described like a reaction to a tragic death of some sort, it also suggests that there has been an overflow of compassion for those who have been targeted by the vandalism. The final time we see this house, 'It's like nothing's ever happened, unless you know to look a little more closely to make out the outline of the word HOME under the layer of blue' (253). The erasure of these words may suggest that the words have been covered over in order to ignore them, yet the fact that the word that remains slightly visible is 'HOME' is comforting—as though the house and its inhabitants are publicly proclaiming their belonging despite attempts to cast them as outsiders.

Autumn's moral takeaway is that everything is ultimately interconnected—time, space, and people form the collage that makes up the world. Smith beautifully and finally considers the interconnectivity of people and the world in one of Daniel's final dream-like sequences, where he sits with his sister and explains to her all of the things he is: 'I'm the butterfly antenna. I'm the chemicals that paint's made of. I'm the person dead at the water's edge. I'm the water. I'm the edge. I'm skin cells. I'm the smell of disinfectant...I'm the ink, the paper, the grass, the tree, the leaves, the leaf, the greenness in the leaf. I'm the vein in the leaf. I'm the voice that tells no story' (191–192). His sister '(Snorts.) There's no such thing' (192), she says. 'Just one lone single leaf, are you?' (192). Daniel explains with ease: 'No. To be more exact. As I've already said. As I've already made clear. I'm all the leaves' (192). Explaining in a different way, he goes on:

> There's always, there'll always be, more story. That's what story is.
> (Silence.)
> It's the never ending leaf-fall.
> (Silence.)
> Isn't it? Aren't you?
> (Silence.) (193)

In this wonderful passage, Daniel links his life to things that are eternal: nature, the cycle of the seasons, and he also suggests that stories themselves are endless. He becomes all things at once—he is skin cells, he is 'all the leaves', he is 'the ink, the paper, the grass, the tree' (191–192). Daniel recognizes that he is connected to all things on earth because all things are made of the same matter, and when everything is stripped down to this simple fact, there is no difference between anything at all. He also reminds his sister, who is dead, that she remains alive in his mind—she is not physically present, and yet she is also still alive. Daniel's words also provide insight into the novel as a whole; through his character, Smith reminds her readers that *Autumn*—a story titled after the fall of leaves that Daniel describes—is also cyclical and infinite, just like the seasons. 'That's the thing about things, they fall apart' (3), Smith writes at the opening of the novel, but in less plain language, Smith also shows us that even when things, even people, fall apart, they endure.

Ali Smith's *Autumn* is a profound and beautiful novel, intended both to capture the current political moment and to escape from the utter dejection that accompanies it. The final lines of the novel indicate rejuvenation even as things are beginning to decay:

> The furniture in the garden is rusting. They've forgotten to put it away for the winter.
> The trees are revealing their structures. There's the catch of fire in the air. All the souls are out marauding. But there are roses, there are still roses. In the damp and the cold, on a bush that looks done, there's a wide-open rose, still.
> Look at the colour of it. (259–260)

The presence of roses, which are not only the quintessential English flower, but also the flower most closely associated with love, emerges here as an image of rebirth and hope for England. As in Geoffrey Hill's *The Book of Baruch by the Gnostic Justin*, rather than remain stagnant in the present moment, Smith allows time to expand and life to explode, and she reminds us that even something as devastating as Brexit cannot prevent the passage of time, which will go on in its cyclical fashion and pull us along with it. Indeed, *Autumn* shows us that art, people, and events are all part of an endless, ongoing cycle. Everything happens simultaneously, and the world is connected by time, space, and its diverse beliefs, like one giant collage. Smith captures the atmosphere in England post-referendum, and depicts Englishness as a thorny, polarized identity, but she also provides the reader with new frameworks for understanding the world that are ultimately hopeful. Even if we can't see or yet believe that time will mend, Smith writes it into existence with *Autumn* — as Daniel says, stories are no less real than reality. Like Geoffrey Hill, Smith reminds us that things disintegrate but they can be restored. She continues to visualize England as just one piece of a global collage, offering a new, more hopeful, and globally interconnected conception of Englishness in the wake of Brexit. Autumn will turn to Winter — a time of darkness and cold, but after Winter comes Spring, and then Summer. As Smith intimates towards in this first of her seasonal quartet, the infinitely repeating passage of a year has the power to revitalize and rebirth all things. Ultimately, hope prevails, and love overcomes hate in these extraordinary times.

* * *

Sam Byers' *Perfidious Albion*: Stuck in Dystopia

Sam Byers is an English author who entered the literary scene in 2013 with his debut novel *Idiopathy*, which earned him media attention and landed him two awards — the Betty Trask Award and the Waterstones 11 Prize. Published in 2018, 2 years after the Brexit referendum, *Perfidious Albion* is Byers' second published novel and was longlisted for both the Orwell Prize for Political Fiction and the Encore Prize. It is a work of dystopian fiction — and a satire — published in a moment of deep uncertainty concerning the Brexit proceedings and the political direction of the Western world. Byers targets specifically the role of the internet and social media as forces that enable and provoke sexist, racist, and nationalistic messages that lead to a polarized society. Indeed, throughout the Brexit campaign, social media and the internet were used as platforms through which to disseminate, in many cases, xenophobic and hateful messages that spurred a click-bait culture within politics. This click-bait phenomenon was exploited during the Brexit campaign by various organizations in ways that threatened the democratic process. The Cambridge Analytica scandal, which involved the analysis of Facebook users' data by parent company SCL Group, according to a whistle-blower, 'likely breached the UK's strict campaign financing laws and may have helped to sway the final Brexit outcome' (Scott). Cambridge Analytica has also been at the centre of controversy in the US, where the illegal data-mining of 50 million Facebook users helped to sway the 2016 US presidential election (Scott). Throughout *Perfidious Albion*, Sam Byers reveals the dangers of the trend towards data-mining as a source of political power, explores how ethical boundaries break down in today's click-bait culture, and offers a frozen, dystopian vision for England and Englishness in a post-referendum world.

Byers' novel is a BrexLit novel not in its engagement with Brexit—the vote is mentioned once throughout the novel—but in its *feeling*. In an interview with Faber & Faber, Byers said: 'I think it's fair to say at this point that Brexit is a feeling as well as an event, and that was one of the questions I was interested in when it came to writing the book' (Faber & Faber). He also suggests that this feeling is specific to the English condition during this time. He muses: 'When I come to look back at it in a few years' time I think this will come to feel like an emotionally very distinct period of English life' (Faber & Faber). Indeed, navigating through Byers' dystopia, it becomes clear that the world of *Perfidious Albion* is intended to be a mirror to our own, and Byers' writing is certainly an emotional response to the turbulent political times we live in.

The title of the novel *'Perfidious Albion'* is an international relations term meaning 'England or Britain considered as treacherous in international affairs' *(OED)*, which immediately marks Byers' work as a state-of-the-nation novel dealing specifically with the problem of Englishness. The novel takes place in 2020 in a small fictional English town called Edmundsbury, which becomes the setting of a conspiracy coordinated by Green, a large tech company, which uses Edmundsbury residents (and their own employees) as lab rats for data-mining experiments without their consent. Rather than creating a product, employees of Green *are* the product—they help the tech giant learn how people behave in certain situations, gathering information to help other companies and individuals target specific people who are likely to react positively to their platforms. Of course, this is akin to the work that Cambridge Analytica did in 2016, and what Google, Facebook, Uber, and other Silicon Valley giants continue to do today. The 'Twitterverse' looms large throughout the novel too, providing a powerful and occasionally dangerous space to air thoughts. The novel follows politician Hugo Bennington—who closely resembles Farage—the leader of political party 'England Always'—which closely resembles UKIP; a journalist named Robert and his partner, Jess, who is a formidable feminist; an old white man named Darkin whose xenophobia is fuelled by the feeling that he has been left behind; and a black woman named Trina who sends an offhand tweet and unintentionally rouses white supremacist ideas into mainstream media. Among others, these characters all interact primarily through cyberspace to demonstrate the quintessential tensions that are rife within English society today, and Edmundsbury becomes a microcosm where Byers and his readers can explore the impact of data-mining, fearmongering, and social media on politics and society. Ultimately, Byers depicts a bleak vision of England, and contemporary Englishness, in the immediate moment.

Edmundsbury is described in the novel as a place that 'North London refugees' fled to, and which 'increasingly existed in the collapsed distinction between creativity and commerce' (Byers 5). These 'refugees' from London are satirically depicted as primarily white men suffering from intense nostalgia for the imagined England of the past. From the outset, the reader is confronted with characters who we are encouraged to dislike and a social space that is overwhelmed by narcissism and a distinctly masculine self-importance. The novel opens at a social event hosted by Jacques DeCoverley, 'a blow-in from the city' who 'was reinventing himself as a deep-thinking rural gentleman for the twenty-first century, wearing wellington boots indoors and waxing lyrical about a "lost" England comprised entirely of hedgerows and loam' (5–6). DeCoverley's move from London—the diverse capital city—to a predominantly white space in the regions of England, coupled with his snobbish nostalgia for a 'lost England', immediately indicates a hostility to progress. DeCoverley starts his night by discussing the meaning of the word 'now' with a journalist named Robert, concluding that 'These are post-present times' (3), before going on to infuriatingly lament his success as a writer: '"I'm rapidly coming to the conclusion that the best thing I could do for my career right now would be to write something wildly unsuccessful. I *pine* for obscurity"...He squinted, momentarily pained by his own significance' (7). The absurd and arrogant tone of this conversation is exasperating, and creates an immediately unpleasant and unwelcoming atmosphere as we enter the text.

Unfortunately, DeCoverley's self-aggrandizing nature is shared by his guests. A group of 'theorist poseurs' attempt to 'decode the encoded fascism of everyday life', including the 'fascism of iced buns' (6), while a man named Lionel Groves revels in his capacity for emotion as others 'used him as a litmus test for what they should be feeling themselves' (11).

The discussion on the 'fascism of iced buns' is both pretentious and ridiculous, and is a botched attempt at sounding deeply philosophical, while the fact that Groves acts as a male 'litmus test' for emotion indicates that both he and those around him are performing emotion rather than truly feeling it. Jess, who is journalist Robert's partner and who spends a significant amount of time researching internet misogyny, surveys the room and despairs at the vision of masculinity that confronts her: 'It was, Jess thought, the age of beatified masculine emotion. Everywhere you looked, men were sweeping up awards for feeling things' (11). Jess' observation implies that the value placed on masculine emotions is higher than the value placed on feminine emotions, and the reader is encouraged to sympathize with her revulsion. This opening scene introduces a hostile environment of male-dominated power and self-importance and lays a dismal foundation for the rest of the novel.

Throughout the novel, the most powerful and controversial figures are all white men. The most notable of these is Hugo Bennington, leader of the fictional political party England Always. We are first introduced to Hugo through the perspective of Darkin, an old white man living precariously in a soon-to-be demolished housing estate. Darkin's political opinions are derived from the pages of a newspaper called *The Record*, which paints 'a near-dystopian vision of England...The country was overrun, under threat, increasingly incapable. Hordes of immigrants massed at its borders. Its infrastructure frayed at the seams. Basic morality was eroding at an alarming rate, worn down by tolerance, permissiveness, turpitude' (24), and describes Hugo Bennington as the 'one, lone politician' they proclaim to be different (24). That Byers describes *The Record*, which publishes stories that very closely resemble those that proliferated during the Brexit campaign, as 'near-dystopian' offers a bleak indication that the world we live in might already be something out of a dystopian novel. Certainly, the image of

'Hordes of immigrants massed at its borders' is reminiscent of the Leave campaign's poster depicting lines of Middle Eastern immigrants supposedly all waiting to enter the UK (see Appendix, Figure 1). Reading *The Record*'s endorsement of Bennington is not intended to move the reader towards supporting him or believing the paper. Rather, given the paper's ludicrous description of England and Bennington's close resemblance to Farage, we are invited to reject and disdain both. However, the paper achieves its intended effect on Darkin. The narrative notes that, 'Like any long-standing *Record* reader, he read not to have his fears assuaged, but to have them confirmed' (24). The reference to confirmation bias here aptly epitomizes a click-bait culture, and offers a new paradigm of journalism that prioritizes reaction over objectivity. While Byers is calling the reader's attention to the dangerous role the media plays in inciting division and fear, he also bleakly reminds us that our reality looks eerily similar.

It is quickly revealed that Bennington is a contributor to *The Record* and that his latest column is a xenophobic rant promoting white nationalist ideas about who is entitled to what in British society. He begins by asking: '*Equality: is it a good or bad thing?*' and '*Is there such a thing as too much equality?*' (25). He goes on to complain about how '*housing is scarcer than it has ever been, yet immigration continues to rise. Unemployment among working Britons still isn't coming down fast enough, yet time and again we hear that companies must have quotas to ensure that for every white Englishman they employ they must also hire three foreigners, two women, and at least one homosexual*' (25). He then goes on to end with a flourish: '*what we have in Britain now is a society that asks those who work to share their earnings with those who scrounge; those who have grown up here to share their hard-fought space with those who have just arrived; and those who deserve their place to share it with those who merely envy it*' (26). First and foremost, Bennington falls into the common trap of using 'Briton' and 'Englishman' interchangeably, displaying once again the Anglo-centrism of discussions such as this one. His opinion piece also contains several assumptions, the most obvious being that white English people (most likely white men in particular) are more deserving and harder-working than their minority counterparts. The language that he uses here of a 'hard-fought space' and people who 'deserve their place' is an ugly representation of the most xenophobic incarnations of English nationalism. Just like Nigel Farage did as leader of the United Kingdom Independence Party (UKIP), Bennington uses his platform as a tool to further a political agenda that serves only two sets of people: himself, and those who look like him.

Hugo Bennington's xenophobia is based on a conviction that racial diversity is incompatible with Englishness, and he uses his voice as a way of 'deliberately fanning the flames of racial hatred' (270) in order to convince others of the same. Both he and his editor, Teddy, seek out opportune moments to do this— one presents itself when Trina, a black woman who works at Green, posts a flippant tweet that reads: '#whitemalegenocide. Lol'. (137) after she is angered by an unpleasant encounter with her white male colleagues. Teddy tells Hugo: 'This tweet was written by someone who is basically just some woman. Some black woman. She's not a somebody…it's not really a thing, but what I'm saying is that it could very easily become a thing, if we wanted it to' (149). Teddy acknowledges that this tweet is not a genuine threat but that, with the right reaction from Hugo, it could be depicted as one, and could bolster the racist message of his platform. He also merrily states that, 'this is even better than a death threat. This is a genocide threat' (150). Hugo is at first sceptical that the tweet is worth responding to, recognizing that: 'It says lol at the end. That doesn't make it sound very threatening' (150). However, Teddy is uninterested in the intention behind the tweet—he is solely concerned with how it can be weaponized for their own political gain, and Hugo is quickly persuaded to take action. After posting his response, it is picked up by internet trolls who respond en masse to Trina's post. By taking the tweet at face value and twisting it into a genuine threat to white men everywhere, Teddy and Hugo purposefully portray Trina as a racial terrorist—a claim that is effortlessly swooped up by his followers. This includes Darkin, who happens to be Trina's neighbour and who becomes convinced that 'on the estate a murderous black woman was whipping up some kind of race war' (211). In this scene, Byers demonstrates how quick and easy it has become to put ideas out into cyberspace that can be picked up and perverted in order to fit a political agenda. The narrative does not depict Trina as dangerous in the slightest, but one moment of anger, albeit misjudged, has the potential to change her life completely.

Even before Hugo enacts his racially-motivated response to Trina's tweet, he recognizes that there has been a shift in how leaders and influential figures capture their base of support: 'Hugo was old enough to remember the days when politics was about reassuring people. But those days were over. Now you had to keep them fearful' (78). Here, Byers subtly calls the reader's mind to the popular phrase 'Project Fear', which was what the Leave campaign dubbed the Remain campaign for its attempts to raise concerns about the economic toll that Brexit would have on the UK. In doing so, he satirically shows that the Leave campaign used the very same strategy of fearmongering that it supposedly rejected in its opponent. The appeal of inciting widespread anxiety lies in its ability to capture the attention, horror and, consequently, the support of people who would otherwise be unlikely to be engaged in the political system.

The attraction to taking this strategy also extends to other careers besides politics in the novel. Over the course of the book, Robert, a journalist for *The Command Line*, sinks into the quicksand of fearmongering and becomes an agent of click-bait as he slowly but surely heeds the advice of his editor, Silas. Silas is adamant that any reaction is better than no reaction, regardless of what Robert says. The first piece of advice he gives to Robert in the novel is: 'You're nobody until somebody hates you, Robert...No-one sucks up anymore. It backfires...better to get in there early with some pre-emptive hatred and get credit for that. Anyway, hatred equals hate-clicks, so, you know, win' (19–20). This logic reframes journalistic success as the number of clicks you get—in other words, how much attention one receives—rather than the accuracy of the information one presents. In a manner similar to Sir Jack in *England, England*, Silas recognizes the power of giving people what they want, as opposed to what they need, and like Darkin reading *The Record*, emphasizes the appeal of echo chambers of information that reinforce existing biases. For Robert, confirming and validating his readers' understandings of the world becomes more important and more fruitful for his career than providing objective analysis of the world—a virtue of journalism that Byers suggests has been lost entirely. The author encourages the reader to feel dismayed by the trend that Robert follows; he freezes us in a hostile and distorted world that apparently resembles our own, and offers us no alternative to the corruption that we witness.

Robert is initially tentative of diving into controversial reporting. He dabbles in feminist thought-pieces but swiftly shrinks away from such discourse. Ultimately, he takes the plunge with an investigative piece on the Larchwood estate featuring resident Darkin as a way of '*humanising* the estate story' (54). Robert is genuinely shocked by the state of Darkin's apartment, describing it to Julia as a 'real *scene* of a flat. Stuff smeared on the windows. Dark...Filthy. Stank' (54) and writes a reactive piece in response to what he witnesses. The resulting article is unintentionally positioned as a defence-piece for old, white men who have been discarded, ignored, and forgotten by the English public. Silas has high praise for Robert's piece, primarily because it is controversial. When Robert cannot see what is controversial, Silas responds: 'About being a man? About being white? About being English? Nor can I, Rob. Nor can you. Nor can the Darkins of the world, am I right? But the point is that it *is* controversial. And that's exactly what this piece is saying' (143). Here, Silas defends the position that white men are oppressed by English society, and he either cannot recognize or purposefully overlooks the problematic understandings of race and opportunity in England on which these ideas rely. Under the pretence of 'starting a conversation' (143), Robert engages in the rhetoric of white supremacy, wherein Englishness equals whiteness, and the greatest threat to the country is '*white male plight*' (150).

Despite his initial hesitance to write articles purely to provoke reaction, Robert is ultimately drawn in deeper, and begins to enjoy the effect his words can have on his readers. When Trina's '#whitemalegenocide' tweet begins to circulate, Silas calls it 'a godsend' (183) and entices Robert with a single promise for writing a responsive article: 'You're about to go supernova' (183). As Robert slips further into the rhetoric of racism and white nationalism, he convinces himself that what he is writing is justified. He assures himself that in his first piece on Darkin, he was simply standing up for a man who 'had been unjustly maligned and ignored in favour of hipper, more attractive causes' (277–278). Yet, even as he does so, he acknowledges that he is no longer 'reporting what was happening...what was happening had come to have less and less bearing on what he thought, until all that mattered...was that he thought at all. Now, what he thought *was* what was happening' (278). In this final statement, Robert recognizes the influence that his willingness to discuss controversial perspectives has— even though the reader knows that he writes not out of genuine belief but out of the desire to provoke a reaction. Eventually, Robert convinces himself that 'Silas was right: hatred, pushback, dissent were all just modified matrices of the only things that meant anything: impact and volume' (278). Robert's assertion that impact and volume are the only meaningful measures of information casts a dismal shadow over the state of the nation, indicating that societal values have been warped to defend the incitement of latent xenophobia and white nationalism because they are popular with a large swathe of the country. The reader is invited to feel deeply disturbed by Robert's willingness to .stir up racial tension, just as they are invited to feel repulsed by Hugo Bennington's political platform. For both Robert and Hugo Bennington, having a voice is more important than what one uses that voice to say. This dismal depiction of how journalism functions—not as an objective source of information, but as a provocative opinion piece—reflects once again the moral and intellectual decay that is widespread in both the novel and the post-referendum England that it reflects.

Even more so than political rhetoric, data-mining becomes an immense source of power in this novel, which similarly disregards both people and ethics. Data cares about data— about clicks and the quantification of human behaviours so that such information might be weaponized. Throughout the novel, a group of masked individuals calling themselves 'The Griefers' threaten residents with claims of holding individuals' data, using phrases like 'We are your face' and 'What don't you want to share' (31) to elicit a fearful public response, yet they have no way of backing up these claims besides a 'sequenced dissolve of faces' on their website (232). The Griefers execute staged public insurrections to reassert their threats, which are effective in stirring up public anxiety about data and data privacy. Both Jess and Deepa, her friend and fellow Green employee, spend much of the novel considering the implications of these threats, and whether the threat is true or simply another tool designed to incite fear. Deepa expresses that she almost wishes they would release data proving that the threat is true, because:

it would be disruptive and awful and shaming and probably sort of violent and maybe offensive...but at least it would be committed and it would be in the name of something, whereas if you go out there with your dicks swinging around going, oh, we're going to go all the way, and then it turns out that not only are you not going all the way but you don't really have any, like, *way* to go, then that's just... shit. (234)

Here, Deepa acknowledges that it is increasingly difficult to distinguish between a genuine threat and an empty threat used to incite fear and expresses frustration that the line between the two has been blurred. She also alludes to the fact that the visceral reaction that occurs in people is the same regardless of whether the threat is real or fake, lending legitimate power to The Griefers whether or not their warnings are genuine. Indeed, Jess explicitly says: 'Whatever they're doing and however or wherever they're doing it, the feelings they're producing in people are real, so you want what they're doing to be real as well, to *merit* the feelings' (234). As has been established, the Leave campaign frequently made unfounded claims about what would happen if the UK remained in the EU, such as that it would receive a colossal influx of Turkish migrants, and would continue to pay huge sums of money to the bloc. Yet, despite the fact that these claims were false, they evoked genuine fear in many people and drove them to vote in certain ways. The insinuation of course is that many are deceived by empty threats, and politicians exploit existing insecurities and fears in order to serve their own agendas. Once again, this scene freezes us in a vision of post-referendum England that is unable to move past the dubious morality of the Brexit campaign, and offers no escape from the dystopia in which we find ourselves living.

As it turns out, The Griefers are not really data terrorists at all, but a group of trained actors employed by tech company

Green as part of an elaborate 'experiment' on the town of
Edmundsbury (366). Green markets itself as a simple tech
company based in Edmundsbury, but Jess, Deepa, and Trina—
the heroines brave enough to hope for a better world—all
suspect otherwise. Before she was let go from her job at Green
after her controversial tweet, Trina was confined to a single
level of Green's office building, and frequently wonders what
goes on above her and why it is a secret. When she is asked to
return to meet with Bangstrom, her slimy boss, the three women
use it as an opportunity to uncover the surreptitious objective of
the company. When Bangstrom makes clear that he is willing to
rehire Trina, she requests a promotion to 'The Field', which is
the name of a computer program that Trina helped to create and
a department within the company—the headquarters of which
are located on the upper level of the building. When Bangstrom
agrees, Trina is granted access to a wealth of knowledge
that was previously shielded from her. She is newly privy
to genuine information about who The Griefers actually are
('performance artists' (365)), and the purpose of having them,
which Bangstrom divulges is simply: 'outcomes' (366). He also
reveals that Edmundsbury was chosen for headquarters because
Green 'needed a stable, contained setting' (366) to harvest data
from the local population:

> Internet naivety is over. You think people are still surprised
> to find out that tweets are public and your data may be used
> for other purposes? Are they fuck. They know that, and they
> live around it. But they still maintain this illusion of division
> between their online and offline lives. So our aim with
> Edmundsbury was pretty basic: make a real-world haven,
> fuck with it, watch what happens. We're not interested in how
> people behave when they feel restricted. We're interested in
> how people behave when they think they're totally free...
> That's where the real data is, and that's where the profit is. A

map of how people react to certain threats, to the unknown, to *disruption*. (367)

This revelation suggests that Green has used an entire population of people, against their will, as guinea pigs in a data-mining experiment—one driven by corporate greed and which relies on the illusion of freedom. If Edmundsbury is a microcosmic example of England during and after the Brexit campaign, this passage is an alarming comparison which suggests that England has been the subject of a dystopian experiment on how people behave when they are under the influence of fear. Although Hugo Bennington and Robert are not part of Green's scheme, they feed into the simulation in alarming yet familiar ways. Their reaction to fear is to exploit it for personal political power, at the expense of the people that they supposedly serve. Ultimately, Byers invites the reader to imagine a world in which people are purposefully subjected to a campaign of fear and monitored for their reaction, and then to consider how closely that world looks like our own.

Perfidious Albion captures the exact political mood that reverberated after the Brexit referendum. While Geoffrey Hill's *The Book of Baruch by the Gnostic Justin* and Ali Smith's *Autumn* are hopeful in their conceptions of time as a restorative force, *Perfidious Albion* freezes us in a terrifying and stagnant vision of England and Englishness—where data is a weapon, where politics is a self-serving endeavour, and where conspiratorial forces seek to exploit the general public. Indeed, the novel ends abruptly with: 'And then' (383), suspending the reader in the middle of a sentence that we expect to go on. As we turn the page, we find 'Error 404: The page you are looking for does not yet exist' (384). The use of this internet code language is clearly relevant to the novel's overarching themes, but it also suggests a complete absence of future. Of course, *Perfidious Albion* is so on the nose that there literally is no future yet—as Robert says, 'what...could be more now than now?' (21) — but the implication of the error code is that we are stuck in this dystopian version of England — that there is no way out. The disturbing ending leaves us with a distinct sense of hopelessness and frustration that we are unable to escape our current moment. However, it can also be read as an urgent call to reject the current trajectory of English politics and society, not only against the pervasive data-mining and fearmongering, but also against a monolithic vision of England that has inspired a new wave of hatred and violence throughout the nation. *Perfidious Albion* is, at its core, a satire, but it is also a warning that, if we do not change our trajectory soon, we too will be frozen in this bleak and perverse state of Englishness.

* * *

Jonathan Coe's *Middle England*: Crisis and Comedy

Jonathan Coe's *Middle England* is the third instalment of a trilogy that began in 2001 with *The Rotters' Club*, closely followed in 2004 by *The Closed Circle*. The series was originally meant to conclude at book two; however, in the wake of the Brexit referendum in 2016, Coe decided to revive his characters to explore, once again, the human impact of a state of political turmoil in Britain, as well as its impact specifically on England and Englishness. Following the chronology of their lives from children growing up in the 1970s to the present, Benjamin and his schoolmates are now in their middle age; some have children, and their parents are all old or have passed away. Because *Middle England* is the last book of a trilogy, Coe is able to use its predecessors as comparative, or mirroring, works, which gives a broader scope for demonstrating the changes that have occurred in England and Englishness over the past 50 years. *The Rotters' Club* is set primarily and almost exclusively in Birmingham, a city hovering in the region commonly referred to as 'Middle

England'. By the time we reach the novel that takes that name, the original characters are dispersed across the country, but their roots remain firmly in their home city, and this continues to define their relationship to the political world around them. All three of the novels deal extensively with politics and the political atmosphere throughout the country during the time periods in which they are set. While *The Rotters' Club* follows the conflicts between trade unions and the government, *The Closed Circle* deals extensively with the New Labour movement in British politics and the post-9/11 West. *Middle England* begins in April 2010 and tracks the fall of Labour to the Conservative/Lib-Dem coalition, all the way through to 2018 and post-referendum Britain. The action of the novel happens against the backdrop of the 8-year newsreel between Gordon Brown's and Theresa May's governments, through the 2012 Olympic Games, the London riots, and the murder of Jo Cox. *Middle England* is itself split into three parts: 'Merrie England', 'Deep England', and 'Old England', each covering a few years and their accompanying political moods. Over the course of the novel, we watch as a microcosmic example of England's perpetual struggle for identity unravels, and the country experiences marked shifts from national cohesion to national division, from acceptance to intolerance, and from futility to hope.

Because the novel was published within 2 years of the referendum and was written as the consequences were still taking shape across the UK, the action of the novel is extremely familiar to the informed reader. As Sam Leith of *The Guardian* notes, 'in that respect, of course, we know what's going to happen because we're living it. This is a book that foretells the present.' Indeed, there are no mysteries in *Middle England* besides those that are closely related to the personal lives of its characters. However, the way in which Coe captures one of the most seismic referenda in modern British history is somewhat surprising: he writes a comedy. Although Coe confronts some of the uglier facets of Britain in the years up to and after the Brexit referendum, he does so — in a very English fashion — with a sense of humour and self-deprecation that settles the reader into a spirit of hopefulness. A review in the *Evening Standard* wrote that 'Coe's light, funny writing makes you feel better' (Butter). The purpose of this novel is not, like Sam Byers' *Perfidious Albion*, to reinforce the dystopian vision of Britain that much of the UK imagined after the referendum, but to lift the reader out of their shock, and prompt them to believe that, one day, they will look back on Brexit and be able to laugh.

The novel opens in the solemn moments after Benjamin Trotter, the central protagonist, leaves his mother's funeral with his grieving father, Colin. Benjamin and Colin drive 'through the heart of Middle England', a drive described as 'a placid, unmemorable journey where the only punctuation marks were petrol stations, pubs and garden centres, while brown heritage signs dangled the more distant temptations of wildlife centres, National Trust houses and arboretums in front of the bored traveller' (Coe 3–4). The morbidity of the funeral coupled with the dreariness of the surroundings creates a gloomy atmosphere almost immediately. In an attempt to distract them from where they have just come from, Benjamin turns on the radio, which is playing Fauré's Piano Trio. Entering Benjamin's mind, the narrative suggests that the music 'seemed to mirror, in sound, the gentle curves of the road, and even the muted greens of the landscape through which it carried them. The fact that the music was recognizably French made no difference: there was a commonality here, a shared spirit. Benjamin felt utterly at home in this music' (4). Opening the novel with a scene in which an English radio station — Radio Three — is playing French music offers an immediate sense of connection with Europe, highlighting how Benjamin's definition of 'home' extends across the English Channel to the Continent. That Benjamin feels the song mirrors the English countryside's landscape is a further emphasis on the fact that Europe and the UK are, in Benjamin's mind, both 'home', each reflecting and complementing the other in this classical music piece. This scene is also a reminder that for almost all of Benjamin's life, the UK has been a member of the EU—it is all he has known, and he is extremely comfortable with it. Colin, on the other hand, a young man during the Second World War, feels no such connection to the music: 'Turn that racket off, can't you?' (4). Opening the novel in this way both points out Benjamin's European—as opposed to solely English—identity, and also immediately indicates a generational divide that separates Benjamin's attitudes to Europe from his father's—a divide that was eventually used to explain voting behaviours across England in the 2016 referendum.

Benjamin switches the radio to Radio Four's *PM* programme, which unlike the calming notes of Fauré, 'plunged [them] into a familiar world of gladiatorial combat between interviewer and politician' (4). The programme is being run in the lead-up to the 2010 general election, and the 'big story seemed to be that the prime minister, Gordon Brown, fighting for re-election, had been caught on microphone describing a potential supporter as 'a sort of bigoted woman', and the media were making the most of it' (4–5). The report involves a statement from a Conservative MP, who 'gleefully' suggests that 'The prime minister has shown his true colours...Anyone who expresses these legitimate concerns is simply a bigot, in his view. And that's why we can never have a serious debate about immigration in this country' (5). This discussion serves as the first intimation of political tension in the novel; the lament that there cannot be a 'serious debate about immigration' serves to foreshadow the future and also to reveal that these conversations were happening, though more quietly, for years before they came to the fore with ferocity in 2015–2016. Indeed, Benjamin and Colin simply turn off the radio to avoid listening to the programme, dismissing it entirely and therefore lending it no power. The muting of the radio is both an indication that in 2010 politics was still something that many felt they could comfortably ignore, and a foreboding moment in which two characters willingly dismiss the bubbling of an ideological conflict that will soon spur immense upheaval across the entire nation.

Despite Benjamin and Colin's dismissiveness, early signs of political unease are rife throughout the 'Merrie England' section, and most suggest a communal anger simmering within the people. Benjamin's friend from school, Doug, now a political journalist in London, discusses his take on the current political landscape with Benjamin:

'I honestly think we're at a crossroads, you see. Labour's finished. I really think so. People are so angry right now, and nobody knows what to do about it...People see these guys in the city who practically crashed the economy two years ago and never felt any consequences—none of them went to jail, and now they're taking bonuses again while the rest of us are supposed to be tightening our belts. Wages are frozen. People have got no job security, no pension plans, they can't afford to take a family holiday or do repairs to the car. A few years ago they felt wealthy. Now they feel poor.' (14)

Here, Doug observes how the 2008 economic crash has contributed to a heightened level of anger and frustration throughout the UK, an anger that is directed towards the government under which the crash happened. While Doug's commentary in this moment relates directly to the impending general election that will, as he predicts, invite a Conservative government led by David Cameron into power, it also tells the reader something about how one's economic situation can drastically shift one's political alliance. As I mention in part one, in their book *The Rise of the Right,* Steven Winlow, Steve Hall, and James Treadwell analyse the conditions that allowed the right-wing group the English Defence League to gain so much support in the lead-up to Brexit, and they explain why so many others felt that 2016 was an opportunity to take back something that has been lost. Like Doug, Winlow, Hall and Treadwell emphasize that the simmering anger throughout Britain is a side effect of our market-driven society, which serves some while crushing others under its weight. Just as we saw the rejection of a marketized society in *Jerusalem* in chapter three, here, three political scientists track these frustrations among those in the real world who are suffering most as a result of the current economic system. At this early stage in the novel, it is already abundantly clear that the economy has become one of the most important issues for the average British person and, consequently, is one of the most significant indicators of the political direction that the country will take.

Another, more menacing, scene of bubbling anger occurs at a Speed Awareness Course, where Sophie, Benjamin's niece, is in attendance. As Sophie sits in the class that is being led by an Asian woman named Naheed, she notices that everyone there has something in common: 'As Sophie listened to the speakers, so different in age, class, gender and ethnicity, all with such different stories to tell, she realized that they were in fact united by one common factor: a profound and abiding sense of injustice' (Coe 37). One driver, Derek, seems particularly afflicted, and interrupts Naheed's advice on road safety to ask: 'I've been driving for forty years...And I've never had an accident. Why should I take lessons from someone like you?' (40). Derek's defiance hints at a sense of his injured pride after being forced to return to an educational environment despite his 'forty years' of experience behind the wheel, but more than this, there is a blatantly racist undertone to Derek's sneer: 'someone like you'. In a manner that is reminiscent of Daniel Gluck's story about a man dressed in a tree costume in Ali Smith's *Autumn* ('people like you generally' (124)), Derek targets Naheed's nationality as a way of undermining her authority, her sense of belonging, and her expertise. In a later conversation with Sophie, Naheed acknowledges this emotional charge as a normalcy: 'One thing you learn in this job—there's a lot of anger out there...it's not always to do with race anyway. People like to get angry about anything' (43). Naheed calmly and coolly observes the general simmering of unpleasant emotion that underlies her everyday experiences and creates a distinct sense of foreboding—while they are not yet disruptive, racial tensions are certainly noticeable.

As we saw in *The Rotters' Club*, class and race immediately form a framework for understanding British politics generally, and Englishness in particular, and this only becomes more pronounced throughout the 'Merrie England' section. Although many characters become more attuned to recognizing these early indications of political unease, there is still a general sense that the country is, as a whole, blissfully unaware of how serious the consequences of this anger, if unchecked, can become. When Sohan, a gay Sri Lankan man, chairs a panel with two writers— one English and one French—the Frenchman, M. Aldebert, suggests that 'The French are an intolerant, judgemental people. Not like the British, I think' (29). When asked to elaborate, he continues: 'In France, we look at the British and we are impressed that, unlike most other European countries, you don't have this phenomenon—a popular party of the far right...You have UKIP, of course, but my understanding is that they are a single-issue party, who are not taken seriously as a political force' (29). Aside from the distinct sense of foreboding that ensues from the four-letter combination: UKIP, Aldebert's speech suggests a calm confidence in the level nature of British political life. He also distinguishes between France and Britain to suggest that Britain is an exception to the current European rule. Aldebert's colleague and white English writer Lionel Hampshire follows up smugly with his own take on Britain's exceptional political nature:

'I'm not an uncritically patriotic person. Far from it. But there is something in the English character that I admire...I mean our love of moderation...We're a pragmatic nation, politically. Extremes of left and right don't appeal to us. And we're also essentially tolerant. That's why the multicultural experiment in Britain has by and large been successful, with one or two minor blips...speaking personally, these are the things I most admire about the British: our moderation, and our tolerance.' (30)

Hampshire's speech about political moderation in Britain seems deeply ironic and comical to the contemporary reader, who, with the benefit of hindsight, can confirm that extremes will in fact dominate the political landscape. It is also amusing that Hampshire interchangeably uses 'English' and 'British', which suggests that he does not know the difference between his subnational territory and the polity of the UK — in other words, that he doesn't know much about his country at all. Just as Jack Forrest suggests that class warfare is over in *The Rotters' Club*, Hampshire's pride in unwavering British tolerance is undercut by events that follow, and is made to seem both naïve and laughable. Indeed, his reverence for the success of the 'multicultural experiment' feels exhausting and depressing in the light of the referendum campaign and its xenophobic aftermath. To talk about Britishness as being equivalent to 'tolerance' is also a line that both inspires laughter and a morbid sense of exasperation that the country might have been so blind to its impending fate, or so unwilling to see itself for what it was and change course.

Sohan's reaction to the conversation that unravels on-stage marks him as a knowing victim of the underlying current of racism that Naheed experiences in her classroom, and he feels anger and frustration at both Aldebert and Hampshire's remarks:

'What a load of self-satisfied bullshit,' said Sohan. But, regrettably, he did not say it on stage [...]

Every day you come face to face with people who are not tolerant at all...They may not say anything aggressive but you can see it in their eyes and their whole way of behaving towards you. And they *want* to say something. Oh yes, they want to use one of those forbidden words on you, or just tell you to fuck off back to your own country—wherever they think that is—but they know they can't. They know it's not allowed. So as well as hating you, they also hate *them*— whoever they are—these faceless people who are sitting in judgement over them somewhere, legislating on what they can and can't say out loud. (30–31)

Sohan's personal experiences as a Sri Lankan man create a sharp divide between himself and the authors who join him on stage. While his home is in England, he recognizes that others cannot reconcile Englishness with anything other than whiteness, offering another indication that race is playing a key role in influencing political attitudes. Furthermore, his ready use of the phrase 'fuck off back to your own country' that became such an indicator of the post-Brexit referendum political atmosphere, used in a scene set in 2010, allows Coe to introduce both the existence and denial of division and tension within England simultaneously. When Sohan acknowledges that the anger of the people is turned from the 'other' to the government—the people who are enforcing policies to protect them—he helps to explain why later, when political figures start to align themselves with those harbouring the rumblings of racism and anger, the locus of their frustration is able to shift so quickly, and indeed violently, onto immigrants and those who do not fit the 'white British' archetype.

The first time in the novel where underlying tensions— specifically racial tensions—rise to the surface is during the London riots of 2011. Though they are not labelled 'race riots' officially, the London riots were unequivocally racially motivated. Coriander, Doug's daughter, is the vehicle through which the reader experiences the riots. She is a white, upper-class, 14-year-old girl who 'lived in a house currently valued by local estate agents at a little over six million pounds, spreading over five floors, tucked away in a hard-to-find backwater between the King's Road and Chelsea embankment' (77). Perhaps unexpectedly, Coriander loathes her privilege, and finds solace only in the voice of Amy Winehouse, who had recently passed away, because 'She *was* the voice of North London' (79), a place which Coriander sees as far more diverse and interesting than Chelsea. Coriander is invited to the London riots by 'AJ, a young and handsome black boy she'd met at a club in Hackney' (79), with a message promising 'Pure terror and havoc' (79). At the riot, chaos does indeed begin to ensue. People are 'smashing up the windows of the bus which had been parked and abandoned when the traffic came to a halt...Two Rastas were trying to get down the street back to their flat but the police weren't letting them through...protesters had now armed themselves with bottles looted from the local Tesco...They ran past a Mazda MX5 which had been set on fire' (80–82). Coriander shares in the anger of her black compatriots, who 'were angry at the killing of Mark Duggan four days before and the years of unfair treatment from the police,' while 'the police were angry at the lawlessness of the protest and the violence they were being threatened with' (82–83). With the chaotic description of the riots, the novel demonstrates that the recent trigger event of Mark Duggan's death is not the only reason for this outburst of violence. The underlying racial tension that has been kept forcibly at bay even before Culpepper and Steve Richard's feud in *The Rotters' Club* is finally boiling over and being recognized for what it is. The riots contribute to the growing sense that the latent issues throughout society—ignored by the white population—are beginning to boil over, and will ultimately lead to an even greater eruption of debates between the racist and anti-racist, xenophobic and accepting, in 2016.

While Coe continues to reveal the deep-set division and anger throughout England and the UK, he also takes time to consider what brings the UK together as a whole. He does so most notably in the final chapter of the 'Merrie England' section—a chapter that follows the novel's characters as they watch the opening ceremony of the Olympic Games in London 2012. In their book *Performing Englishness: Identity and Politics in a Contemporary Folk Resurgence*, Trish Winter and Simon Keegan-Phipps suggest that the Olympic opening ceremony is, in essence, 'a performance celebrating the national identity of the host nation' (Winter and Keegan-Phipps 4). Considering the complex definition of nationhood when it refers to the conglomerate of the UK, there was serious debate about which aspects of national identity should be performed at the London Olympics. Morris dancing, for example, is a traditional English folk dance, and as early as 2005 there was a debate surrounding its inclusion (Parkinson). In the end, it made only a brief appearance in the closing ceremony as a 'figure of fun within a celebration of British humour, rather than as representing traditional culture *per se*' (Winter and Keegan-Phipps 4). Winter and Keegan-Phipps argue that 'national identity is understood not as something that is naturally given or pre-existing, but as something that is made', specifically through performative acts such as folk dance and music (Winter and Keegan-Phipps 12). Benedict Anderson similarly claims that nationalisms can be understood as 'imagined communities', which are created and displayed to a group of people who then consider themselves connected in a unique way. Connecting these two notions of nationhood to the case of Britishness, J. Storey claims:

There is nothing natural about nationality. One is not born

British, one becomes British...The performance of nationality creates the illusion of a prior substantiality—a core national self—and suggests that the performative ritual of nation-ness is merely an expression of an already existing nationality. However, our nationality is not the expression of the location in which we are born, it is performatively constructed in processes of repetition and citation, which gradually produce and reinforce our sense of national belonging. (Storey 19)

In view of these theories, the true purpose of the Olympic ceremony is not to celebrate the sporting event about to take place, though of course it does this as well, but rather to celebrate the host nation—to play songs signifying national greatness, perform traditional dances, and recall the most successful Brits to ever live—and ultimately to fortify a sense of collective identity among its people. The 2012 Olympics provided the UK with an opportunity to reinforce an idealized version of what it means to be British—importantly, *not* just English, Scottish, Welsh, or Irish—to all of its citizens, and indeed to the entire world. It was a project of unity and patriotism intended to keep the imagined community bound together as one.

In an extensive and gripping scene, Coe writes about the experience of his characters as they sit to watch the opening ceremony in 2012, demonstrating just how quickly such a performance can entrance even the most critical and unpatriotic character, serving to invigorate, sustain, and perpetuate a collective form of nationalism. What results is a case study in the unifying power of performative narratives of nationhood and nationally broadcasted television. The chapter begins:

At nine o'clock on the evening of Friday, 27 July 2012:

Sophie and Ian were sitting together on the sofa in their flat, watching the Olympic opening ceremony on television.

Colin Trotter was alone at home in Rednal, sitting in

his armchair, watching the Olympic opening ceremony on television.

Helena Coleman was alone at home in Kernal Magna, sitting in her armchair, watching the Olympic opening ceremony on television.

Philip and Carol Chase, along with Philip's son Patrick and his wife Mandy, were sitting in the living room of their house in King's Heath, a Chinese takeaway on their laps, watching the Olympic opening ceremony on television.

Sohan Aditya was alone in his flat in Clapham, lying on the sofa, watching the Olympic opening ceremony on television and texting his friends about it.

Christopher and Lois Potter, in the midst of their subdued walking holiday in the Lake District, were watching the Olympic opening ceremony on the television of their rented cottage.

Doug Anderton, his daughter Coriander and his son Ranulph were all sitting in separate rooms of their house in Chelsea, watching the Olympic opening ceremony on different televisions.

Benjamin was alone in the mill house, sitting at the desk in his study, making cuts and revisions to his novel, while listening to a string quartet by Arthur Honegger. (Coe 129)

In this passage, with the exception of Benjamin, we have a wide array of individuals with widely different views, in widely different locations across England (or in different rooms in the same house), all tuned in to exactly the same programme, imagining themselves as a community. It once again reminds us of Benedict Anderson's theory about how the emergence of print capitalism and national newspapers disseminated a cohesive form of imagined community nationalism, because these forms provided 'the technical means for "re-presenting" the *kind* of imagined community that is the nation' (Anderson

25). In the same way, we see here that Coe's characters from across the country all tune in to the same TV channel, and they all fall deeply into an emotional, patriotic reverence for Britain.

Everyone except Benjamin is shown to emerge from the ceremony with a passionate sense of connection to their fellow Brits, with many characters having experiences that feel to them like an enlightenment. Indeed, as Philip watches the ceremony, he becomes excited at a Pink Floyd reference that he 'and a few million others' (Coe 130) would understand, and he calls Benjamin to tell him to turn on the TV and watch as Mike Oldfield, an English composer, plays *Tubular Bells* (134). Similarly, Sohan and Sophie exchange excited texts about '*Pandemonium*' and '*Humphrey Jennings*' (131). (Sohan is so puzzled and inspired by the ceremony that he later commits his career to the study of Englishness.) Doug, who makes a living analysing and criticizing British politics, feels:

> the stirrings of an emotion he hadn't experienced for years— had never really experienced at all, perhaps, having grown up in a household where all expressions of patriotism had been considered suspect: national pride...at this moment he felt proud, proud to be British, proud to be part of a nation which had not only achieved such great things but could now celebrate them with such confidence and irony and lack of self-importance. (132)

Even Coriander, who frequently expresses disdain for almost everything, after watching a scene about Tim Berners-Lee, exclaims: '"What? The *British* invented the internet?...That's amazing"...She took out her BlackBerry and took a picture of the image on the screen, then wrote *I come from an awesome country* and tweeted it to all 379 of her followers' (138). In all of these reactions, there is a sense of national belonging that overrides individualism—they even share their personal reactions with close friends or followers during this time, creating an even greater sense of community and national belonging. The Olympic ceremony becomes not just a celebration of sports, but a celebration of Britishness, and it ignites a sense of unity that is otherwise absent from the novel. The only character who does not fall into a flurry of excitement is Benjamin. Even after Philip implores him to watch, Benjamin turns on the TV but does not concentrate on it, his mind drifting to other places. He chooses to listen to Arthur Honegger, a Swiss composer, above watching the Olympic opening ceremony and indulging in the display of Englishness, which marks Benjamin, in multiple ways, as a neutral bystander to the nationalism that surrounds him.

As we enter the second section of the novel: 'Deep England', the unity inspired by the Olympic ceremony falls away entirely, and we enter a far more recognizable world: one that is dominated by the threat of UK fragmentation and withdrawal from the EU. 'Deep England' is a satirical term coined to describe, according to *The Guardian*, the Brexiteer Englanders who 'believe that life was better before the evils of industrialisation, foreign competition and, you know, immigration' ('This is "Deep England"'). With such people in mind, the action of the novel reopens in 2014 to tell the reader that '"Yes Scotland" had now secured one million signatories to its campaign for an independent Scotland ahead of the referendum in September; that the number of British people needing emergency supplies from food banks had already risen by one-fifth this year; and that the BBC was being accused of a cover-up over its role in the recent police raid on Sir Cliff Richard's home following sexual assault allegations' (Coe 154). Where 'Merrie England' was a section full of blissful denial despite simmering tension, the reader can immediately sense that 'Deep England' will be quite the opposite. Indeed, the section begins by revealing a far more visible atmosphere of xenophobia and anti-foreign sentiment. As Sohan and Sophie have drinks in London's newest high-rise building, the Shard,

Sohan comments: '"London doesn't belong to Londoners anymore...This building where we're standing. London's latest star attraction. You think it's British? Ninety-five percent of it is owned by the state of Qatar...Walk anywhere in central London these days and the chances are you're treading on foreign soil'" (143–144). Sohan's reflections on the international character of London, while not necessarily derisive in tone, highlight a general feeling among the population that they are being taken over—that there is a malevolent 'foreign' force and that global capital is overtaking the cultural integrity of London.

Not only foreign investment, but foreign people, or at least people who appear foreign, are the targets of similar attacks. When Sophie and her husband Ian are on a cruise ship filled with retired English couples, Sophie tells her table about Ian losing his bid for promotion at work to his colleague Naheed. A fellow passenger, Mr Geoffrey Wilcox, comments:

'Hmm. Naheed—so I'm guessing this is...an Asian lady, am I right?'

'That's right.' [...]

'Look,' he said. 'I don't want to cause trouble. But your husband here is feeling bad about not getting the job, and all I'm saying is, he shouldn't blame himself' [...]

'We all know what it's like nowadays,' said Mr Wilcox.

'"What it's like?"'

'This country. We all know the score. How it works. People like Ian don't get a fair crack of the whip anymore.' (165–166)

Mr Wilcox's observation concerning 'People like Ian' is a blatant reference to the colour of Ian's white skin. He is suggesting that there is a culture of favouritism towards people like Naheed who belong to ethnic minorities that precludes white English people from moving up in the world. Geoffrey continues: 'We don't look

after our own anymore, do we?...If you're from a minority—
fine. Go to the front of the queue. Blacks, Asians, Muslims, gays:
we can't do enough for them. But take a talented bloke like Ian
here and it's another story' (166). Geoffrey's speech holds a
very dangerous assumption about race in England. First, he has
received no information to suggest that Ian is 'talented', other
than his physical appearance, i.e., his whiteness. Second, he is
suggesting that when a black, Asian, Muslim, or gay person is
hired it has nothing to do with *their* talents, but rather is a result
of their ethnic identity or sexuality. This is the rhetoric of 'they
are stealing your jobs'—a totally ironic frustration experienced
by white people when they are no longer granted a supremacy
that they believe they are entitled to. Geoffrey's statements
suggest that an encroaching belief that the foreign 'other' is
the root of white men's problems is gaining ground, and Coe
goes on to demonstrate how easy it is to get swept up in the
xenophobic rhetoric that has begun to take hold.

While Sophie is deeply concerned by Geoffrey's assumptions
about Naheed's promotion, Ian slowly becomes more convinced
of his own victimhood—a difference of opinion that eventually
drives them apart as a couple. Ian's gradual snowball into
anger appears to fit O'Toole's notion of 'self-pity'—the only
emotion that can reconcile both a belief in one's superiority
and the feeling that one is being oppressed (O'Toole 3). Initially
unconvinced by Geoffrey's comments, when Geoffrey turns out
to be right in an earlier speculation that two women travelling
together on the ship were 'lezzers' (Coe 161), Ian experiences a
moment of reflection: 'if Mr Wilcox had been right about those
two, why shouldn't he be right about other things as well' (171)
meaning about Naheed. From this moment, Ian develops an
extremely short fuse for anything 'politically correct' ('PC').
When Sophie is suspended from her lecturing job due to a
student complaint about 'transphobic remarks made by Sophie
during a seminar' (243), Ian becomes exasperated at how she

handles the situation. Sophie sees everything as nothing more than a 'misunderstanding' (282) and defends her student on account of having 'respect for minorities' (282). Ian shoots back:

'Will you *stop* being so bloody...PC about all of this!'

Sophie sat back and smiled. 'There we are. I wondered how long it would take before those two little letters were introduced into the conversation.'

'Meaning?'

'Do you have any idea, Ian, how often you accuse me and everyone else of being too "PC" for your liking these days? It's become your obsession. And I don't even think you know what it means.'

'I know exactly what it means. What you call respect for minorities basically means two fingers to the rest of us. OK, so protect your precious...transgender students from the horrible things people say about them. Swaddle them in cotton wool. What happens if you're white, and male, and straight, and middle class, hmm? People can say whatever the fuck they like about you then.' (282–283)

Ian's outburst is another sharp indication that the rhetoric of white male plight is creeping to the surface of the everyday. The rumblings of class and racial tensions have been felt since *The Rotters' Club*, but here they both leap to the fore simultaneously, and the conflicting beliefs between families, friends, and partners threaten the stability of relationships all across the UK. Ian's anger also stems from the blow to his confidence that occurs when he doesn't receive the job promotion, which suggests he is lashing out against the system of political correctness that he deems responsible. In a sense, Ian's anger is sad—he cannot see that the opportunity denied to him has been historically denied to minority groups for decades—centuries even—and rather than admit that Naheed may be equally, if not more, qualified for the position he lost, he uses her as a scapegoat for his own failure. In a final, stinging condemnation of Sophie's behaviour, Ian tells Sophie that in the upcoming referendum, '"Leave is going to win. Do you know why?... People like you," he said, with a note of quiet triumph. And then he repeated, with a jab of his finger: "People like *you*"' (284). In this nasty scene, the reader witnesses the vicious polarization that the Brexit campaign unleashed on the country through the experience of a married couple. Once again, the phrase 'people like you' indicates a world increasingly defined by sides and binaries: white or non-white, Leave or Remain, and so on. The forcefulness of Ian's words and gestures demonstrates that he and Sophie have become completely alienated from each other, and their relationship shatters. From a human perspective, watching the savage political battle between Leave and Remain break apart a married couple is extremely depressing, and reveals just how powerfully divisive the Brexit campaign was.

Meanwhile, it becomes clear throughout 'Deep England' that Englishness is unstable and unclear, and Coe demonstrates that England is a place that lacks a firm, stable identity. When Sophie, Ian, and a Chinese businessman named Mr Hu set out to play a round of golf on a Sunday morning, Mr Hu is delighted with the opportunity to partake in an activity that is so quintessentially English. Excitedly, he comments to Sophie: 'This is where golf should be played,' he said, gesturing around him. 'In England. England's "green and pleasant land".' They walked on. 'You teach at university, right? So you know about William Blake?...This poem, "Jerusalem" — it's very beautiful' (207). Mr Hu's reference to Blake's poem is a reminder of Jez Butterworth's play *Jerusalem* and suggests that the depiction of Englishness invoked in both the poem and the play is felt as much abroad as on home soil, though of course, as explored in chapter three, such a depiction is primarily based on myths and fallacies. Mr Hu continues to show interest in English traditions, comically unaware that he identifies many aspects of English culture that are either outdated or that simply never happened. Noticing a picture of 'a dozen or so red-coated, top-hatted riders cantering through fields and leaping over hedges in pursuit of a recalcitrant fox,' Mr Hu says:

> 'Now this,' said Mr Hu, 'is something I would really like to see. A traditional British hunt. Perhaps for my next visit, Mr Bishop, you could arrange it? Purely as a spectator, of course.' [...]
> 'I'm afraid that fox-hunting is now regarded as a criminal activity in this country...It's been banned for quite a number of years.'
> 'Banned? How strange. I didn't realize...Of course, the British are famous for their love of animals.' (212)

This amusing exchange demonstrates that even a businessman from China can long for the kind of England that one finds in a period drama—the kind that does not exist, and perhaps never really existed as we imagine it today. The dialogue here is also reminiscent of the theme park in Julian Barnes' novel *England, England*, which was developed in order to preserve mythological figures such as Robin Hood and depict them as true English heroes, ultimately creating a new version of England which satisfies the world's muddled and romanticized vision of Englishness. Ultimately, we see that no one, whether English or not, seems have a sense of Englishness, or indeed England, that does not rely on myth and mendacity.

While 'Deep England' portrays how the experiences of everyday people began to drastically shift in the lead-up to the referendum, it also satirically portrays the very events that trigger this change of atmosphere to take place—namely, David Cameron's re-election campaign and the release of the Conservative Party manifesto. When London-based journalist

Doug sits with his friend and fellow political pundit Nigel (not Farage), who is involved with Cameron's campaign, Nigel sits extremely smug in the steady assurance that the Conservatives will win: 'The *confidence*, Douglas, the *enthusiasm* — that's what's off the scale. Dave's ready for this fight, and do you know why? Because he knows he is going to win' (181). When Doug retorts: 'He hasn't been reading the opinion polls, then?' (181), Nigel responds dismissively: 'We never take any notice of opinion polls. They're always wrong' (181). As we now know, the opinion polls indicating a Remain win in the referendum were heralded as accurate, making Nigel's confidence deeply ironic. Doug and Nigel go on to read the section of the 2015 manifesto that forever changed British politics: 'Page seventy-two of the manifesto: "Real change in our relationship with the European Union"..."Only the Conservative Party will deliver real change and real choice on Europe, with an in-out referendum by the end of 2017"' (182). Doug's concern over the political gamble represented by a referendum on EU membership is swiftly swatted aside by Nigel, who makes the blasé yet assured statement: 'the bottom line is, it's not going to happen' (185). When Doug asks: 'Why not?', Nigel replies: 'Because there's no way he's going to win an overall majority. All the opinion polls say so. Don't you ever look at them, Douglas? You really should.' (185). This scene between Doug and Nigel is intended as more than mere backstory. In this sardonic moment where Nigel completely contradicts his earlier assertion that he never pays attention to opinion polls, the reader is invited to feel frustrated, yet also to revel in how wrong he will turn out to be. This scene ultimately satirizes Cameron and his party's decision to include a referendum on the EU in the Conservative manifesto without considering the real consequences of that decision were things to turn out unexpectedly, and Coe offers the reader an element of comic relief from what is otherwise an infuriating series of events.

The comedy continues when Doug and Nigel next meet, after the date of the referendum is officially announced: 'A few weeks earlier, David Cameron had visited Brussels to negotiate a new deal with the European Union, hoping to extract concessions which would give Britain exceptional status—even more exceptional than it had already—and pacify the country's seemingly ever more vocal army of Eurosceptics' (264). The word 'exceptional' here reminds us of Arthur Aughey and English exceptionalism, and Coe clearly satirizes Cameron's greedy attempts to make Britain even more powerful within the bloc. When the date of the referendum is announced as '23 June—the second day of the Glastonbury Festival, as it happened' (264), Doug sardonically asks Nigel: 'Well, then, that's a hundred thousand young people who won't be bothering to vote, isn't it?' (265). Reassuring Doug, Nigel replies that 'Dave has foreseen every eventuality,' though *not* including, 'the one where he loses and we have to leave the EU' (265). Nigel concedes that what he means is: 'Every *probable* eventuality, I should say' (265). Once again, Coe's satire depicts Nigel and the entire Conservative Party's obliviousness to the chain of events that were to occur as a result of their actions. The comedy of this scene culminates in a laugh-out-loud-worthy mistake that the Conservative Party has been making up to this point by thinking that Brexit was called 'Brixit' (265). The novel depicts Nigel, David Cameron, and the Conservatives as a group of airheads unable to even get the name of their own referendum right, and the reader, while horrified, is encouraged to feel almost glad that the absurd and wanton confidence of this character will be karmically repaid—albeit in a way that affects us all. In this way, Coe's satirical portrayal of Cameron's manifesto promise provides an opportunity for the reader to relieve their frustration and pain through humour, thus creating a more light-hearted atmosphere to a deeply troubling event that was still very much consuming conversation at the time the novel was published.

In *The Rotters' Club*, the reader was exposed to the human trauma of the IRA's attacks in Birmingham through the experience of Lois Trotter and her boyfriend, Malcolm. In *Middle England*, the trauma of the Brexit campaign is also crystallized in a tragic death, this time the real murder of Jo Cox, a Labour MP Remainer who was brutally murdered in the street. Importantly, Lois, also a victim of a nationalist attack, is the character through whom we experience it. As Lois is going about her day, Lois hears news 'which brought her afternoon to a halt':

A member of parliament had been attacked in her constituency; attacked in the street as she walked to her local library, where she had been intending to hold a surgery.

Lois had never heard of the MP. Her name was Jo Cox. She was the MP for Batley and Spen, a constituency in Yorkshire. A young woman. The attack sounded horrific. She had been both shot and stabbed by her assailant. As he attacked her he had shouted some wild, seemingly incoherent words which were later reported to have been a cry of 'Britain first. This is for Britain.' (308)

Jo Cox's death shocked the entire nation and was a turning point in the debate that exposed the sinister consequences of rousing English nationalists by portraying it as an identity that rejects tolerance and inclusivity. An act of homegrown terrorism had been inspired by a debate on the mainstream political stage—a debate that was consuming people's whole lives. Now, through Lois, we watch as the fierce Brexit campaign claims the life of a young woman who sought to defend what she thought was right. This was, as the assailant's cries reveal, a nationalist attack, and when it is reported that Jo Cox died from her injuries, Lois experiences a fit of panic and horror as she is reminded of her own personal experience of violence at the hands of a nationalist organization:

> 'No, no, no, no, *NO!*' she wailed, and threw herself down
> on the sofa. Her body was racked with sobs. 'No!' she kept
> saying, again and again. 'No, no *NO!*' then she stood up and
> yelled at the TV screen: 'You stupid people!' She strode over
> to the window and looked out at the quiet street and shouted,
> louder than ever: *'You stupid people–letting this happen!'*...for
> the next few minutes she was kicking furniture, throwing
> cushions, pounding the walls with her fists. She smashed
> a vase and soaked the carpet with water. How long the fit
> lasted, she couldn't say. Eventually she blacked out. (309)

In this harrowing scene, we watch Lois as she is both reminded
of her own trauma and disgusted at the sight of similar violence.
Her screams are deeply upsetting, especially because the reader
barely hears Lois' voice at all since Malcolm's murder in *The
Rotters' Club*, and when we do, she is portrayed as a relatively
meek character. The intensity with which she experiences Jo
Cox's murder ripples through the reader as their own reminder
of the shock of this event, and they are invited to feel deep
sympathy and melancholy for the life-shattering effects of a
debate being conducted by characters like Nigel, who ignore
the consequences and laugh off the severity of the promises that
they make.

As we enter the final part of the novel titled 'Old England',
one might be reminded that in *England, England*, this is the name
given to what is truly England after the theme park replaces it
in terms of global relevance. In Barnes' novel, Old England is a
decaying, deteriorating, and now historically irrelevant place.
In *Middle England*, it is portrayed similarly, though 'Old' here
also appears to double in meaning by referring to the elderly
population. We enter part three after the referendum has
happened—the narrative skips over the day of the referendum

itself, except for showing Colin Trotter place his 'Leave' vote and dying on the same day. Colin's timely death is an overt statement about the voting trends that resulted in an overall Leave result. The narrative suggests that in his old age, Colin has placed a vote that will never affect him—an ageist but frankly true statement that lends legitimacy to the anger of the younger population who have been dumped in a situation that many of them didn't vote for. Colin's death is also reminiscent of David Cameron's decision to resign after the referendum results came in; he created an awful situation and then left others to pick up the pieces.

'Old England' opens like 'Merrie England' did—with a funeral, this time Colin's. As Benjamin and Lois prepare to scatter their father's ashes, Benjamin places his iPod on a nearby bench and starts loudly playing 'The Lark Ascending', a melody composed by Englishman Ralph Vaughan Williams:

> Almost at once, the gentle, modal chords rose up, unmistakeably English: Benjamin closed his eyes and for a few seconds lost himself in the music, music which he had heard thousands of times but would never tire of, music which spoke to him in the subtlest, most persuasive way of his roots, his sense of self, his feeling of profound attachment to this landscape, this country (316)

Benjamin's attachment to the 'unmistakably English' melody he plays is notable in comparison with the 'recognizably French' (4) music that made him feel so at home while winding through the English countryside at the beginning of the novel. The shift from feeling at home in music from another European country to feeling profoundly attached to an English melody suggests a kind of isolationism and contraction of what home means for English people post-Brexit referendum. Despite how it seems, Benjamin does not feel the allure of isolationism himself. As he and Lois leave, Benjamin reflects on the music again:

> He thought about Vaughan Williams: his conception of music as 'the soul of a nation', the way he had uncovered so many old English folk tunes, helping to rescue a whole tradition almost from oblivion, and yet there was no contradiction, no tension even, between this deep cultural patriotism and his other political beliefs, which seemed to have been so liberal and progressive. He thought about how badly this country, this crisis-riven country, stood in need of figures like that at the moment...(318–319)

Here, Benjamin reflects on the English composer Ralph Vaughan Williams' legacy as a musician and suggests that the patriotism of Williams' English music did not preclude him having a liberal progressive attitude. Considering his 'crisis-riven country', Benjamin's musings here suggest that English patriotism, which is cast in such a negative light in the wake of the referendum, can and should be used to unite, rather than divide, people. In other words, Benjamin does not think that taking pride in one's country should be mutually exclusive from embracing the rest of the world. His attitude suggests a disappointment with the referendum result, despite having not been particularly invested in the debate as it was happening. His reflection also demonstrates the kind of person Benjamin wants to be: patriotically English and a global citizen, all at once—a new and far more hopeful vision of Englishness.

Unlike Benjamin, Sophie is unable to feel hopeful in the wake of the referendum, and in fact feels extremely dejected by the isolationism that the referendum symbolized. If Colin represents 'Old England', Sophie represents Young England, and she speaks to the emotions of many young voters who felt betrayed by the Leave outcome. Sitting on a bench in Hartlepool, a place just south of Durham, Sophie reflects on her identity and her Englishness:

> this was England after all — her country — but she felt wholly
> estranged from this corner of it. For the last ten years, despite
> the time she had spent in the Midlands, her heart had always
> been in London. She considered herself a Londoner, now,
> and from London she could not only travel by train to Paris
> or Brussels more quickly than she could come here, but she
> would probably feel far more at home on the Boulevard
> Saint-Michel or Grand-Place than she did sitting on this
> bench. (369)

Of course, Sophie's young age contributes greatly to the way
she identifies herself in contrast with Benjamin, as does her
attachment to London, as opposed to Benjamin's Birmingham.
As we know, London was one of the few metropolitan areas
in England to overwhelmingly vote Remain in the referendum,
demonstrating a commitment to a multi-ethnic society and a
globally connected world. Sophie demonstrates that being a
'Londoner' is an international identity — one that is inherently
connected to the European nations that Brexit has scorned.
For Sophie, isolationism is claustrophobic, and she is able to
distinguish between being English and being a Londoner in
a way that suggests they are irreconcilable identities post-
referendum. It seems that the identity of a Londoner is more
European than it is English.

Sophie's anger at the Leave vote is not solely a sense of
personal dejection. As we saw in the middle section of the novel,
the Brexit debate drove her and her husband Ian apart as he
became more consumed by the rhetoric of the Leave campaign.
In the third and final section, we learn that Sophie and Ian
have been attending counselling to heal their marriage: 'A very
specific form of counselling, in fact. Post-Brexit counselling'
(325). While the absurd fact that a whole new type of therapy

was created to deal with the polarizing effects of the Brexit referendum is almost amusing, it also demonstrates how much people needed this type of support in its immediate aftermath. Despite this apparently bleak scenario, the presence of therapy at all does demonstrate a collective attempt to heal the divides that had set in—a hopeful sign.

Later in the novel, Sophie reflects on her separation from Ian:

> from every rational point of view, the trigger for her separation from Ian looked crazy. A couple might decide to separate for all sorts of reasons: adultery, cruelty, domestic abuse, lack of sex. But a difference of opinion over whether Britain should be a member of the European Union or not? It seemed absurd. It was absurd. And yet Sophie knew, deep down, that it had not so much been a reason as a tipping point. Ian had reacted (to her mind) so bizarrely to the referendum result, with such gleeful, infantile triumphalism (he kept using the word 'freedom' as if he were the citizen of a tiny African country that had finally won independence from its colonial oppressor) that, for the first time, she genuinely realized that she no longer understood why her husband thought and felt the way that he did. At the same time, she herself had been possessed by the immediate sense, that morning, that a small but important part of her own identity—her modern, layered, multiple identity—had been taken away from her. (326)

Here, once again, Sophie considers the way the referendum has jeopardized her global sense of identity, and she recognizes that in a sense, she blames Ian for the part he played in allowing that to be taken away. She also highlights her frustration at Ian's 'triumphalism', comparing him to a member of 'a tiny African country that had finally won independence from its colonial oppressor'. The reader is encouraged to read these lines with the same scepticism as Sophie: the hypothetical comparison between an English liberation movement and an African liberation movement is both appalling and amusing, because of course it is British oppression that African countries had to liberate themselves from in the first place. The incredible reversal that takes place in Ian's mind—which is presumably shared by those who think like him—that English people were the ones who were being oppressed in the new order that the EU offered is a frustrating and historically jumbled understanding of England's place in the world. Just as Johnny Byron, the supposed English protector in *Jerusalem*, pushes back against the forces of globalization that England helped to create in the first place, here Sophie considers Ian's beliefs to be an equally ironic conception of Englishness that is extremely powerful, but deeply flawed.

In the final chapter of the novel, we are geographically resituated to Benjamin and Lois' new home together in France. Their move is primarily a chance to start a life away from the chaos of Brexit, which has proven extremely draining for them both, and to live together as a family. Grete and Lukas, a Polish couple who used to work for Ian's mother, have also left England and come to France, having concluded that 'there are other countries now where life might be easier for us' (385). Grete takes on the role of housekeeper while Lukas works nearby, and they live on the same grounds as Benjamin and Lois with their young daughter. Their new home is the location of the final scene of the novel, where they have invited friends and family to visit for a housewarming gathering. The first to arrive is Sophie, who travels from London, and the next is Benjamin's friend and struggling entertainer Charlie who arrives with his wife, Aneeqa. Claire Newman, Benjamin's friend from school and a central character in *The Rotters' Club*, arrives next with her husband, Stefano. The final arrival is one of Benjamin's writing students, Alexandre, who has travelled a shorter distance from

Strasbourg. As they all gather for a meal, Benjamin surveys around the table and begins a speech: 'Six English people...two Lithuanians, a Frenchman and an Italian all had dinner together one beautiful evening in September. Sadly, this is not the set-up for a joke...But what it is—if anything—what it represents, what it *symbolizes*, I should say...' (415). As Benjamin trails off, Claire picks up the speech on his behalf: 'We get the message... It's a wonderful example of European harmonization' (415). Benjamin heartily agrees with Claire, and continues his semi-drunk rambling:

> '*Exactly*,' said Benjamin, striking the table for emphasis. 'That's exactly what I'm trying to say. What could be more inspiring, what could be a more powerful...metaphor... for the spirit of cooperation—international cooperation— which prevails, which *has* prevailed—which *ought* to prevail, if...if we, as a nation, hadn't made this...regrettable, but understandable—in *some* ways understandable...'
> 'Sit down and shut up,' said Lois.
> 'I will not,' said Benjamin. 'I have something to say.' [...]
> Then, in a tone of belligerent triumph, he said, '*Fuck Brexit!*' and sat down to a round of applause. (415)

Benjamin's spirited and uplifting appeal to his friends and family to remain confident in the project of internationalism in spite of the Brexit referendum result is a moment of hope and happiness that the reader is encouraged to share in. This scene pulls us away from the political turmoil that continued to dominate the landscape in 2018 when *Middle England* was published, and grounds us in an extremely heartening example of a group of people defying the resounding message of the referendum. Although this scene takes place in France—in Europe—and therefore seems to suggest that this kind of harmonization requires a removal from England in its current state, there is still an element of hopefulness, that even despite all of the hideous xenophobia and polarization that have occurred over the last 4 years of the novel, humanity will prevail, and the spirit of Englishness is up to the people—not to politicians.

On top of Benjamin's speech, the novel closes on the ultimate note of hopefulness. As Sophie begins to drive away from Benjamin and Lois' home, Lois reveals to Benjamin that Sophie is pregnant (421). Benjamin is elated at this news:

> His heart thumping, his spirits soaring as the news gradually permeated his weary, addled consciousness, Benjamin raised his arm at the receding car and began to wave in quick frantic movements. But his niece was not looking back. Her eyes were fixed on the road ahead as she accelerated down the lane, one hand on the steering wheel, the other resting on her swollen belly: home, for now, to Sophie and Ian's tentative gesture of faith in their equivocal, unknowable future: their beautiful Brexit baby. (421)

This final reveal of the novel is a promise of new life, new hope, and a new future, not only for Sophie and Ian, but, more broadly, for the entire country. Rarely do we see the words 'beautiful' and 'Brexit' paired alongside each other, yet to close the novel in this way indicates that this child—this new life and a symbol of the next generation—will be able to heal a divided relationship, and a divided England.

Coe's *Middle England* is a stunning example of how literature can both mirror and meditate on the present moment simultaneously, inviting sympathy, anger, and amusement from the reader all at once. Unlike the first two books in his series, the action of *Middle England* ends in the exact year the book is published, rooting the story distinctly in our politically turbulent present, when the Brexit negotiations were still being painfully turned over and over, providing people with no real opportunity to move on from the 2016 referendum. Despite, or perhaps because of, the emotional exhaustion of Brexit, *Middle England* provides the reader with an opportunity to escape their own personal experiences of the referendum by plunging them into the lives of a plethora of characters—some who will share the readers' views, and others who won't. In this way, the novel is an exercise in human understanding and an opportunity to heal from the polarization of the current moment. While Coe does not shy away from the ugliest facets of Brexit and the troubling effects that it has had on many people's lives, he also does not seek to exacerbate them by offering no hope for the future. As Sarah Butter of the *Evening Standard* writes of *Middle England*, 'Brexit and outrage may dominate but Coe finds humanity' (Butter). Indeed, Coe sets out to capture the political mood and deal with some of the secondary consequences of the referendum—strained marriages, broken friendships, violent interactions—yet he does so with an equally distinct sense of balance, compassion, and hope. *Middle England* is comparable to Geoffrey Hill's *The Book of Baruch by the Gnostic Justin* and Ali Smith's *Autumn*; although the spirit of defeatism and hopelessness that is so familiar in our society today is rife, Coe does not let this consume the novel entirely. In spite of the chaos, there is room for silence, and there is room for the future.

* * *

Ian McEwan's *The Cockroach*: Another *Metamorphosis*: The Government Against the People

Ian McEwan's novella *The Cockroach* is a political satire and an unapologetic condemnation of the government that attempts to deliver the promise of the Brexit referendum—to leave the EU. The novella follows a conceit in which cockroaches inhabit the body of the British Conservative prime minister and his entire cabinet (as well as the President of the US), and together they work to deliver a new economic system called 'Reversalism', standing in for the 'Leave' campaign. The opposition to Reversalism is 'Clockwise economics' ('Remain') and is deemed a 'dead hand' (McEwan 47), even though it is the system used throughout the rest of the world. McEwan depicts the debate between the two economic systems as being absurd and totally devoid of legitimate reason or humanity—symbolized, of course, by the insect-inhabited bodies of the people in charge. While Sam Byers' *Perfidious Albion* and Jonathan Coe's *Middle England* are both satirical sketches of Brexit-Britain, McEwan takes on the political landscape in an exceptionally unforgiving manner. Perhaps written to capture the rage of the Remainers throughout the nation, *The Cockroach* certainly has no time for objectivity in the wake of Brexit, and in that sense is a valuable testimony to the incredibly polarized nature of Englishness in our time. McEwan demonstrates a clear bias throughout the book, made all the more evident by his previous success as a novelist who writes disdainfully about the upper class and politics. However, given the binary nature of England at the time McEwan was writing, the reader should also remain aware that this biased account is one that much of the nation will derive immense, smug pleasure from reading.

Before engaging with the work of the text, it is important to fully grapple with the conceit that it follows, especially with regard to the premise of Reversalism. The idea is explained at length:

Let the money flow be reversed and the entire economic system, even the nation itself, will be purified, purged of absurdities, waste and injustice. At the end of a working week, an employee hands over money to the company for all the hours that she has toiled. But when she goes to the shops, she is generously compensated at retail rates for every item she carries away. She is forbidden by law to hoard cash. The money she deposits in her bank at the end of a hard day in the shopping mall attracts high negative interest rates. Before her savings are whittled away to nothing, she is therefore wise to go out and find, or train for, a more expensive job. The better, and therefore more costly, the job she finds for herself, the harder she must shop to pay for it. The economy is stimulated, there are more skilled workers, everyone gains. (25–26)

Aside from reading as an absurd economic system—and one that would imaginably lead to incredible hoarding of things as opposed to money—Reversalism is literally an indication that politicians, and the people in the world of the book who voted for it, want to do everything backwards. McEwan's imaginary system takes the way that we live and flips it on its head—something that the politicians and Reversalists are hopeful will immeasurably improve lives, but that seems perfectly capable of doing the opposite. The use of an economic system to symbolize Brexit is also notable here, since one of the primary indicators of voting Leave was socioeconomic status, and because the impact on the economy was a key point of contention throughout the debate. The literal backwardness of changing the economic system in this way mirrors the way that Remainers perceive Brexit as a backward step for the UK when it leaves the EU and turns inwards on itself. Reversal is the opposite of progress, and McEwan means to emphasize this point throughout the novella.

Upon reading the very first line of the novella, *The Cockroach* reveals itself as a spin on Franz Kafka's *The Metamorphosis* (1915), which depicts the life of a man named Gregor who wakes up and finds himself transfigured into a giant insect. *The Metamorphosis* starts as follows: 'One morning, when Gregor Samsa woke from troubled dreams, he found himself transformed in his bed into a horrible vermin' (Kafka 1). In an almost identical opening, *The Cockroach* begins: 'That morning,

Jim Sams, clever but by no means profound, woke from uneasy dreams to find himself transformed into a gigantic creature' (McEwan 1). While Kafka's character Gregor Samsa has gone from human to 'vermin', Jim Sams is vermin—a cockroach— who becomes human. Similarly, while Gregor's transformation is often read as resulting from a desire to escape responsibility from the world, Jim's transformation from cockroach to human oppositely posits him in the highest position of responsibility in the United Kingdom—into the role of prime minister.

Reflecting on how he came to control the body of the prime minister, Jim recalls that after exiting the gutter where he lives, 'Mounting the pavement, as he did, he submitted to the collective spirit. He was a tiny element in a scheme of a magnitude that no single individual could comprehend' (6). The use of the phrase 'collective spirit' is reminiscent of the idea of the will of the people—that they have spoken as one and must be respected—a notion often referred to post-referendum as the impetus for getting Brexit done. Following the conceit, this language suggests that the 'collective spirit' of Reversalism (thereby Brexit) created an invisible force that drove cockroaches into positions of human power—a harsh criticism indeed. As Jim becomes accustomed to his new human form while lying in bed, he is reassured by his ability to recall how he got to where he is: 'It was good to know that his brain, his mind, was much as it had always been. He remained, after all, his essential self' (8). Here, far from suggesting that the transformation from cockroach to politician is a bizarre and extremely unfamiliar one, Jim suggests that even in his insect form, his mind works much the same as it is working now. This could either be read as an appreciation for the intelligence of cockroaches, or, more likely, a denigration of politicians who can be easily imitated by a cockroach. Jim's transformation immediately conveys the idea that there is a lack of humanity in British politics (led by an English prime minister), as he is essentially not human in this novella.

Jim's attempts to adjust to his human form and new role as prime minister are tentative yet internally confident throughout the novella. When an aide comes to his attic room to make sure that he is awake, she reveals: 'It's Wednesday. Cabinet at nine. Priorities for government and PMQs at noon' (10). Jim's internal monologue reveals a familiarity with this recurring human event:

> Prime Minister's Questions. How many of those had he crouched through, listening enthralled from behind the rotten wainscoting in the company of a few thousand select acquaintances? How familiar he was with the opposition leader's shouted questions, the brilliant non sequitur replies, the festive jeers and clever imitations of sheep...But was he adequately prepared? No less than anyone else, surely. (10)

The sardonic description of PMQs here makes this sacred British political tradition look like a playground fight between children—a description that should not be completely rejected, but which sharply undermines the severity and significance of this weekly occurrence. The mention of 'sheep' here is comical given that cockroaches, who are literally pheromonally programmed to follow and find each other, still see politicians as sheep in the sense that they are easily influenced or led. This line also invokes a further use of animal imagery within the conceit of the novella, again dehumanizing politicians. The idea that this cockroach, who has watched PMQs be conducted by a different species, is no less prepared than anyone else, further undercuts the intelligence of politicians, literally suggesting that an insect could step in without anyone noticing. For those readers who are, understandably, frustrated by the jeering that takes place weekly in the House of Commons, this description is comical and deeply satisfying, while for those who sit in the

House, it is incredibly demeaning.

In his new position of power, Jim begins the process of weeding out those in his party who disagree with the move towards Reversalist economics in order to create a united cabinet. He starts by firing Simon, a fellow cabinet member who raises concerns about the state of the country: 'The country's tearing itself apart. We had that ultra-Reversalist beheading a Clockwise MP in a supermarket...time to call it off' (16–17). In this barely concealed, brutal reference to Jo Cox's murder, McEwan depicts a country similarly gripped by extremism and opposition, using Simon's character as a kind of whistle-blower. After a moment of reflection, Jim dismisses Simon from his job: 'I want your resignation letter on my desk within the half hour and I want you out of the building by eleven' (18). The abruptness of this decision suggests a new, hard-headed intolerance for those who do not support Reversalism within Jim's government, and reveals a concerning disregard for how the debate between two economic systems is impacting—now violently—the lives of British people.

Though Simon's immediate dismissal is harsh, others are more cruelly dealt with. Benedict St John, the foreign secretary, watches with growing alarm as Jim's cabinet grows more emboldened, and begins a 'secret cabal' among the backbenchers 'to help the opposition defeat the Reversalism bill when it came back to the Commons' (67). To deal with Benedict's scheme, Jim solicits the help of a woman named Jane Fish, who 'belonged mostly in the no-nonsense faction' (72) of politics and 'had been a passionate Clockwiser until, respectful of the will of the people, she became a passionate Reversalist. She was admired for speaking well for both' (72). While Jane Fish is not portrayed as a particularly powerful political figure in the novella, she does bear some resemblance to former PM Theresa May, who initially campaigned for Remain before switching her tune and stepping into office vowing to follow through with Brexit. Jim and Jane work together on a manuscript to be published in *The Guardian*—a manuscript, it turns out, that accuses Benedict of 'harassment, bullying, obscene taunts and inappropriate touching that led by turns to verbal abuse' (77). The news spreads quickly and gives Jim the necessary excuse to remove Benedict from his position. The viciousness of this accusation and the willingness of the prime minister to disseminate a lie of this scale into the public sphere leads the reader to wonder what other lies he might be capable of spreading for his own sake, and it stands to reason he could lie to the public about anything else that serves him. Jim's lie makes the reader distrustful of his motives not only with regard to controlling who remains in his immediate circle, but also with regard to his larger goal of introducing a Reversalist economy to Britain.

The vicious plot against Benedict is alarming in itself, but it is even more so because Benedict is the only member of the cabinet who remains his true human self. In Jim's very first cabinet meeting in his new body and role, he is understandably nervous about appearing plausible to his fellow humans. However, he quickly has a joyous revelation, realizing that he is not the only cockroach who has inhabited the body of a human:

> It was in those few seconds, as he met the bland gaze of Trevor Gott, the chancellor of the Duchy of Lancaster, then the home secretary, attorney general, leader of the house, trade, transport, minister without portfolio, that in a startling moment of instant recognition, an unaccustomed, blossoming, transcendent joy swept through him, through his heart and down his spine. Outwardly he remained calm. But he saw it clearly. Nearly all of his Cabinet shared his convictions. Far more important than that, and he had not known this until now, they shared his origins...It had never occurred to him that the mighty burden of his task was shared, that others like him were heading towards separate

ministries to inhabit other bodies and take up the fight. A couple of dozen, a little swarm of the nation's best, come to inhabit and embolden a faltering leadership. (20)

In this passage, Jim somehow sees through the human exterior of others and recognizes that their true form is the same one that he left behind that morning—a cockroach. Furthermore, this passage also seems to allude to the real-life commonalities that exist between politicians—for example, that many traditionally emerge from educational institutions such as Eton and Oxbridge—though in this case their shared backgrounds are that they are all vermin. While this depiction of who inhabits high-ranking roles in the government lacks nuance, it does reflect a popular and genuine belief about the prerequisites for power in the UK—a belief that many throughout the UK find deeply frustrating, and which McEwan clearly criticizes. As Jim continues to scan the room, he also feels the presence of a 'traitor at his side' (20): 'When Jim had looked into the eyes of Benedict St John, the foreign secretary, he had come against the blank unyielding wall of a human retina and could go no further. Impenetrable. Nothing there. Merely human. A fake. A collaborator. An enemy of the people. Just the sort who might rebel and vote to bring down his own government. This would have to be dealt with' (21). The description of Benedict's eyes as an impenetrable wall suggests not only a lack of depth to his character, but also an inability on Jim's part to understand him. Perhaps obviously, McEwan depicts Benedict as human to cast him as the 'good guy' in Jim's government—he is the only one willing to take a stand against Reversalism and attempt to bring down what he sees as a dysfunctional and dishonest leadership. In other words, he has his humanity. On the other hand, Jim and his fellow cockroaches are fundamentally not human, which suggests that their motives and actions are to the detriment of other people (which by the end of the text, they are). By expelling

Benedict from their midst, Jim empowers his cockroach-cabinet to achieve their goals without the interference of someone with humanity—a sharp critique of what and who it takes to deliver something like Brexit.

Once Jim has successfully weeded out the dissenters and is left only with his fellow cockroach-humans, the path towards Reversalism is confirmed, but when he is asked to explain why they are pursuing this end in the first place, Jim is unable to provide a satisfactory answer. In a private meeting with the chancellor in Berlin, Jim is asked, through an interpreter: 'Why are you doing this? Why, to what end, are you tearing your nation apart? Why are you inflicting these demands on your best friends and pretending we're your enemies? Why?' (86). It is notable that this question comes from the chancellor of Germany—one of the largest powers in the European Union. In the context of the book, Reversalism, like Brexit, has major implications for Britain's relationship with the EU in economic terms, but this question is still a very thinly veiled reference to the real-world Brexit scenario. Without verbally responding, Jim turns over thoughts in his mind: 'Because. Because that's what we're doing. Because that's what we believe in. Because that's what we said we'd do. Because that's what people said they wanted. Because I've come to the rescue. Because. That, ultimately, was the only answer: *because*' (86–87). Each utterance of 'because' becomes less and less meaningful over the course of this internal monologue, ending with only the word by itself. In each sentence there is an attempt at logic, but they are all ultimately unconvincing, and the final '*because*' betrays that there is simply no reason at all for Reversalism. It is just something that is happening because. The lack of purpose betrayed by Jim's thoughts once again reflect the real-world Remain position that Brexit is a meaningless endeavour that has no clear advantages. It also excludes the possibility that there could be any sound reasoning to wanting Brexit to happen in the first place, which is an equally popular position for Remainers. Robert Shrimsley of the *Financial Times* lamented McEwan's novella in his book review for this very reason. He writes: '[*The Cockroach*] simply symbolised the self-righteous inability to understand the half of the country that does not have the innate good sense to agree with McEwan' (Shrimsley). Indeed, McEwan's writing here feeds into the polarizing narratives that separate Leave from Remain and reads sanctimoniously, offering no real attempts to understand that the Leave campaign could have had any logical premise, or to heal from the hatred that Brexit unleashed.

Just as Jim is unable to articulately explain why his government has continued to forge a path for Reversalism, he is equally unwilling to remain trapped in the prime minister's body to see it through, triumphantly returning to his cockroach form. Once the bill for Reversalism is signed into law, Jim instructs that 'All Cabinet members were to leave their borrowed bodies tidily at their ministry desks, ready for the return of their rightful owners' (McEwan 95), and they return to the gutters. Before they leave Downing Street, the cockroaches all assemble in their true forms to celebrate what they have accomplished, and this meeting reveals why McEwan elected to have it be cockroaches, as opposed to any other insect, that possess the government. Addressing his colleagues and kin, Jim proclaims:

'Our kind is at least three hundred million years old. Merely forty years ago, in this city, we were a marginalised group, despised, objects of scorn or derision. At best, we were ignored. At worst, loathed. But we kept to our principles, and very slowly at first, but with gathering momentum, our ideas have taken hold. Our core belief remained steadfast: we always acted in our own best interests. As our Latin name, *blattodea*, suggests, we are creatures that shun the light. We understand and love the dark...we have lived alongside humans and have learned their particular taste for

that darkness...whenever it is predominant in them, so we
have flourished. Where they have embraced poverty, filth,
squalor, we have grown in strength...When that peculiar
madness, Reversalism, makes the general human population
poorer, which it must, we are bound to thrive.' (97–98)

Jim's speech is on the surface comical, as the reader imagines
a group of cockroaches bemoaning their marginalization from
human society. However, there is a deeply sinister undertone
here that attacks the politicians who delivered Brexit, as well
as the general population who voted for it. The imagery of
this scene is extremely atavistic—the speech is given 'behind a
wastepaper bin' (96) and longs for a darker time, both literally
and figuratively. Jim's primary message is one of survival: that
the cockroaches are an ancient species and must ensure that the
conditions in which they thrive are kept so that they continue to
live for millions more years. He suggests that the progress made
in human society is making the world uninhabitable for them,
as they require 'poverty, filth, squalor'—all of which humans
seek to eradicate in favour of progress and prosperity. The idea
that these cockroaches wish to turn back the clock to a world
such as this is an extremely harsh criticism of the Leave position
by McEwan. He portrays Euroscepticism as something far more
menacing, and suggests that a government that seeks to deliver
Reversalism—that seeks to deliver Brexit—does so knowing
that it is against the best interest of the people.

Where McEwan is criticizing politicians, Jim's remark that
'Merely forty years ago, in this city, we were a marginalised
group' dates back exactly to 1979 (since the year of the book's
publication)—the year that Margaret Thatcher became prime
minister—and the year that the UK's relationship with the
EU started to become strained under her leadership. Indeed,
Thatcher's term incited Euroscepticism within government that,
as Jim suggests, has been 'gathering momentum' ever since.

As Jim's monologue suggests, the victory of the Eurosceptics equivalates to a giant step backwards; back towards the dirty conditions that favour cockroaches while doing a disservice to humans. McEwan's message, here, is literally that Brexit will make us poorer, and does more for insects than it does for people. With regard to the population of Leave voters, there is also an insinuation here that they are in some way barbarous—that they are willingly and knowingly voting for their own demise and to reverse the progress made by the more civilized members of society, i.e., Remainers. Once again, these accusations against those pushing the Brexit agenda read as an emotional and polarizing response to the ongoing push to leave the EU, and capture a snapshot of how divided the country continues to be, even 3 years on from the referendum vote.

Ultimately, *The Cockroach* suggests that the only explanation for the actions of politicians who continue to push for Brexit is that they have been possessed by cockroaches who seek to halt human progress and return to the filth of years past. The nostalgia of the novella is not for better times, as is the common rhetoric, but for worse times that will allow these insects to best survive. Of McEwan's final message, Robert Shrimsley writes: 'Even now, you can hear the cackles across London, in the living rooms of Lewisham and the semis of Surbiton. Yes! Yes! Brexit is nothing more than a wicked populist plot to sow division, drive down living standards and so promote the social conditions in which extremists may thrive' (Shrimsley). Shrimsley's derisive observation that this story re-asserts the liberal perspective of Londoners—one of England's only Remain dominated regions—shames McEwan's novella for feeding into a polarizing narrative, and frames it as an emotional response to Brexit that precludes any attempt to understand the opposite side. Shrimsley even calls McEwan's novella an 'essay', as opposed to a work of literature, further expressing his concern about the one-sided nature of the text. Certainly, where Jonathan Coe's

Middle England gives voice to a plethora of perspectives that the Brexit debate inspired in the British population, *The Cockroach* privileges one as the right one. Certainly, it reveals a deep disdain for the form of Englishness that currently confronts the nation. In the same way as *Perfidious Albion*, McEwan's novella serves as a snapshot of just how polarized—just how *angry*—post-Brexit referendum Britain has become. Its dire message is intended to encourage the reader to look towards an alternative version of Englishness—one that will unite rather than divide, and one that, most of all, retains its humanity.

PART THREE

PART EIGHT

Chapter Five

Conclusion: Reimagining Membership

It is frankly difficult to conclude something that hasn't finished happening yet. BrexLit is by no means a literary phenomenon that has seen its last day, and it is unlikely that it will for the foreseeable future. As the UK continues to learn its place in the new world order it has created for itself, literature will continue to emerge in response. However, the immediacy with which BrexLit was published demonstrates a fierce desire to grapple with the political moment in which English people find themselves—one defined by division and uncertainty not only about the future of their country, but also about their collective identity. I argue that each of the literary texts covered in part two, whether published pre- or post-referendum, offers a unique conception of Englishness, but what unites all of them is that they zealously scrutinize an identity that often goes unexamined. For English people, it is in their interest *not* to investigate Englishness—to avoid confronting its history of violence and colonialism, and to ignore the implications of internal conflicts over race and class on a supposedly collective identity. However, the authors and texts I have covered refuse to follow suit. Where pre-Brexit referendum texts sought to problematize the form of Englishness that has emerged in the past 2 decades, BrexLit texts, in many cases, attempt to resolve it. In all of the eight texts I have covered, Englishness is depicted as an enigma not because no identity exists at all, but because the identity that has traditionally been sought by many English people is steeped in myth and conveniently obscures England's true past.

In chapter three, I examined how *England, England, The Rotters' Club* and *Jerusalem* both seek to portray an England that is struggling to achieve a collective identity, and how each author highlights an array of problems associated with that endeavour. In Julian Barnes' *England, England,* in order for Englishness to be experienced in a satisfying and cohesive way, Sir Jack designs a fictional re-interpretation of England in the form of a theme park, which eventually supersedes 'Old England' in terms of its global relevance. Jonathan Coe's *The Rotters' Club* offers the reader a coming-of-age story: through Benjamin's attempts to understand himself as an individual and as an Englishman, Coe directs the reader towards the problems associated with Englishness, where identity is defined by ongoing race and class warfare and the English inability to think of themselves from a perspective beyond their own borders. In Jez Butterworth's *Jerusalem,* England is a mystical and enchanted land, and its elucidation of Englishness as a force of anti-modernity is spectacularly hypocritical. *England, England* and *Jerusalem* both portray an Englishness that satisfies mystical, mythical fantasies about England and its history, but which ignores England's brutal history of violence and global conquest. The assertion of that flawed, collective identity is portrayed as absurd in both texts, and the reader and the theatrical audience, respectively, are asked to simultaneously indulge in and criticize these interpretations of Englishness, though *Jerusalem* offers more opportunity for indulgence out of the two. Meanwhile, *The Rotters' Club* more closely guides the reader through the formation of a young man's English identity in the 1970s, offering a more realistic depiction of the challenges of Englishness. Despite their differences, these three texts all engage with the market-driven era in ways that point towards the economy as a key factor for the resurgence of English nationalism, and they all reveal the problematic upshots of longing for a more exclusive English identity—an impulse that they prove was becoming ever more powerful in the lead-up to the Brexit referendum.

Amidst the turmoil of the referendum, BrexLit shows us something significantly different. When the future of the UK changed on June 23, 2016, so did the literature about English identity; rather than simply problematizing Englishness, authors now in many cases sought to resolve it. For Geoffrey Hill, tracing the historical destruction and rebuilding of London in *The Book of Baruch by the Gnostic Justin* becomes a way of demonstrating the resilience of London as a metaphor for the strength of Englishness, and although the poet's concerns about the future of his country are resonant, Hill's humour imbues the reader with a renewed sense of hope for the future. Similarly, Ali Smith's *Autumn* offers the reader what they least expect in the immediate wake of the vote: a heart-warming, unconventional story of an intergenerational friendship, and an affirmation of time as a healing mechanism for the division that seeps through the novel. Jonathan Coe's *Middle England* offers a diverse range of perspectives of England and Englishness in a fictional reimagining of the events leading up to and after the referendum, but he too ends the novel on a point of hope—a gathering of friends from across Europe, and the revelation that one of the protagonists is pregnant with her first child. Hill, Smith, and Coe linger not on the disappointment and loss associated with Brexit but rather allow their readers to look towards a positive vision of the future. On the opposite end of the spectrum, Sam Byers' *Perfidious Albion* and Ian McEwan's *The Cockroach* are satirical and deeply pessimistic visions of Englishness—the former rooted in the appeal of populism and data conspiracies, and the latter depicting a corrupt, cockroach-infested government that works against the best interest of the people. Even though they were published 2 and 3 years after the referendum, respectively, neither *Perfidious Albion* nor *The Cockroach* offers the reader any real hope or vision for the future, and while they reject the current incarnations of English nationalism, they offer no better alternative, even while insinuating that there is one.

Consequently, I find that there are two distinct strains of BrexLit: one rooted in hope and the other in hopelessness. Yet despite their differences, BrexLit texts all reject the current dominant form of nationalism that confronts England. Rather than depicting an England that confirms a gratifying, yet deeply flawed, form of Englishness as in *England, England* or *Jerusalem*, BrexLit portrays an England that has lost sight of itself, and exposes it instead as, in David Wheatley's words, a 'nation out-of-kilter' (Wheatley). All of the texts in chapter four perform a kind of demystification, asking the reader to leave pre-referendum nationalism and this out-of-kilter nation behind. However, while Byers and McEwan stop there, Hill, Smith, and Coe offer the reader an opportunity for realignment. The hope with which they end their literary texts offers a new foundation for Englishness that allows it to remain a part of the world. *Middle England* ends with a vision of European, multicultural harmony, while *Autumn* reminds England sternly yet compassionately that it is just one part of the collage that makes up the world. Although the Brexit referendum resulted in the UK relinquishing its membership of the EU, BrexLit offers a reimagination of what membership can mean for England in this new era. It invites the reader to recognize the possibility of an English identity based on inclusion and humility, and to consider that being one-among-many powers is not a threat to English dominance but, rather, a chance to participate in the global whole—to contribute to the collage of nations and identities that make up the world. Just like Benjamin Trotter, the reader can leave the pages of these novels feeling that Englishness does not have to be mutually exclusive from a global, liberal identity. The opportunity to reframe Englishness as an identity that will *remain* a part of the world despite the Leave vote is what makes these BrexLit texts so deeply powerful.

This book has been dedicated to revealing the power of

BrexLit to both expose the rifts in English society and detoxify Englishness in the wake of one of the most toxic events in its recent history. All BrexLit texts were published with haste, responding immediately to the state of the nation after the referendum vote—something that I claim is one of their greatest strengths. However, there has been some recent debate on whether texts published in moments of crisis are worthwhile at all. In an article written for the *New York Times* in March 2020 about literature in the time of coronavirus, Sloane Crosley says: 'From an artistic standpoint, it's best to let tragedy cool before gulping it down and spitting it back into everyone's faces…Art should be given a metaphorical berth as wide as the literal one we're giving one another' (Crosley). Crosley's suggestion that art should not attempt to grapple with a crisis as it is happening is based on the notion that 'get-it-while-it's-hot literature' is 'limited' somehow, and that those texts published immediately are 'born of ego or competition or fear' (Crosley). Why, she asks, 'do we continue trying to interpret our nightmares as they happen?' (Crosley). My answer is that literature is intended to interpret the world in which we live. Like all forms of art, literature offers us an exceptional opportunity to step outside of our lived experience and to reconsider our relationships to the world, and to ourselves. In the case of BrexLit, the immediacy of the response is both an attempt to document this incredible and turbulent period, and also to understand its impact on the nation and its people. Sure, novels written long after a critical event like Brexit with the benefit of hindsight might be able to capture a perceptibly more overarching picture, as they will have had more time to let the implications of the UK leaving the EU simmer. But without the literature that documents *the moment*— as Sam Byers suggests, the *feeling*, of Brexit as it happened—the art that comes out of it will undoubtedly lose some of its charge. Since 2015, the UK has experienced a period of turmoil and fast-paced change, and the accompanying, unparalleled confusion surrounding Englishness naturally drove authors towards their chosen art form in an attempt to resolve it. In the most wonderful sense, BrexLit is a vehicle for understanding what has been least visible to us during this English crisis. While some of the texts I have covered—most notably *Perfidious Albion* and *The Cockroach*—are arguably egoistic and self-indulgent, they are also invaluable explorations of how Englishness has been complicated by the political shock of Brexit.

Writing this as an Englishwoman has been an adventure towards better understanding something that I had never been able to articulate. Englishness, to me, had never been something I thought much about; it had always seemed to be nothing more than a series of stereotypes: 'stiff upper lip' and enjoying a well-formed queue. However, the literature covered in part two of this book provides an opportunity to reflect on the ways in which English identity is created, challenged, and reinforced, and in this exceedingly difficult and troubling period of change, that is both a disconcerting and empowering endeavour. Without a doubt, more than being simply the only way to interpret the contemporary English nightmare, BrexLit, as with all literature, allows readers to connect, empathize, and contend with something rife with confusion and uncertainty. Though it will not immediately heal the polarized state of English politics, nor will it instantly repair the damage done to the lives of people and citizens that Brexit has failed, it certainly has the power to inspire reflection on both, and it motivates English people in particular to ask themselves who they *really* want to be in this new and unknown future. BrexLit seeks to re-examine the nature of Englishness, and offers readers an extraordinary opportunity to step outside of the chaos, reflect, and, in many cases, heal from the dismal anxiety of the present .

Appendix

Nigel Farage standing in front of the Leave campaign's poster
'Breaking Point'.

Boris Johnson standing in front of the Leave campaign's red bus
plastered with a promise to use the money channelled into the EU for
the NHS instead.

Pauline Boty, 'Untitled (Sunflower Woman),' 1963.

Acknowledgements

First and foremost, I would like to thank Jeff Strabone for his resolute support of this project from start to finish. Without his expertise, questions, and keen eye for grammatical error, this book would have been completely impossible.

I must also thank Steven Shoemaker and David Patton, who both willingly shared their knowledge with me throughout the writing process and whose feedback I greatly value and appreciate.

Thank you to Jake and the Kingfisher crew for putting me up, and putting up with me, through a pandemic so that I could finish my degree and this project in-country—I appreciate you all and your kindness more than you know.

Finally, I would like to thank my entire family, and my parents in particular, for their support of this project and my education as a whole. By example, they have shown me the meaning of hard work, and they have encouraged my love of English and writing without reservation. Their unwavering support of me travelling across an ocean to study at Connecticut College has further pushed me to work hard in everything that I do. None of us could have predicted that leaving England would be what piqued my interest in Englishness, but my time away from home undoubtedly offered me a new perspective that not only enabled me to write this book, but has also allowed me to better understand myself. For that I am truly grateful.

Author Biography

Dulcie was born and raised in London, England, where she attended Wimbledon High School. In 2016, Dulcie moved across the Atlantic to study at Connecticut College, a liberal arts college in the US, where she read English, Philosophy, and Government, and swam competitively.

Dulcie has been interested in the intersection between literature and politics since she conducted an independent project in her final year of school, examining how literature published during and about the Spanish Civil War preserved memories and stories that would otherwise have been lost due to the Pacto de Olvido ('Pact of Forgetting'). When it came to choosing a university dissertation, she knew that she wanted to continue to explore the role of literature in documenting and challenging contemporary politics, which is how she discovered the term and genre of 'BrexLit'. In a hugely ambitious project, Dulcie tackled the problem of English identity in the age of Brexit—how English nationalism has developed, why it is unique, and what literature published pre- and post-Brexit referendum has to say about it. The result was a graduate level thesis that was nominated by her department for the Oakes and Louis Ames Prize, awarded to the student with the best honours thesis at the college.

Dulcie currently works as a Communications Executive at Denford Associates in London, England.

Note to Reader

Thank you for the time and energy you have given to reading this book. I sincerely hope that you enjoyed it, and that you have taken something away from it that you did not have before you began reading. Writing *BrexLit: The Problem of Englishness in Pre- and Post-Brexit Referendum Literature* is my proudest achievement to date, but I do not imagine that it is perfect. I'm incredibly excited to see all of the future work that emerges on the subject of BrexLit—for I am confident that more will follow—and hope that those authors who tackle it next challenge my arguments and thus bolster and sustain the conversation surrounding these, and other works of literature, and their intersection with contemporary British politics. If you are still with me and would like to stay updated with my future work, please visit my website www.dulcieeveritt.com and sign up for my newsletter.

References

Aitken, Ian. 'Now Wilson has to tackle Left'. *The Guardian*, June 7, 1975. Retrieved from: static.guim.co.uk/sys-images/Guardian/Pix/pictures/2015/6/4/1433414893468/Europhoria-7 May-1975-001.jpg. Accessed April 29, 2020.

Akala. *Natives: Race & Class in the Ruins of Empire.* London: Two Roads, 2019. Print.

Anderson, Benedict. *Imagined Communities: Reflections on the Origin and Spread of Nationalism.* Rev Ed. New York: Verso, 2016. Print.

Aughey, Arthur. *Nationalism, Devolution, and the Challenge to the United Kingdom State.* London: Pluto Press, 2001. E-book.

Aughey, Arthur. *The Politics of Englishness.* Manchester: Manchester University Press, 2007. Print.

Barnes, Julian. *England, England.* Random House: New York. 1998. Print.

Barnes, Julian. *Conversations with Julian Barnes.* Edited by Vanessa Guignery and Ryan Roberts. Mississippi: University Press of Mississippi, 2009. E-book.

Barnett, Anthony. *The Lure of Greatness: England's Brexit & America's Trump.* London: Unbound, 2017. Print.

Barton, Laura. 'Why I love Jez Butterworth's Jerusalem'. *The Guardian*, October 25, 2011, www.theguardian.com/stage/theatreblog/2011/oct/25/why-i-love-butterworths-jerusalem. Accessed February 18, 2020.

Baudrillard, Jean. *Simulation and Simulacra.* Translated by Sheila Faria Glaser. Ann Arbor: The University of Michigan Press, 1994. E-book.

Black, Jeremy. *English Nationalism: A Short History.* London: Hurst, 2018. Print.

Brantley, Ben. 'This Blessed Plot, This Trailer, This England'. *The New York Times.* April 21, 2011, www.bbc.com/news/uk-wales-48692863. Accessed February 11, 2020.

'Brexit "major influence" in racism and hate crime rise'. *BBC News*, June 20, 2019, www.bbc.com/news/uk-wales-48692863. Accessed April 15, 2020.

Brown, Matt. 'Where to See Roman London'. *Londonist*, October 18, 2016, www.londonist.com/2015/08/where-to-see-roman-london. Accessed April 16, 2020.

Butter, Susannah. 'Charting the way we came to live in uncertain times'. *Evening Standard*, October 25, 2018, www.standard.co.uk/lifestyle/books/middle-england-by-jonathan-coe-review-a3971281.html. Accessed April 3, 2020.

Butter, Susannah. 'Brexit takes centre stage in Jonathan Coe's new novel *Middle England'*. *Evening Standard*, October 31, 2018, www.standard.co.uk/lifestyle/books/brexlit-takes-centre-stage-in-jonathan-coes-new-novel-middle-england-a3976771.html. Accessed April 3, 2020.

Butterworth, Jez. *Jerusalem*. New York: Theatre Communications Group, 2009. Print.

Byers, Sam. *Perfidious Albion*. London: Faber & Faber, 2018. Print.

Cavendish, Dominic. 'Jerusalem: Why no fuss about this radical play?' *The Telegraph*, February 23, 2010, www.telegraph.co.uk/culture/theatre/7265867/Jerusalem-why-no-fuss-about-this-radical-play.html. Accessed February 18, 2020.

Childs, Peter. *Julian Barnes*. Manchester: Manchester University Press, 2011. E-book.

Churchill, Winston. 'European Unity: Something That Will Astonish You'. *Winston Churchill Blood, Toil, Tears and Sweat: The Great Speeches*. Edited by David Cannadine. New York: Penguin Classics, 2007 [1989]. Print.

Cobain, Ian, Nazia Parveen, and Matthew Taylor. 'The slow-burning hatred that led Thomas Mair to murder Jo Cox'. *The Guardian*, November 23, 2016, www.theguardian.com/uk-news/2016/nov/23/thomas-mair-slow-burning-hatred-led-to-jo-cox-murder. Accessed April 15, 2020.

Coe, Jonathan. *The Rotters' Club*. London: Penguin Books, 2014 [2001]. Print.

Coe, Jonathan. *Middle England*. London: Penguin Random House, 2019. Print.

Cohen, Jeffrey Jerome. 'Old English Literature and the Work of Giants'. *Comitatus: A Journal of Medieval and Renaissance Studies*, 24(1): pp. 1–32. Retrieved from https://escholarship.org/uc/item/5jt8f7dd. Accessed March 26, 2020.

Coogan, Tim Pat. *The IRA*. New York: St Martin's Press, 1970. Print.

Crosley, Sloane. 'Someday, We'll Look Back on All of This and Write a Novel'. *New York Times*, March 17, 2020, www.nytimes.com/2020/03/17/books/review/sloane-crosley-pandemic-novel-coronavirus.html. Accessed April 20, 2020.

Day, Jon. 'Brexlit: the new landscape of British fiction'. *Financial Times*, July 28, 2017, www.ft.com/content/30ec47b4-7204-11e7-93ff-99f383b09ff9. Accessed November 20, 2019.

Defoe, Daniel. *The True-Born Englishman: A Satire*. Leeds: Alice Mann, 1836 [1701]. Print.

Dickens, Charles. *A Tale of Two Cities*. New York: Charles Scribner's Sons, 1899. E-book.

Downes, Kerry. 'Wren, Sir Christopher'. *Oxford Dictionary of National Biography*, September 23, 2004, doi.org/10.1093/ref:odnb/30019. Accessed April 18, 2020.

'Election 2015: Conservative manifesto at-a-glance'. *BBC News*, April 15, 2015, www.bbc.com/news/election-2015-32302062. Accessed April 11, 2020.

English Defence League. English Defence League, www.englishdefenceleague.org.uk. Accessed December 15, 2019.

'EU Referendum: Birmingham votes Brexit by a whisker'. *BBC News*, June 24, 2016, www.bbc.com/news/uk-politics-eu-referendum-36616108. Accessed April 26, 2020.

Faber & Faber. 'Sam Byers discusses whether *Perfidious Albion is a Brexit novel'*. *Youtube*, April 4, 2019, https://www.youtube.

com/watch?v=ZCwN1cbmO2E. Accessed April 19, 2020.

Foley, James and Pete Ramand. *Yes: The Radical Case for Scottish Independence*. London: Pluto Press, 2014. JSTOR, DOI: 10.2307/j. ctt183p60d. 13. Accessed March 31, 2020.

Gervais, David. *Literary Englands: Versions of 'Englishness' in Modern Writing*. Cambridge: University of Cambridge Press, 1993. Print.

Gilroy, Paul. *There Ain't No Black in the Union Jack*. Oxford: Routledge Classic, 2008. Print.

The Gnostic Bible. Edited by Willis Barnstone and Marvin Meyer. Boston: New Seeds Books, 2003. E-book.

Grierson, Jamie. 'Stephen Lawrence: a timeline of events since the teenager's murder'. *The Guardian*, August 11, 2020. Accessed August 26, 2020.

Healy, Patrick. 'Putting the Juice in "Jerusalem"'. *The New York Times*, April 7, 2011. Accessed February 11, 2020.

Hill, Geoffrey. *The Book of Baruch by the Gnostic Justin*. Edited by Kenneth Haynes. Oxford: Oxford University Press, 2019. Print.

Hobsbawm, E. J. *Nations and Nationalism Since 1780*. Cambridge: Cambridge University Press. 1990. Print.

Hogan, Karina Martin. 'Baruch'. *The Apocrypha: Fortress Commentary on the Bible Study Edition*. Edited by Gale A. Yee, Hugh R. Page, and Matthew J. M. Coomber, Minneapolis: Fortress Press, 2016, pp. 1027–1034.

'How the regions voted in the referendum'. *The Guardian*, June 7, 1975. Retrieved from: static.guim.co.uk/sys-images/Guardian/ Pix/pictures/2015/6/3/1433346595960/Voting-7-June-1975-009. jpg. Accessed April 29, 2020.

Hunt, Alex. 'UKIP: The story of the UK Independence Party's rise'. *BBC News*, November 21, 2014, www.bbc.com/news/uk-politics-21614073. Accessed April 15, 2020.

Kafka, Franz. *The Metamorphosis*. Translated by David Wyllie. Stockholm: Wisehouse Classics, 2015. E-book.

Kavenna, Joanna. '*Autumn* by Ali Smith review—a beautiful, transient symphony'. *The Guardian,* October 12, 2016, www.theguardian.com/books/2016/oct/12/autumn-ali-smith-review. Accessed April 21, 2020.

Kingsnorth, Paul. *Real England: The Battle Against the Bland.* London: Portobello Books, 2008. Print.

Lyall, Sarah. 'From Ali Smith, It's the First Great Brexit Novel'. *New York Times,* February 17, 2017, www.nytimes.com/2017/02/17/books/review/autumn-ali-smith.html. Accessed April 21, 2020.

McEwan, Ian. *The Cockroach.* New York: Anchor Books, 2019. Print.

McGee, Luke. 'A legacy of failure: Theresa May was a disaster as Prime Minister'. *CNN,* May 26, 2019, www.cnn.com/2019/05/24/uk/theresa-may-legacy-of-failure-analysis-intl-gbr/index.html. Accessed April 16, 2020.

Miller, Vaughne. '"Ever Closer Union" in the EU Treaties and Court of Justice case law'. *House of Commons Library.* November 16, 2015, commonslibrary.parliament.uk/research-briefings/cbp-7230/. Accessed April 29, 2020.

Mutter, Reginald P. C. 'Daniel Defoe'. *Encyclopaedia Britannica.* 2020. Accessed January 31, 2020.

Orwell, George. *Notes on Nationalism.* London: Penguin Books, 2018. E-book.

O'Toole, Fintan. *Heroic Failure: Brexit and the Politics of Pain.* New York: Apollo, 2018. Print.

Oxford English Dictionary Online, Oxford University Press, https://www-oed-com.peach.conncoll.edu/. Accessed March 4, 2020.

Pagels, Elaine. *The Gnostic Gospels.* New York: Vintage Books, 1979. E-book.

Parekh, Bhikhu. 'Feeling at Home: Some Reflections on Muslims in Europe'. *Harvard Middle Eastern and Islamic Review* 8 (2009): pp. 51–85.

Parkinson, Justin. 'Morris dancing for the Olympics?' *BBC*

News, October 17, 2005, www.news.bbc.co.uk/2/hi/uk_politics/4349088.stm. Accessed April 1, 2020.

Perraudin, Frances. 'Conservatives election manifesto 2015—the key points'. *The Guardian*, April 14, 2015. www.theguardian.com/politics/2015/apr/14/conservatives-election-manifesto-2015-the-key-points. Accessed April 11, 2020.

'Race and religious hate crimes rose 41% after EU vote'. *BBC News*, October 13, 2016, www.bbc.com/news/uk-politics-37640982. Accessed April 15, 2020.

Rocks, Christopher. 'Productivity trends in London: An evidence review to inform the Local Industrial Strategy evidence base'. *GLA Economics*, September 2019, https://www.london.gov.uk/sites/default/files/productivity-trends-in-london-final.pdf. Accessed August 31, 2020.

Rylance, Mark. Interview with Andrew Marr. *The Andrew Marr Show*, 2010. Accessed February 14, 2020. https://www.youtube.com/watch?v=JrdKme_QU48.

Schnapper, Pauline. 'The Elephant in the Room: Europe in the 2015 British General Election'. *Revue Française de Civilisation Britannique*, 20.3 (2015): pp. 1–10. DOI: 10.4000/rfcb.613. Accessed April 11, 2020.

Scott, Mark. 'Cambridge Analytica helped "cheat" Brexit vote and US election, claims whistleblower'. *Politico*, March 27, 2018, www.politico.eu/article/cambridge-analytica-chris-wylie-brexit-trump-britain-data-protection-privacy-facE-book/. Accessed April 20, 2020.

Servini, Nick. 'Tony Blair: I steamrolled devolution for Wales'. *BBC News*, September 11, 2007, www.bbc.com/news/uk-wales-politics-41199659. Accessed March 31, 2020.

Seymour, Richard. 'The British have invaded 90% of the world's countries. Ha ha?' *The Guardian*, November 6, 2012, www.theguardian.com/commentisfree/2012/nov/06/british-invaded-90-per-cent-world. Accessed April 1, 2020.

Shrimsley, Robert. '*The Cockroach* by Ian McEwan—cathartic but tin-eared Brexit satire'. *Financial Times*, September 27, 2019, www.ft.com/content/54ec1dfc-df93-11e9-b112-9624ec9edc59. Accessed April 6, 2020.

Smith, Ali. *Autumn*. London: Penguin Books, 2016. Print.

Smith, Helena. 'Shocking images of drowned Syrian boy show tragic plight of refugees'. *BBC News*, September 2, 2015, https://www.theguardian.com/world/2015/sep/02/shocking-image-of-drowned-syrian-boy-shows-tragic-plight-of-refugees. Accessed September 26, 2020.

'Stephen Lawrence murder: A timeline of how the story unfolded'. *BBC News*, April 13, 2018, www.bbc.com/news/uk-26465916. Accessed April 16, 2020.

Stewart, Heather and Rowena Mason. 'Nigel Farage's anti-migrant poster reported to police'. *The Guardian*, June 16, 2016, www.theguardian.com/politics/2016/jun/16/nigel-farage-defends-ukip-breaking-point-poster-queue-of-migrants. Accessed April 29, 2020.

Taylor, Adam. 'Map: The rise and fall of the British Empire'. *The Washington Post*, September 8, 2015, www.washingtonpost.com/news/worldviews/wp/2015/09/08/map-the-rise-and-fall-of-the-british-empire/. Accessed April 1, 2020.

'The Islamic veil across Europe'. *BBC News*, May 31, 2018, www.bbc.com/news/world-europe-13038095. Accessed April 21, 2020.

'The ley of the land'. *The Guardian*, May 12, 2000, www.theguardian.com/theguardian/2000/may/13/weekend7.weekend1. Accessed April 1, 2020.

'This is "Deep England": warm ale, village greens and cheeky milkmen'. *The Guardian*, April 11, 2017, https://www.theguardian.com/politics/shortcuts/2017/apr/11/deep-england-brexit-britain. March 17, 2020.

TLDR News. 'How UKIP Made Brexit Without Any Power—Brexit Explained'. *YouTube*, May 6, 2019, www.youtube.com/watch?v=9HG7eJPC6WU. Accessed April 1, 2020.

'UK results: Conservatives win majority'. *BBC News*, December 12, 2019, www.bbc.com/news/election/2019/results. Accessed April 16, 2020.

Varagine, Jacobus de. *The Golden Legend: Reading on the Saints*. 2 vols. Translated by William Granger Ryan. Princeton: Princeton University Press, 1993. E-book.

Wall, Stephen. *A Stranger in Europe: Britain and the EU from Thatcher to Blair*. Oxford: Oxford University Press, 2008. E-book.

Warrell, Helen. 'Eastern European migration to the UK in 5 charts'. *Financial Times*, July 10, 2017, www.ft.com/content/14b558c8-6585-11e7-8526-7b38dcaef614. Accessed April 29, 2020.

Webber, Douglas. 'The Brexit Crisis'. *European Disintegration? The Politics of Crisis in the European Union*. London: Red Globe Press, 2019. E-book.

'What was the IRA?' *Boston Herald*, November 9, 2019, www.bostonherald.com/2019/11/09/the-ira/. Accessed March 21, 2020.

Wheatley, David. 'The Book of Baruch by the Gnostic Justin by Geoffrey Hill review—the last judgments'. *The Guardian*, May 3, 2019, www.theguardian.com/books/2019/may/03/the-book-of-baruch-by-the-gnostic-justin-geoffrey-hill-review. Accessed April 13, 2020.

Winlow, Simon, Steve Hall, and James Treadwell. *The Rise of the Right: English Nationalism and the Transformation of Working Class Politics*. London: Policy Press, 2017. Print.

Winter, Trish and Simon Keegan-Phipps. *Performing Englishness: Identity and Politics in a Contemporary Folk Resurgence*. Manchester: Manchester University Press, 2013. E-book.

World Population Review. 'United Kingdom Population 2020 (Live).' worldpopulationreview.com/countries/united-kingdom-population/. Accessed April 29, 2020.

Further Reading

Black, Jeremy. *English Nationalism: A Short History.* London: Hurst, 2018.

Norris, Pippa and Ronald Inglehart. *Cultural Backlash: Trump, Brexit, and Authoritarian Populism.* Cambridge: Cambridge University Press, 2019.

O'Toole, Fintan. *Heroic Failure: Brexit and the Politics of Pain.* New York: Apollo, 2018.

O'Toole, Fintan. *Three Years in Hell: The Brexit Chronicles.* New York: Apollo, 2020.

Sobolewska, Maria and Robert Ford. *Brexitland: Identity, Diversity and the Reshaping of British Politics.* Cambridge: Cambridge University Press, 2020.

Wall, Stephen. *Reluctant European: Britain and the European Union from 1945 to Brexit.* Oxford: Oxford University Press, 2020.

CULTURE, SOCIETY & POLITICS

The modern world is at an impasse. Disasters scroll across our smartphone screens and we're invited to like, follow or upvote, but critical thinking is harder and harder to find. Rather than connecting us in common struggle and debate, the internet has sped up and deepened a long-standing process of alienation and atomization. Zer0 Books wants to work against this trend. With critical theory as our jumping off point, we aim to publish books that make our readers uncomfortable. We want to move beyond received opinions.

Zer0 Books is on the left and wants to reinvent the left. We are sick of the injustice, the suffering and the stupidity that defines both our political and cultural world, and we aim to find a new foundation for a new struggle.

If this book has helped you to clarify an idea, solve a problem or extend your knowledge, you may want to check out our online content as well. Look for Zer0 Books: Advancing Conversations in the iTunes directory and for our Zer0 Books YouTube channel.

Popular videos include:

Žižek and the Double Blackmain

The Intellectual Dark Web is a Bad Sign

Can there be an Anti-SJW Left?

Answering Jordan Peterson on Marxism

Follow us on Facebook
at https://www.facebook.com/ZeroBooks and Twitter at https://
twitter.com/Zer0Books

Bestsellers from Zer0 Books include:

Give Them An Argument
Logic for the Left
Ben Burgis
Many serious leftists have learned to distrust talk of logic. This is
a serious mistake.
Paperback: 978-1-78904-210-8 ebook: 978-1-78904-211-5

Poor but Sexy
Culture Clashes in Europe East and West
Agata Pyzik
How the East stayed East and the West stayed West.
Paperback: 978-1-78099-394-2 ebook: 978-1-78099-395-9

An Anthropology of Nothing in Particular
Martin Demant Frederiksen
A journey into the social lives of meaninglessness.
Paperback: 978-1-78535-699-5 ebook: 978-1-78535-700-8

In the Dust of This Planet
Horror of Philosophy vol. 1
Eugene Thacker
In the first of a series of three books on the Horror of Philosophy,
In the Dust of This Planet offers the genre of horror as a way of
thinking about the unthinkable.
Paperback: 978-1-84694-676-9 ebook: 978-1-78099-010-1

The End of Oulipo?
An Attempt to Exhaust a Movement
Lauren Elkin, Veronica Esposito
Paperback: 978-1-78099-655-4 ebook: 978-1-78099-656-1

Capitalist Realism
Is There No Alternative?
Mark Fisher
An analysis of the ways in which capitalism has presented itself
as the only realistic political-economic system.
Paperback: 978-1-84694-317-1 ebook: 978-1-78099-734-6

Rebel Rebel
Chris O'Leary
David Bowie: every single song. Everything you want to know,
everything you didn't know.
Paperback: 978-1-78099-244-0 ebook: 978-1-78099-713-1

Kill All Normies
Angela Nagle
Online culture wars from 4chan and Tumblr to Trump.
Paperback: 978-1- 78535-543-1 ebook: 978-1-78535-544-8

Cartographies of the Absolute
Alberto Toscano, Jeff Kinkle
An aesthetics of the economy for the twenty-first century.
Paperback: 978-1-78099-275-4 ebook: 978-1-78279-973-3

Malign Velocities
Accelerationism and Capitalism
Benjamin Noys
Long listed for the Bread and Roses Prize 2015, *Malign Velocities*
argues against the need for speed, tracking acceleration
as the symptom of the ongoing crises of capitalism.
Paperback: 978-1-78279-300-7 ebook: 978-1-78279-299-4

Meat Market
Female Flesh under Capitalism
Laurie Penny
A feminist dissection of women's bodies as the fleshy fulcrum of
capitalist cannibalism, whereby women are both consumers and
consumed.
Paperback: 978-1-84694-521-2 ebook: 978-1-84694-782-7

Babbling Corpse
Vaporwave and the Commodification of Ghosts
Grafton Tanner
Paperback: 978-1-78279-759-3 ebook: 978-1-78279-760-9

New Work New Culture
Work we want and a culture that strengthens us
Frithjoff Bergmann
A serious alternative for mankind and the planet.
Paperback: 978-1-78904-064-7 ebook: 978-1-78904-065-4

Romeo and Juliet in Palestine
Teaching Under Occupation
Tom Sperlinger
Life in the West Bank, the nature of pedagogy and the role of a
university under occupation.
Paperback: 978-1-78279-637-4 ebook: 978-1-78279-636-7

Ghosts of My Life
Writings on Depression, Hauntology and Lost Futures
Mark Fisher
Paperback: 978-1-78099-226-6 ebook: 978-1-78279-624-4

Sweetening the Pill
or How We Got Hooked on Hormonal Birth Control
Holly Grigg-Spall
Has contraception liberated or oppressed women?
Sweetening the Pill breaks the silence on the dark side of hormonal
contraception.
Paperback: 978-1-78099-607-3 ebook: 978-1-78099-608-0

Why Are We The Good Guys?
Reclaiming Your Mind from the Delusions of Propaganda
David Cromwell
A provocative challenge to the standard ideology that Western
power is a benevolent force in the world.
Paperback: 978-1-78099-365-2 ebook: 978-1-78099-366-9

Most titles are published in paperback and as an ebook.
Paperbacks are available in traditional bookshops. Both print and
ebook formats are available online.
Follow us on Facebook
at https://www.facebook.com/ZeroBooks
and Twitter at https://twitter.com/Zer0Books